WALKING THE WALK

For Karen,
with every blessing.
Sept. 2013.

WALKING THE WALK

The Rise of King David for Today

A dramatic exposition of 1 Samuel 16:1 –
2 Samuel 5:10

Pete Wilcox

Paternoster:
thinking faith

MILTON KEYNES ● COLORADO SPRINGS ● HYDERABAD

First published 2009 by Paternoster
Paternoster is an imprint of Authentic Media
9 Holdom Avenue, Bletchley, Milton Keynes, Bucks, MK1 1QR, UK
1820 Jet Stream Drive, Colorado Springs, CO 80921, USA
Medchal Road, Jeedimetla Village, Secunderabad 500 055, A.P., India
www.authenticmedia.co.uk

Authentic Media is a division of IBS-STL U.K., limited by guarantee, with its
Registered Office at Kingstown Broadway, Carlisle, Cumbria CA3 0HA.
Registered in England & Wales No. 1216232. Registered charity 270162

British Library Cataloguing in Publication Data

A catalogue record for this book is available from the
British Library

ISBN-13: 978-1-84227-648-8

Cover design by James Kessell for Scratch the Sky Ltd.
(www.scratchthesky.com)
Print Management by Adare
Printed and bound in Great Britain by J. F. Print, Sparkford

The Lord said,
'Walk before me,
as David your father walked.'
1 Kings 9:4

Contents

Introduction

It used to be said that three subjects were taboo in polite conversation: sex, religion and politics. Take these out of the David story, and not much remains (except violence, on the battlefield and off it). The story of David is a story about power: about the use and abuse of power in his relations with women (sex), with God (religion) and with kings (politics).

The story of David is therefore full of relevance for today: to individuals exercising power in their personal relationships and seeking to develop into the people they were created to be; to the church, exercising power as an institution and (at least in the West) seeking to renew its structures in the wake of a considerable loss of influence in society; to institutions of government, exercising social, political, economic and military power and seeking the welfare of the people on whose behalf they rule.

The story of David is lengthy. He is a prominent character in the Bible: his name occurs over eight hundred times in the Old Testament and over fifty times in the New. He is introduced for the first time in 1 Samuel 16 and dominates not just the following fifteen chapters of that book, but the whole of 2 Samuel (another twenty-four chapters), and even the first two chapters of the first book of Kings. The story thus spans forty-two chapters of Scripture in all.

Apart from Jesus himself, there is no figure in the Christian Scriptures to whom as much narrative space is devoted. The story of Jesus may be more than twice as long, but it is one story, told four times. The story of David is one single continuous narrative. It does, however, fall into two halves. 'The rise of King David' (the subject of this book) runs from 1 Samuel 16:1

to 2 Samuel 5:10 – from his anointing by Samuel to the moment he achieves kingship over all Israel. 'The fall of King David' (the subject of a sequel) then runs from 2 Samuel 5:11 to 1 Kings 2:12 – from the moment of his accession to the moment of his death.

Power is the key theme in both parts of the story. Specifically in relation to David's rise, the theme of power is explored in this exposition in relation first, to subversion; second, to corruption; and third, to divine providence.

The story of David's rise: power and subversion

The Bible is a political book with a subversive message. On almost every page, by bearing witness to the power and kingdom of God, Scripture calls into question every earthly empire (and every cosmic force). It ridicules riches, mocks military might and pours scorn on princes: from the anti-Babylonian shape of Genesis 1 (which took shape during the period of the Exile and tells the story of creation in such a way as to assert the authority of the Lord God not just over primordial chaos, but by implication also over the rival god Marduk) to the lampooning of Rome (as 'the Beast' of military might and 'the Harlot' of economic oppression) in the book of Revelation; from the Pauline assertion that 'Jesus [not Caesar] is Lord', to the assertion of Jesus to Pilate, in the Gospel of John, that even the most ruthlessly powerful of governments would have 'no power . . . unless it had been given from above'. It is one of the great ironies and tragedies of church history that the Bible, which was almost entirely written by and for persecuted communities, has so often been used as a tool of oppression.

The story of the rise of David, often read merely as a case study in personal faith and holiness, stands in this subversive tradition. It is first and foremost about the subjection of every human power (especially political power – the power of kings and armies) to the gracious will and purpose of God. At least in the first part of the narrative (the story of David's rise) the reason for this is clear: David is weak. He enters the story as a nobody. When he fights Goliath, it is as the underdog. When he enters

Saul's service, it is as an underling. In the first part of the story David consistently confronts those who are more powerful than himself. In this position of relative weakness David trusts in God. By doing so he bears witness to a higher power. Throughout the course of the narrative from 1 Samuel 16 to 2 Samuel 5, his appeals to God Most High have the effect of challenging – even taunting – worldly power. Despite every apparent earthly advantage, the kings of both Israel and Gath are unable to resist this young man with his naïve faith and trust in God.

The subversive strand is also evident in the part played by women. On the face of it this is a thoroughly male story. All the major players are male: Samuel, Saul, Goliath, Jonathan, Abner and Joab. Most of the minor players are male too: Jesse and all his sons, Achish, Ahimelech, Abiathar, Abishai, Asahel, Ishbaal. But the narrative also features three significant women: Michal, Abigail and the witch of Endor. What is striking is that their interventions in the narrative are exceptionally effective. They are also consistently both cunning and entirely in tune with the will and purpose of God. As a result of their guile these women influence the shape of the story to an extent out of all proportion to their status and influence.

More subtly, there is also Zeruiah (1 Sam. 26:6ff.). The fact that she, too, is a woman is easily missed. It is unusual for male offspring (such as Joab, Abishai and Asahel) to be defined in relation to their mother. But these three violent men are consistently called 'the sons of Zeruiah'. And while '-iah' names in the Bible are almost always male (Jeremiah, Isaiah, Obadiah, Micaiah), Zeruiah is a woman – and a sister (or half-sister) of David (1 Chr. 2:16; 2 Sam. 17:25). Rather as Matthew carefully includes four dubious women (including a Moabite, an adulteress and one who seduced her father-in-law) in his genealogy of Jesus, and thus subverts any sense that Jesus was born of a line merely of the great and the good, so the inclusion of this woman undermines any assumption that machismo rules.

The story of David's rise: power and corruption

There is, however, another side to the story. Even in this first half of the narrative, before David's accession to the kingship, the corrupting potential of power is felt.

When David is face to face with kings Saul and Achish there is no doubt where the worldly power lies. Likewise, when he fights hand to hand with Goliath: in the evident mismatch every worldly advantage is with the Philistine. But in the story of David's rise there is one conflict in which the balance of power is not so one-sided. In 1 Samuel 25 David is pitted against Nabal. Nabal is the richer man, with the higher social status. But David has the greater military might. Soberingl, it is in this episode of the story that David's darker side emerges most obviously. He is not immune to the corrupting nature of power and is only saved from evil intentions by Nabal's wife. The episode hints how David's personality will develop after his accession, when he is mightier in worldly terms than his opponents.

There is an inevitability about this for David, as there was for Saul – Israel's first king. From the moment when Israel expresses the wish to have a king (like other nations), the dangers are spelt out. When the elders of Israel come to the prophet Samuel with the request that a king should rule over them, he is not pleased (1 Sam. 8:6). When the Lord instructs Samuel to go along with the proposal, the instruction is theologically loaded: 'Listen to the voice of the people in all they say to you; for they have not rejected you, but they have rejected me from being king over them' (1 Sam. 8:7; 12:17). Ideally, the implication is, the Lord alone rules as king over Israel. Yet if the people wish for a king like other nations, they will get a king like the other nations. In 1 Samuel 8:10–18, Samuel (reporting all the words of the Lord) warns the people what it will be like to have such a king. Six times the phrase is repeated, 'he will take'. It is the nature of human kingship to grab, just as it is in the nature of divine kingship to give. There is something programmatic about the statement: 'These will be the ways of the king who will reign over you: he will take your sons . . . He will take your daughters . . . He will take the best of your fields . . . He will take one-tenth of your grain . . . He will take your male and female slaves . . . He will take one-tenth of your flocks'. But the people are not to be dissuaded: 'We are determined to have a king over us, so that we also may be like other nations, and that our king may govern us and go out before us and fight our battles.'

This is the context in which Saul becomes the first king – and David, as it were, God's loyal opposition. Saul is not obviously a bad man. On the contrary he was a 'handsome young man . . . he stood head and shoulders above everyone else' (1 Sam. 9:2). He was chosen by God (1 Sam. 9:15; 10:1) and had a God-given heart (1 Sam. 10:9). He was capable of being possessed by the Spirit of God and of taking his place among the prophets (1 Sam. 10:10–12, 11:6). He was decisive in a crisis (1 Sam. 10:7–11, 12:2–3) and magnanimous in victory (1 Sam. 10:27; 11:13).

But Saul is quickly corrupted by his power. Even before David makes his first appearance on the scene, three incidents occur which show this. At one level his offences appear to be trivial, or at least religiously ritual and technical: first (in 1 Sam. 13) he presumes to offer to the Lord a burnt-offering which was Samuel's prerogative to offer; then (in 1 Sam. 14) he commits 'a very rash act' by laying on his troops a reckless and unnecessary oath ('Cursed be anyone who eats food before it is evening and I have been avenged on my enemies'); and finally (in 1 Sam. 15), he erects 'a monument for himself', fails to carry out the (admittedly harsh-seeming) commands of the Lord and 'swoops down' on enemy spoil. What emerges here is the portrait of a man flushed with self-importance. He erects a monument not for the Lord, but for himself; and comes to regard the Philistines not as the enemies of his kingdom, but as his own personal foes. Power turns him into an insecure man, anxious about the outward appearance of things (1 Sam. 15:30). 'Power tends to corrupt': it not only inflates self-esteem, but simultaneously undermines it.

It is in relation to this corrupt and unstable Saul (desperate to hang onto power and inclined to see threats everywhere), that David is defined in 'part one' of his story. First he serves in Saul's court, yet provokes him; then he flees from him, yet humiliates him; and finally he succeeds him, yet defends his house.

The story of David's rise: power and providence

Thirdly, the story of David's rise is an exploration of the relationship of power and divine providence. No matter how corrupt or wicked human agents may be in this narrative, no matter how mixed human motives, the will and purpose of God are served.

One of the prominent literary motifs in the story is the repeated references to 'hand'. The word occurs forty-nine times in the narrative and is almost always a symbol of power – specifically of military might. When David first approaches Goliath 'his sling was in his hand' (1 Sam. 17:40). Repeatedly, Saul is portrayed with 'his spear in his hand' (1 Sam. 18:10; 19:9; 22:6).

Just over half the references (twenty-six in all) are to the hand of David. For all his weakness, relative to Goliath and Saul, it is with the actions of David that this story is most concerned. Eleven of these references are to Saul, and the rest to a variety of agents, such as Ahimelech, Abiathar, Nabal and Abigail. Conspicuously not one of these references is to the 'hand of the Lord'.

It is often the way in Scripture that the work of God is hidden. The will and purpose of God are 'providential': they are worked out in and through natural (mostly human) agency. At points in the story, this is explicit: up against Goliath David does not primarily claim, 'I will strike you down and cut off your head', but 'the LORD will deliver you into my hand' (1 Sam. 17:46). The point is important enough for David to reiterate it: 'the LORD does not save by sword and spear; for the battle is the Lord's and he will give you into our hand' (1 Sam. 17:47). David understands, as Goliath plainly does not, that human hands are only ever powerful contingently or derivatively. They have power only in so far as it is given from above. Individuals and institutions that understand this are in a position to work with God; those that fail to understand it are doomed to work (or at least to risk working) against God. So the Lord can promise David (in 1 Samuel 23:40), 'I will give the Philistines into your hand' (1 Sam. 24:10; 26:8, 23). And conversely, when eventually Saul loses his grip on his crown, it will be because 'the Lord has torn the kingdom out of [his] hand' (1 Sam. 28:17).

It is in deference to the providence of God that David is so careful throughout the story not to raise his hand against the

Lord's anointed (1 Sam. 24:6; 24:10–13; 26:9–11, 23), so swift to act against those who do so (2 Sam. 1:14; 2 Samuel 4:11) and so relieved to be restrained (by Abigail or by the Lord?) 'from blood-guilt and from taking vengeance with [his] own hand' (1 Sam. 25:26, 33; compare 2 Samuel 3:28). David's determination not to have 'innocent' blood on his hands (or, for that matter, the determination of the narrator to portray David as free of shedding 'innocent' blood) is the result of his faith in the providence of God. He expresses this faith most fully when, with Saul at his mercy, he states, 'As the LORD lives, the LORD will strike him down, or his day will come to die, or he will go down into battle and perish. The LORD forbid that I should raise my hand against the LORD's anointed' (1 Sam. 26:10–11).

There is, however, an undeniably arbitrary aspect to the providence of God in this story. Like the chief suspect in a murder mystery, David finds himself the beneficiary of the sudden, violent and immensely convenient death of his opponents. This happens not once but repeatedly. When first Saul and Jonathan, then Abner and finally Ishbaal are killed, the narrative goes to great lengths to assert David's innocence (in Abner's case, almost comically). The providence of God is at work. The narrative is even – less predictably – careful to preserve him from violence towards Nabal. Yet there is a cheerful lack of concern (and an absence of squeamishness troubling to a Christian reader; though compare 1 Chronicles 28:3) about his responsibility for the massacre of Amalekites, Geshurites and Gerzites, as well as for the bloody execution of Goliath, the Amalekite messenger, Rechab and Baanah.

There is a similar lack of squeamishness in regard to the deviousness of the 'goodies' in the story. Michal deceives her father into thinking that David is in her bed, when she has helped him to escape (1 Sam. 19:12–17); Jonathan tells an outright lie to his father in order to protect his friend (1 Sam. 20:28–29); David himself first feigns madness before the King of Gath (1 Sam. 21:13) and later cons him shamelessly into regarding him as a loyal ally (1 Sam. 27:8–12) – and also, disastrously, misleads the priest of Nob as to his circumstances (1 Sam. 21:2, 8). In none of these situations is the deceit in any way condemned in the text.

Even the Lord is implicated. The story opens with Samuel pleading that he cannot visit Bethlehem openly without provoking the suspicion and hostility of Saul: 'Then tell him you are only visiting to perform a sacrifice', the Lord advises (1 Sam. 16:2). It's true that Samuel does in fact then arrange a sacrifice in Bethlehem. But the dissimulation remains. What is the Christian reader to make of this – especially the English Christian reader, culturally conditioned to regard anything sly and underhand as cheating?

Two points are worth noting. In the first place, such incidents simply serve to underline the grace of God. It is characteristic of God, in Scripture, to choose and use sinners as his servants; and their sinfulness proves to be no obstacle to the providence of God. The good will and purpose of God are furthered as much in the Bible by human shortcoming as by human saintliness. Secondly, in the story of David's rise deceit is generally practised by the weak. Those who are confronted with opponents more powerful than themselves resort to the only strategies available to them. The narrative seems to accept and even celebrate such incidents as resourceful and cunning. Similar deceitfulness on the part of the more powerful party in a conflict is not celebrated or even tolerated – at least in part two of the story, when David sets out to cover up his adultery by attempting to deceive Uriah the Hittite in 2 Samuel 11.

There is a larger, but equally inscrutable, aspect to the providence of God in the story. It is ultimately a mystery why David is preferred to Saul, why Saul is rejected as king over Israel and David is chosen in his place. Superficially it is simply a question of good and evil. Evil is associated with Saul (1 Sam. 16:14–16; 18:10; 19:9; 20:7–9; 23:9; 24:17), good with David (16:18; 19:4; 24:17–19; 25:15). Indeed the evil plotted by Saul is typically evil 'against David' (1 Sam. 20:9; 23:9). But it is 'an evil spirit from the Lord' (1 Sam. 16:14–15) which troubles Saul, and it is the good 'that [the Lord] (1 Sam. 25:30) has spoken' which determines David's destiny. The narrative does not attempt to explain why David is forgiven his failings (which seem as great as Saul's), when Saul is not. These loose ends in the story serve a purpose: the narrative is pointing beyond itself to a larger world of meaning. Not every question is capable of being answered within the world of this story. This is by no means the only time the Bible asserts the ultimate incomprehensibility of God's providence, from a human point of view.

The story of David's rise: 'A dramatic exposition'

The story of David is sometimes described by scholars as 'the David cycle'. This is a helpful term. There are similar cycles of stories in the Bible, for example about Joseph (in Genesis 37 – 50) and about Elijah (in 1 Kings 17 – 2 Kings 2). A 'cycle' in this sense is a series of connected and continuous narratives about a central figure, in which the component parts nevertheless have their own coherence and integrity – like episodes in a TV drama series (or like individual parts in a 'cycle' of 'Medieval Mystery Plays').

This is how the David story is approached in the chapters that follow. Each 'episode' is treated as a drama in its own right, made up often of several distinct 'scenes'; but with due attention to its place in the unfolding of the narrative as a whole. The narrative sequence and chronology are respected – and interrogated for meaning. (In a similar vein, see my exposition of Genesis 37 – 50 in *Living the Dream: Joseph for Today*, published by Paternoster in 2007.)

Generally speaking, a chapter in this book corresponds to a chapter of the biblical text. In each chapter special effort has been made to follow the contours of the Bible passage, attending carefully to its shape and structure. The text has been read realistic-ally, attending to the literary details in the story. Like a novel this text has to be taken at face value, if its meaning is to be appropriated. There has been a certain amount of reading between the lines of the text, but always with the aim of enabling the narrative to have its full dramatic impact.

To assist in this task, the biblical text (divided up into 'episodes' and 'scenes') is printed together with the commentary. The translation is the 'anglicized' *New Revised Standard Version* – chosen for the balance it achieves between a closeness to the Hebrew text on the one hand; and a fluency of contemporary English on the other.

But what is offered here is also 'a theological exposition' – and to be specific, a Christian theological exposition. This does not mean that in the following chapters every opportunity has been taken to draw parallels between David and Jesus. There is a long tradition of this kind of 'typology' in the church. The aim in this book has been a little different. This book asks what the Word of the Lord might be through this story today, and attempts to answer the question 'in the light of Christ'. What do we learn from this text, in other words, given the nature of God as he has made himself known in Jesus Christ? In the concluding paragraphs of each chapter I have tried to indicate – with the interests of preachers particularly in mind – the lines along which each episode might be applied today.

There is little here in the way of interaction with other interpreters of the text (there are no footnotes) or with current academic scholarship. During the last two hundred years or more, much has been written about the development of this text as part of the biblical canon. It is clear that the text has a history: it took shape over time, almost certainly at first in an oral culture as a spoken tale. It wasn't written in a single sitting by a single author. But the form it now has, it has had for at least two thousand years, and what is offered here is a reading of this text in this form. Readers wishing to pursue questions of source criticism should turn to the standard commentaries. In particular where this book comments on the Hebrew text, its observations are derived from the insights of others.

In my own reading of the story I have been especially helped by the interpretations of Robert Alter, Walter Brueggemann, John Goldingay, Eugene Petersen and Andrew Watson – and readers who know their work will doubtless discern my indebtedness, which I am glad to acknowledge. I would also like to record my heartfelt thanks to the three people who – at some cost to themselves – most encourage me to persist in writing: Cathy, Jonathan and Tom.

This book is dedicated, with gratitude and affection, to the staff, congregation and volunteers of Lichfield Cathedral – and particularly to three outstanding clergy colleagues (Adrian Dorber, Wealands Bell and Chris Liley) with whom it is a pleasure to work.

Pete Wilcox
Lichfield Cathedral
The Feast of the Transfiguration, August 2008

ACT ONE

David in the service
of Saul

1 Samuel 16 – 19

Chapter One
(1 Samuel 16:1–23)

David and Samuel

Introduction

It's a mistake to think that appearances are decisive. Yet most of us are prone to judge others by how they look; and most of us are prone to think (or fear) that we are also judged that way. A whole advertising business is based on this assumption – and an entire capitalist economy rests on it too. Everything from cosmetics to cars, from fitness regimes to fashion accessories is sold on the basis that human beings judge by outward appearances. Nothing is sold, still less advertised, on the basis that the Lord judges by the heart. But of all the sentences in the story of David the most arresting (and in terms of a contemporary western culture, the most necessary) is this: 'human beings look on the outward appearance, but the Lord looks on the heart'.

This first 'episode' in the David cycle is a drama in four scenes. Through the first three, Samuel anoints David as a future king; in the last, David enters the service of Saul, the existing king.

The start of the story of David may seem abrupt: the Lord has rejected Saul from being king over Israel and has provided for himself a king from among the sons of Jesse the Bethlehemite. But the moment has been brewing for some time.

The rejection of Saul is not announced for the first time here. Saul himself has already been told explicitly, twice, by the prophet Samuel, that he has been rejected by the Lord (1 Sam. 15:23, 26). He has known for even longer that his successor has been identified by God (1 Sam. 13:13–14 and 15:28). The language of rejection is particularly loaded. Later in this chapter (verse 7), the Lord will tell Samuel that Eliab, Jesse's oldest son, is not his anointed: 'I have rejected him'. More significantly, much earlier in the story (in 1 Samuel 8), when the elders of Israel first come to Samuel and urge him to give them a king and Samuel responds by praying to the Lord, the Lord tells him, 'Listen to the voice of the people in all that they say to you; for they have not rejected you, but they have rejected me from being king over them' (cf. 1 Sam. 10:19).

So the opening words of 1 Samuel 16 are only a shock in so far as the answer to the question which the Lord puts to Samuel ('How long will you grieve over Saul?') turns out to be 'Not long'. In three simple scenes Samuel responds to the word of the Lord by visiting Bethlehem and anointing David there as king. Saul has done unworthily the task to which he had been called, and David is anointed in his place to do the same task worthily. The surprise is that although it is 'not long' before Samuel ceases to grieve over Saul, it will be many years before the newly anoin-ted David eventually succeeds Saul as king. However, while Saul will continue to be king to the end of the biblical book the church knows as '1 Samuel', it is clear from 1 Samuel 16:1 that the story is now in fact about David.

Scene One (verses 1–3): Saul is rejected

> *1 The Lord said to Samuel, 'How long will you grieve over Saul? I have rejected him from being king over Israel. Fill your horn with oil and set out; I will send you to Jesse the Bethlehemite, for I have provided for myself a king among his sons.' 2 Samuel said, 'How can I go? If Saul hears of it, he will kill me.' And the Lord said, 'Take a heifer with you, and say, "I have come to sacrifice to the Lord."' 3 Invite Jesse to the sacrifice, and I will show you what you shall do; and you shall anoint for me the one whom I name to you.'*

The first speaking part in the drama of David's rise to power belongs to the Lord. It is not always the case in a drama that the first speaker is the most significant. On this occasion, however, there is a theological appropriateness both in the fact that the first two words in the story are 'the Lord' (for although the narrative is indeed a story about David, it is still more a story about God); and that the Lord speaks. The God with whom this narrative is concerned is above all a speaking God, who has a definite will and purpose for his people and wills to make his will known. And yet, even in this narrative it will be a comparative rarity for the Lord to speak to humankind unbidden. Most of what the Lord will say, he will say to those who 'inquire of the Lord'. Here the dialogue with Samuel is initiated by the Lord and not by the prophet.

The second speaking part belongs to Samuel, the prophet of God. Of all the members of the people of God, it is above all Samuel's responsibility to discern the will of God. He is God's first confidante, God's chief servant, the one with the greatest access to the presence and mind of God. But the story begins with the Lord apparently rebuking his servant. Samuel is grieving, because the man he had (at God's prompting) anointed as Israel's first king has proved a failure, and because he (Samuel) cannot see what to do next. He cannot see beyond Saul; and God speaks to move him on. His grief is to stop. Samuel is to fill his horn with oil and to set out for Bethlehem.

Kingship in Israel is not an a-religious matter – government is never an a-religious matter – but of deep concern to God. In the theocracy of Israel, it was God who rejected Saul and now instructs Samuel to anoint a successor (on the rejection of Saul, see chapter 13): 'I have provided for myself a king among Jesse's sons'. It's a striking phrase. The Lord does not say, 'I have provided a king for my people', but 'for myself'. (Literally, in fact, the Hebrew is 'I have seen for myself'. It means 'I have provided for myself', but this is the first instance in the Hebrew of a series of words of 'seeing' and 'looking' which are a feature of this first episode of the drama mostly lost in English translation.) There is an allusion here to the anointing of Saul in 1 Samuel 8. He was anointed 'for us' (i.e. for the elders of Israel, verse 5) and 'for them' (the people of Israel, verse 22). David by contrast is first and foremost and from the beginning to be a king 'for Yahweh'.

The prophet however demurs. 'How can I go?', he asks, 'Saul will discern that something is going on and he'll be furious.' It will emerge that Samuel's fear is well founded. Saul is quick to be angry and perfectly capable of murder; but it is nevertheless a surprise to discover that a prophet of God – who surely understands where power truly lies – is afraid of the king; though later in the story it will be Saul who is afraid of Samuel (1 Sam. 28:20).

It is typical of the grace of God throughout Scripture that Samuel's fear is accommodated. The Lord works with his cautiousness. In fact the Lord invites Samuel to dissemble. He instructs his prophet that he is not to let the real purpose of his visit to Bethlehem be known; rather, Samuel is to say that he has come to make a sacrifice to God. Given the recent history between king and prophet, this was an issue over which Saul was unlikely to challenge Samuel. In chapter 13, Saul had impatiently offered a sacrifice he had been instructed to wait until Samuel was present to offer; and he had been rebuked for it. In chapter 15, Saul had spared from destruction Amalekite animals he had been instructed to destroy utterly; and again he had been rebuked for it. So the Lord provides not only a king for himself, but the perfect excuse for Samuel to visit Bethlehem. But whatever Saul and the elders of Bethlehem may think, Samuel and the reader understand that his primary mission is to anoint one of the sons of Jesse.

Samuel is not the only one to dissemble in this way in the story of David, with the apparent approval (or at least the connivance) of the God of Israel. To an extent puzzling to a Christian reader, David himself and also Jonathan will lie, or evade the truth – usually in speaking to Saul. Yet they remain on the side of truth.

Scene Two (verses 4–5): Samuel and the elders of Bethlehem

> *4 Samuel did what the Lord commanded, and came to Bethlehem. The elders of the city came to meet him trembling, and said, 'Do you come peaceably?' 5 He said, 'Peaceably; I have come to sacrifice to the Lord; sanctify yourselves and come with me to the sacrifice.' And he sanctified Jesse and his sons and invited them to the sacrifice.*

Samuel does as he is told. To do as the Lord commands is a key virtue in this whole story. 'Godliness' consists essentially in seeking God's will, and in discovering it, doing it. So the prophet comes to Bethlehem, to be met by an anxious delegation of elders of the city.

Plainly they are frightened. Even four verses into the narrative, the reader understands that (as with Samuel's own fear hinted at in verse 2) the elders are afraid of the king. The fear of Saul (and Saul's own fear) is a key motif in this story. Perhaps the elders of Bethlehem have heard of the estrangement between Samuel and Saul related in 1 Samuel 15. Do they know of his ruthlessness, and his readiness to slay even his own son (1 Sam. 14:44)? When they ask, 'Do you come in peace?', they mean not 'Are you angry with us and are you here to punish us?', but 'You haven't come here to cause trouble have you? Please tell us you're not going to do anything that will bring Saul's wrath down on us and cause him to punish us'.

But Samuel reassures them: 'It's peace. I've come for a feast, to offer a sacrifice to the Lord.' The narrative specifies without explanation that Samuel 'sanctified Jesse and his sons' and invited them to the feast. The details are sparse. The reader is not told what this 'sanctification' involved, or whether sanctifying them in this way set them apart from the other residents of Bethlehem. There is no indication of how Samuel sought out Jesse, or whether it raised questions in the minds of the elders when he did so. Maybe Jesse was one of the elders of the city who came out to meet the prophet.

Scene Three (verses 6–13): David is anointed

6 When they came, he looked on Eliab and thought, 'Surely the Lord's anointed is now before the Lord.' 7 But the Lord said to Samuel, 'Do not look on his appearance or on the height of his stature, because I have rejected him; for the Lord does not see as mortals see; they look on the outward appearance, but the Lord looks on the heart.' 8 Then Jesse called Abinadab, and made him pass before Samuel. He said, 'Neither has the Lord chosen this one.' 9 Then Jesse made Shammah pass by. And he said, 'Neither has the Lord chosen this one.' 10 Jesse made seven of his sons pass before Samuel, and Samuel said to Jesse, 'The Lord has not chosen any of these.' 11 Samuel said to Jesse, 'Are all your sons here?' And he said, 'There remains yet the youngest, but he is keeping the sheep.' And Samuel said to Jesse, 'Send and bring him; for we will not sit down until he comes here.' 12 He sent and brought him in. Now he was ruddy, and

had beautiful eyes, and was handsome. The Lord said, 'Rise and anoint
him; for this is the one.' 13 Then Samuel took the horn of oil, and anoin-
ted him in the presence of his brothers; and the spirit of the Lord came
mightily upon David from that day forward. Samuel then set out and
went to Ramah.

To anoint a future king was a dangerous task and Samuel was
presumably eager to get the thing over and done with as quickly
as possible. But the will of God is seldom straightforward and
Samuel finds himself detained longer than he would have
wished. When Jesse's sons are presented to him, they are predictably in age order: first the oldest, then the next and so on
(compare 1 Sam. 17:13). If only Jesse had had just two sons!
Instead seven of them are presented in turn to Samuel. The first
three are named.

First up is Eliab. He is a man of particular stature, with real
presence and natural charisma – reminiscent of Saul himself who
'stood head and shoulders above everybody else' (1 Sam. 9:2).
But there was a mismatch between Eliab's outward appearance
and his innermost self. It seems certain to Samuel that this is 'the
Lord's anointed'. (This is a key title in the story. It will prove to
be David's habitual way of referring to Saul: 1 Sam. 24:6, 10; 26:9,
11, 16, 23; 2 Sam. 1:14, 16). But no: Samuel is misled by Eliab's
appearance, and something about him is somehow not pleasing
(or is insufficiently pleasing) to the Lord. The Lord has rejected
him, just as he rejected Saul. Eliab is linked to his king in this
unfortunate respect, as well as in respect of his good looks.

Here the story of David touches on one of the great truths of
the Bible. Human judgments are prone to rest on outward
appearances: this is the world of politics and the playground. By
contrast, the Lord looks on the heart. That is in fact all the Lord
looks at. It is an extraordinarily liberating thing (although a thing
extraordinarily difficult to hold onto) that the Lord simply does
not look on the outward appearance – whether that is taken to
mean a person's physical appearance, or more general attributes,
such as achievements and abilities, status and wealth. Where the
real worth of a human being is concerned, such things are funda-
mentally misleading: the real worth of a human being is the state
of the heart. A contrite and humble heart is a pleasing thing to

God – so pleasing that it outweighs all else. Eliab had many things going for him, but apparently not a heart fit for God's service.

Still less detail is offered as to why Abinadab and Shammah (Jesse's second and third sons) did not make the grade. They are presented in turn to Samuel, and in both cases he is told, 'Neither has the Lord chosen this one.' But they are at least named: by contrast, their four younger brothers are completely anonymous. They are lumped together by the narrator. At the end of the parade of seven sons, Samuel is simply told, 'The Lord has not chosen any of these.'

By this point Jesse seems to have gathered that something significant is happening. Thus when Samuel asks him: 'Are these all your sons?', his reply suggests he cannot believe that David could possibly be the solution to any dilemma that Samuel might have. 'There is still the youngest', he says, 'but he is keeping the sheep'. The 'but' there doesn't just mean 'But he can't come: I need one son to watch the family business'; it means, 'But you needn't bother with him. He's not even worth his place at the feast. As the youngest, he's fit only to be watching the sheep.'

David is the eighth son in a culture where seven means perfection and completion (though compare 1 Chron. 2:13–15). If Eliab, Abinadab, Shammah and the others are wanting, David (in fact unnamed to this point) is surely not going to make good what is lacking. He's just a menial shepherd. He is the youngest in a culture where age is revered. But this is the witness of all Scripture: from the beginning, it has been God's way to confound human convention and to choose and use the marginalized, the outcast and the youth: Abel was younger than Cain, Isaac than Ishmael, Jacob than Esau, Joseph than almost all his brothers. (This is the first of many points at which the story of David echoes the story of Joseph.) David was such a nonentity that it apparently did not even occur to his father to present him to Samuel. It is even surprising that the family of Jesse was considered by God suitable for his service: they were descended not only from Boaz via Obed, but therefore from Ruth the Moabite. But it is characteristic of God 'to choose what is foolish in the world to shame the wise . . . [and] what is the weak in the world to shame the strong. God chose what is low and despised in the

world, things that are not, to reduce to nothing things that are'.
(1 Cor. 1:27–28).

So David is summoned. The meal cannot start until he arrives.
When he does arrive, it is disconcerting (in the light of verse 7) to
find that his physical appearance is in fact attractive: he has good
skin tone and beautiful eyes, and was handsome. For looks then,
David was the match of any of his older brothers. But when the
Lord says to Samuel, 'This is the one. Anoint him', the reader
understands that his heart was also in the right place.

Two things follow in a sacrament: an outward and visible sign
is accompanied by an inward and invisible grace. Samuel anoints
David with oil ('in the presence of his brothers', the text states
rather bluntly), and the Holy Spirit comes on him in power. There
is genuine dramatic force in the fact that the narrative names
David here for the first time. Before this moment, he is just 'him',
'the youngest'. He is 'David' only immediately after the anointing, precisely at the moment the Spirit of God comes upon him.
It is only ever in the presence of God that any of us is most fully
and truly ourselves. (In point of fact Saul's anointing had also
come more or less in the context of a feast and sacrifice – 1 Sam.
9:22 – and had also resulted in him being possessed by the Spirit
of God – 1 Sam. 10:10.)

David's destiny (and indeed behaviour) is decisively shaped
by this outpouring of God's Holy Spirit. The experience was not
momentary or even short-lived: the Holy Spirit came mightily on
David, 'from that day forward'.

What the seven older brothers made of this semi-public affir-
mation the reader is not told; but Eliab's resentment towards him
in the very next chapter (1 Sam. 17:38) may be some kind of a
clue. On the other hand, it was not only kings who were anointed in David's day and there was no inevitable implication for
any witnesses that they had seen the identification of their next
monarch.

Afterwards Samuel left Bethlehem and returned to Ramah.
There was no immediate and dramatic sequel to the anointing.
Rather there followed an interlude, in which the ordinary routines
of life were re-established. It was from Ramah that Samuel had
come to Bethlehem (1 Sam. 15:34), and as soon as his mission was
complete, it was to Ramah that he returned. He returned to his

ordinary duties, and presumably so did David. For Jesse and the elders of Bethlehem there was doubtless some puzzlement about exactly what had transpired. David's anointing was public, but not publicized. There remained something discreet, even secretive, about it. It would be many years before his destiny was fulfilled and David entered into kingship. In fact, it would be some months even before David's destiny developed in any way at all. This is often the way with the will and purpose of God: there is waiting.

Scene Four (verses 14–23): David enters Saul's service

The fourth scene of the drama is carefully connected in the narrative, to the first three. Four strands tie this scene to its predecessors: the first is the reference to 'Jesse the Bethlehemite' (in verses 1 and 18); the second is the reference to 'the sheep' (in verses 11 and 19); the third is reference to 'the spirit of the Lord' (coming mightily on David in verse 13 and by contrast departing from Saul in verse 14); and the fourth is the language of 'seeing/providing' (in verses 1 and 7, and 15–17 and 19). There are two points to the passage: the first is to bring David into relationship with Saul; and the second is to introduce David's musical gift.

14 Now the spirit of the Lord departed from Saul, and an evil spirit from the Lord tormented him. 15 And Saul's servants said to him, 'See now, an evil spirit from God is tormenting you. 16 Let our lord now command the servants who attend you to look for someone who is skilful in playing the lyre; and when the evil spirit from God is upon you, he will play it, and you will feel better.' 17 So Saul said to his servants, 'Provide for me someone who can play well, and bring him to me.' 18 One of the young men answered, 'I have seen a son of Jesse the Bethlehemite who is skilful in playing, a man of valour, a warrior, prudent in speech, and a man of good presence; and the Lord is with him.' 19 So Saul sent messengers to Jesse, and said, 'Send me your son David who is with the sheep.' 20 Jesse took a donkey loaded with bread, a skin of wine, and a kid, and sent them by his son David to Saul. 21 And David came to Saul, and entered his service. Saul loved him greatly, and he became his armour-bearer. 22 Saul sent to Jesse, saying, 'Let David remain in my service, for he has found favour in my sight.' 23 And whenever the evil spirit from God came upon Saul, David took the lyre and played it with his hand, and Saul would be relieved and feel better, and the evil spirit would depart from him.

The opening verse of scene four is puzzling to a Christian reader: in what sense is the Lord said to 'torment' Saul with 'an evil spirit'? It's worth noting that the phrase 'an evil spirit from God' is used both by the narrator in verse 14 and by the king's courtiers in verse 15. Whatever the phrase meant, the narrator was confident enough to attribute it to others, as well as to use it in narration.

In the Hebrew Scriptures generally there are no secondary causes: all that is, is attributed to God. What the Christian church usually calls 'the Old Testament' would rather run the risk of implying that God is the author of hardship and even disaster, than risk suggesting that God is not the author of all things. Thus verse 14 reads as if there are two halves of one process, one negative ('the spirit of the Lord departed from Saul'), and one positive ('an evil spirit afflicted him').

But it may be that 'an evil spirit' is an unduly 'New Testament' rendering of the Hebrew term. It has been suggested that the Hebrew might more appropriately be translated 'bad spirit' or 'bad temper' (or even 'bad mood'): 'bad' rather than 'wicked', because although the Old Testament often attributes bad things to God, it hesitates to attribute wickedness to him; and 'temper' (or even 'mood') rather than 'spirit', because the Old Testament tends not to use the language of demon possession in quite the same way as the New Testament. It tends rather to speak about people being dominated by unhealthy (but entirely natural) emotions such as jealousy or deceit (compare Jdgs. 9:23, where the Lord 'sends an evil spirit between' two parties, apparently sowing discord between them).

When the text states that the evil spirit 'tormented' Saul, the language suggests a deep depression. Saul's servants diagnose the problem and prescribe a treatment: the king is advised to search for a skilful musician – so that when the king is overcome with melancholy, the musician can play soothing music on the lyre and Saul 'will feel better'. Saul accepts the prescription (and by implication presumably the diagnosis) and tells his servants to provide (literally, 'to see') such a person for him (compare verse 1).

The servant recommends 'the son of Jesse the Bethlehemite'. There is profound development in the way David is presented here, such that an interval of time is implied since the end of scene three. The son of Jesse is not just musical ('skilful in playing', verse 18) – although presumably that would have been sufficient in the circumstances. He has a reputation for much more. He is known to be a brave fighter ('a man of valour, a warrior'), a charismatic ('a man of good presence') and a formidable public speaker ('prudent in speech'). He is a prodigy in fact. If that were not enough, he is also blessed: 'the Lord is with him'. These words are a refrain in the story. Again and again we are told, 'the Lord was with David'. (There is another link here with the story of Joseph, Gen. 39:2, 21, etc.; compare also 1 Sam. 18:12, 14, 28; 2 Sam. 5:10.) The term chiefly appears to mean that David enjoyed success, and that this success was a mark of the Lord's favour. But it must have been like a knife-wound to Saul to hear that 'the Lord was with David', when he himself has just been told by Samuel (even if he has not yet come to terms with the full implications) that the Lord had rejected him (1 Sam. 15:26).

Nevertheless Saul summons David – and summons him by name. This is striking because in verse 18 the servant only referred to him as 'a son of Jesse the Bethlehemite'. Until now only the narrator has called David by name. Given the way in which the story will develop, it is at the same time ironic and yet entirely appropriate that Saul should do so here (and in verse 22).

But David is still with the sheep. Saul sends a message to Jesse to request that David be sent to his court. And David is sent (compare 'sent', 'send', 'sent' in verses 19–20), bearing gifts, and entered Saul's service. The gifts he brings are bread, and a skin of wine and a kid – which might have alarmed Saul if he had remembered their association in 1 Samuel 10:3. Yet Saul loved David. This state of affairs was destined not to last long, but has to be taken at face value at this point. Indeed, in terms of the story line it is hugely important. It is possible that David's name meant 'Beloved'. That is his nature in this narrative: he was loved by everybody. At this point, before there are any grounds for jealousy, Saul is simply reacting to what he sees: an infinitely attractive young man – perhaps someone who reminded Saul of himself at an earlier stage. Lots of others in the story will be said to have loved David. But Saul was first.

And sure enough, when David plays his music, Saul finds relief. The Hebrew word for relief [*rawach*] is an unmistakable pun on the Hebrew for evil spirit [*ruach*].

Conclusion

The opening episode of the David story invites the reader to ponder what it is a person 'sees'. In the first three scenes, what Samuel sees in the sons of Jesse and what the Lord sees are too entirely different things. Outward appearances can be deceptive, as Saul and the elders of Bethlehem would one day discover. The sacrifice offered by Samuel was a decoy. The real purpose of his visit lay elsewhere.

In the final scene Saul is urged to see things for what they are. 'See now, an evil spirit is tormenting you', his servants tell him. One of them recalls having seen an exceptional musician and human being – who proves to find favour in Saul's sight. So David, the youngest of the sons of Jesse, the unlikely saviour, finds himself thrust into the presence of the king, as the solution to the king's most pressing problem.

This is David's destiny: to be the solution to the problems, not just of Saul but of Israel. It is not clear whether or not he can see it for himself. It is often easier to see the calling of others than our own.

Chapter Two
(1 Samuel 17:1–58)

David and Goliath

Introduction

What is any one person able to do? Most of us underestimate what is possible for us and need to be reminded not just that 'nothing is impossible with God' (Luke 1:37), but that God works in and through ordinary human beings. At a crucial moment in this episode, Saul (judging by appearances), looks at David and says, 'You are not able to fight against this Philistine . . . you are just a boy.' But there are no 'justs' with God.

The story of David and Goliath has a claim to being the best known of all Bible stories. It is the source of an English idiom (to the extent that it is a cliché for a sports journalist to describe a cup-match as 'a real David and Goliath battle'). Even those who have never read the Bible know the outcome.

If there has been some passage of time since David's anointing (or even since David entered Saul's service as musician – and the text at 1 Samuel 16:18 seems to imply some passage of time between the start of that chapter and the end), it is a sufficiently short period for David's youth still to be a prominent feature. He is still 'just a boy' (verse 33), 'only a youth' (verse 42), 'a young man' (verses 55, 58), 'a stripling' (verse 56). He is probably in his mid or late teens.

The episode is in three scenes: before, during and after the battle. Of these, the battle-scene is by far the longest.

Scene One (verses 1–11): Goliath terrorizes Israel

1 Now the Philistines gathered their armies for battle; they were gathered at Socoh, which belongs to Judah, and encamped between Socoh and Azekah, in Ephes-dammim. 2 Saul and the Israelites gathered and encamped in the valley of Elah, and formed ranks against the Philistines. 3 The Philistines stood on the mountain on one side, and Israel stood on the mountain on the other side, with a valley between them. 4 And there came out from the camp of the Philistines a champion named Goliath, of Gath, whose height was six cubits and a span. 5 He had a helmet of bronze on his head, and he was armoured with a coat of mail; the weight of the coat was five thousand shekels of bronze. 6 He had greaves of bronze on his legs and a javelin of bronze slung between his shoulders. 7 The shaft of his spear was like a weaver's beam, and his spear's head weighed six hundred shekels of iron; and his shield-bearer went before him. 8 He stood and shouted to the ranks of Israel, 'Why have you come out to draw up for battle? Am I not a Philistine, and are you not servants of Saul? Choose a man for yourselves, and let him come down to me. 9 If he is able to fight with me and kill me, then we will be your servants; but if I prevail against him and kill him, then you shall be our servants and serve us.' 10 And the Philistine said, 'Today I defy the ranks of Israel! Give me a man, that we may fight together.' 11 When Saul and all Israel heard these words of the Philistine, they were dismayed and greatly afraid.

It was in order to deal with the Philistine threat that Saul was first appointed (1 Sam. 9:16). But he has signally failed: the Philistines are not just gathered for battle – they are gathered on Israelite territory, 'at Socoh, which belongs to Judah'. They are already an occupying power, and are threatening to overrun Israel.

The two armies are lined up on either side of a valley. But there is no actual fighting. It is a stand off – though it's 'Advantage Philistines': partly because they are already standing on Israelite soil; partly because they are something of a superpower, armed with iron (1 Sam. 13:19–22); and partly because they have a champion.

Goliath is a giant. His height 'was six cubits and a span' (about ten feet tall; or a more readily imagined seven feet tall if an alternative reading – four cubits – is preferred). Even Saul, who stood head and shoulders above his peers, is small by comparison. Everything about Goliath is huge. His equipment is unfeasibly heavy: his coat of chain mail weighed about 5,000 shekels (or 125 pounds) and his spear six hundred shekels (or 15 pounds). His kit is so cumbersome that he requires a shield-bearer to go before him. If there was scarcely a sword or a spear on the Israelite side, Goliath's arsenal must have seemed terrifying.

Goliath established a daily ritual, the effect of which was to traumatize the Israelite army. He would come out in front of the ranks of his own army and shout across the valley at the Israelite forces. He would taunt the enemy, inviting them to choose from among themselves a champion, to take him on in single combat. Rather than committing hundreds or thousands to battle, Goliath suggests that he and one Israelite fight representatively. If Goliath is killed, the Philistines will become slaves to Israel. If Goliath is victorious, the Israelites must surrender to the Philistines and serve them. The challenge would have been frightening had it only been issued once. But it was issued again and again: morning and evening Goliath took his stand for forty days. The Israelites must have grown to feel more cowed as day after day Goliath's challenge went unheeded and they were forced to acknowledge that they did not have his equal among them.

Saul and all Israel were dismayed and greatly afraid. Saul's only responsibility at this point in the story is to resist the Philistines. As the one who stood 'head and shoulders' above his peers, he was better placed than any to take up Goliath's challenge, even (or especially) as he the king. But he is paralyzed by fear. He stands helpless and in need of a saviour.

Scene Two (verses–50a): David slays Goliath

12 Now David was the son of an Ephrathite of Bethlehem in Judah, named Jesse, who had eight sons. In the days of Saul the man was already old and advanced in years. 13 The three eldest sons of Jesse had followed Saul to the battle; the names of his three sons who went to the battle were Eliab the firstborn, and next to him Abinadab, and the third Shammah. 14 David was the youngest; the three eldest followed Saul, 15 but David went back and forth from Saul to feed his father's sheep at Bethlehem.

16 For forty days the Philistine came forward and took his stand, morning and evening.

17 Jesse said to his son David, 'Take for your brothers an ephah of this parched grain and these ten loaves, and carry them quickly to the camp to your brothers; 18 also take these ten cheeses to the commander of their thousand. See how your brothers fare, and bring some token from them.'

19 Now Saul, and they, and all the men of Israel, were in the valley of Elah, fighting with the Philistines. 20 David rose early in the morning, left someone in charge of the sheep, took the provisions, and went as Jesse had commanded him. He came to the encampment as the army was going forth to the battle line, shouting the war cry. 21 Israel and the Philistines drew up for battle, army against army. 22 David left the things in charge of the keeper of the baggage, ran to the ranks, and went and greeted his brothers. 23 As he talked with them, the champion, the Philistine of Gath, Goliath by name, came up out of the ranks of the Philistines, and spoke the same words as before. And David heard him.

24 All the Israelites, when they saw the man, fled from him and were very much afraid. 25 The Israelites said, 'Have you seen this man who has come up? Surely he has come up to defy Israel. The king will greatly enrich the man who kills him, and will give him his daughter and make his family free in Israel.' 26 David said to the men who stood by him, 'What shall be done for the man who kills this Philistine, and takes away the reproach from Israel? For who is this uncircumcised Philistine that he should defy the armies of the living God?' 27 The people answered him in the same way, 'So shall it be done for the man who kills him.'

28 His eldest brother Eliab heard him talking to the men; and Eliab's anger was kindled against David. He said, 'Why have you come down? With whom have you left those few sheep in the wilderness? I know your presumption and the evil of your heart; for you have come down just to see the battle.' 29 David said, 'What have I done now? It was only a question.' 30 He turned away from him towards another and spoke in the same way; and the people answered him again as before.

31 When the words that David spoke were heard, they repeated them before Saul; and he sent for him. 32 David said to Saul, 'Let no one's heart fail because of him; your servant will go and fight with this Philistine.' 33 Saul said to David, 'You are not able to go against this Philistine to fight with him; for you are just a boy, and he has been a warrior from his youth.' 34 But David said to Saul, 'Your servant used to keep sheep for his father; and whenever a lion or a bear came, and took a lamb from the flock, 35 I went after it and struck it down, rescuing the lamb from its mouth; and if it turned against me, I would catch it by the jaw, strike it down, and kill it. 36 Your servant has killed both lions and bears; and this uncircumcised Philistine shall be like one of them, since he has defied the armies of the living God.' 37 David said, 'The Lord, who saved me from the paw of the lion and from the paw of the bear, will save me from the hand of this Philistine.' So Saul said to David, 'Go, and may the Lord be with you!'

38 Saul clothed David with his armour; he put a bronze helmet on his head and clothed him with a coat of mail. 39 David strapped Saul's sword over the armour, and he tried in vain to walk, for he was not used to them. Then David said to Saul, 'I cannot walk with these; for I am not used to them.' So David removed them.

40 Then he took his staff in his hand, and chose five smooth stones from the wadi, and put them in his shepherd's bag, in the pouch; his sling was in his hand, and he drew near to the Philistine. 41 The Philistine came on and drew near to David, with his shield-bearer in front of him. 42 When the Philistine looked and saw David, he disdained him, for he was only a youth, ruddy and handsome in appearance. 43 The Philistine said to David, 'Am I a dog, that you come to me with sticks?' And the Philistine cursed David by his gods. 44 The Philistine said to David, 'Come to me, and I will give your flesh to the birds of the air and to the wild animals of the field.' 45 But David said to the Philistine, 'You come to me with sword and spear and javelin; but I come to you in the name of the Lord of hosts, the God of the armies of Israel, whom you have defied. 46 This very day the Lord will deliver you into my hand, and I will strike you down and cut off your head; and I will give the dead bodies of the Philistine army this very day to the birds of the air and to the wild animals of the earth, so that all the earth may know that there is a God in Israel, 47and that all this assembly may know that the Lord does not save by sword and spear; for the battle is the Lord's and he will give you into our hand.'

*48 When the Philistine drew nearer to meet David, David ran quickly
towards the battle line to meet the Philistine. 49 David put his hand in
his bag, took out a stone, slung it, and struck the Philistine on his forehead; the stone sank into his forehead, and he fell face down on the
ground.*

*50 So David prevailed over the Philistine with a sling and a stone, strik-
ing down the Philistine and killing him; there was no sword in David's
hand. 51 Then David ran and stood over the Philistine; he grasped his
sword, drew it out of its sheath, and killed him; then he cut off his head
with it.*

Scene two begins with the arrival of David on the battlefront. In
a quirk which betrays the complex pre-literary origins of the
story, he is introduced in full, as if for the first time: David is 'the
son of an Ephrathite of Bethlehem in Judah, named Jesse, who
had eight sons', as every reader of chapter 16 knows full well. In
fact this is the only time in the whole narrative (including part
two), when David is identified as an Ephrathite. It is significant
only because Ephrath was a woman – the wife of Caleb. This is
the only matrilineal clan in Israel. It is also the fist time a woman
has been named in this story in which women will go on to play
a significant role.

Jesse's three oldest sons (Eliab, Abinadab and Shammah: precisely those who were named in chapter 16) have joined Saul's
army. David, the youngest, was his father's errand boy: he would
'go back and forth' between Bethlehem and the battlefront. There
may be an acknowledgement in verse 15 of the role assigned to
him at the end of the previous chapter as Saul's armour-bearer
(1 Sam. 16:21), when the text says that David went back and forth
'from Saul' to his father's flocks in Bethlehem.

On one occasion, his father asked him to take provisions for
the older brothers and for their commander, and to report back
on their welfare. (There is a parallel here with Joseph, who in
Genesis 37:14 is despatched by his father Jacob to search out his
brothers 'to see if it is well with [them] . . . and bring word back'.)
Supplying an army with provisions was a haphazard business
and soldiers were dependent not only on their king for food, but
also on their family. Jesse knows that his sons' welfare also

depends on the goodwill of their senior officer and does not neglect the commander of their thousand. David leaves Bethlehem with his load of bread, grain and cheeses. He sets off early in the morning, leaving the sheep in someone else's care. He arrives as a day's martial posturing was getting underway: the Israelite army was lining up, to shout its battle cry at the enemy across the valley. The cry will have provoked as much mirth as fear among the Philistine ranks in the circumstances.

When David arrives in the camp he leaves his provisions 'in charge of the keeper of the baggage'. There is a contrast here with Saul, who has previously been said to hide among the baggage (1 Sam. 10:22).

David found his brothers and, as he chatted with them, out came Goliath. To David's shame and horror, the sight struck fear into the Israelite ranks and they fled. The mental image is striking. Even separated from Goliath by the width of a ravine, the Israelites flee. David is doubly outraged. He is outraged that an uncircumcised Philistine should dare to defy the armies of the living God; and he is outraged that no one has been found on the Israelite side ready to do battle with him.

The first words on David's lips in this narrative are a pair of curiously contrasting questions. On the one hand, he asks, 'Who is this uncircumcised Philistine, that he should defy the armies of the Living God?' That David should see Goliath in relation not just to the Israelite army but to the Living God is encouraging, and typical of one side of his character, which was profoundly spiritual. On the other hand, his first question is, 'What shall be done for the man who kills this Philistine and takes away the reproach of Israel?' That David should also see Goliath in relation not just to Israel but to himself and his destiny is less impressive and typical of another side of his character, which was profoundly self-interested. In answer, David is told that such a man stands to gain great riches from the king, and the hand of his daughter in marriage. Precisely these two aspects of his character come into focus again at the end of the story.

When his oldest brother overhears him, he is not best pleased. Of course, Eliab is implicated in David's disappointment that not one of the Israelites responded to Goliath's challenge. When he asked, 'How dare he defy the armies of the living God?', he could equally have said, 'How dare you permit him to defy the armies of the living God?' A combination of his fear of the Philistine and his embarrassment before his kid brother provokes Eliab's contempt. After weeks of feeling pushed around by someone bigger than himself, he can't resist the opportunity to take it out on someone smaller. He doesn't acknowledge the provisions David has brought with him or his father's need for news. Instead he accuses David of presumption, in forsaking his primary obligation (belittling, in the process, his responsibility to care for 'those few' sheep, or 'that flock-let'; verse 28) in order to taste the excitement of the battlefield. David's response betrays years of such contempt. In the cry of the youngest child the world over, he says, 'What have I done now? It's only a question!' David's treatment by his brothers is reminiscent here of Joseph's. David's brothers, like Joseph's, are unable to acknowledge the destiny of their younger one. It is not uncommon for the youngest in a long line of children to have to fight, in the family home, for a fair share and to develop not just martial instincts but artful cunning. His upbringing – as well as his shepherding – prepared David well for the battle that was to follow.

The skirmish with Eliab is the prelude to the principal battle with the mightier Goliath – but David is victorious here also. He ignores his eldest brother's rebuke and turns to another soldier to ask about the situation for a second time. Indeed, he persists to such an extent that he eventually catches the attention of those around him, and his interest is relayed to the king, who sends for him.

David at once volunteers to take on Goliath himself. When, in verse 32, David speaks first in Saul's presence ('Your servant will go and fight this Philistine'), this was surely a breach of protocol. Saul duly deflects the offer: David is just a boy. But the boy is determined. He is not afraid to fight. He may be young, but he is an experienced warrior: as his father's shepherd, he has had to protect the flock against lions and bears. He has fought these by himself and has struck them down, and the Philistine holds no fear for him. He is plainly confident in himself and his abilities: 'your servant has killed both lions and bears, and this Philistine shall be like one of them, for he has defied the armies of the Living God' (verse 36). The repeated servility ('your servant') fails to mask the assertion of David's own confidence and strength.

But David is also confident in the Lord his God. When Saul makes no response to his initial speech (is he lost for words?), David, apparently having paused for breath, continues: 'The Lord, who saved me from the paw of the lion and the paw of the bear, will save me from the hand of this Philistine.' David has a strong relationship with the Living God, forged in the wilderness, in the challenges of his shepherding. His experience of fighting lions and bears has somehow been done in the presence of God, in the strength and the name of God: those battles were the place where his relationship with God was tried and refined and have fitted him for this day. He does not claim that by his experience and skill he will be victorious in the battle; but that he will be delivered out of danger by the Lord. He calls the Living God now, by his personal name: Yahweh. In so doing, David has placed his own personal experiences of deliverance alongside those national, historical experiences through which the identity of Israel as Yahweh's people was forged. David apparently already glimpses that his encounter with Goliath will be both a personal deliverance and a national one.

David's speech convinces the king – and illustrates what a courtier had noted: that David is 'prudent in speech' (1 Sam. 16:18). 'Go,' says Saul, 'and may the Lord be with you.' Saul is now taking his lead from David, not merely strategically in accepting David's plan to take on Goliath; but spiritually in speaking of Yahweh. David's trust in God has persuaded Saul, and has rekindled Saul's faith in the Lord.

The difficulty is that Saul and the Israelites can only imagine one kind of battle, and that is a kind that is fought on Goliath's terms: hand to hand, face to face, with identical sets of weapons. But in such a battle, all the advantages would lie with Goliath: he is taller and stronger than any of them, and his weapons are bigger and heavier. On those terms, there could be only one winner. They are able to rationalize to themselves that this is not a contest about bravery, simply, because the battle being offered is not to be fought on a level playing field. Saul and the Israelites believe this is a situation in which discretion is the better part of valour.

Only David has the capacity to see things differently. He can see how Goliath's great asset (his enormous size) is also a mortal liability. What Goliath may have in size, he lacks in agility; his size will make him a big target. Conversely, what David lacks in size, he more than makes up in both mental and physical nimbleness.

Seeing that David is determined, Saul seeks to give him two things. First he gives him a royal blessing: 'Go,' he says, 'and may the Lord be with you.' There is an irony here: it is precisely the fact that the Lord is with David (as the reader already knows to be the case) that will ultimately provoke Saul to hate David. Secondly, Saul (still thinking in a blinkered and conventional way about the forthcoming combat) clothes David in his own armour: a helmet and a coat of mail and a heavy sword. Having strapped it all on, David attempts to walk; but he can't. The armour is meant for a much bigger man; but in any case, David has no experience of wearing such a thing. At least, that is how the narrative presents the matter here: it runs a little counter to the notice in 1 Samuel 16:21 that David became Saul's armour bearer. In such a role, David must surely have been used to handling weaponry. But handling Saul's armour, or even wearing his own, is different from wearing Saul's armour. Or this may be another small inconsistency in the narrative. In either case, wisely and boldly, David takes all the armour off again.

This is a profoundly significant moment. It takes courage to take off armour that belongs to the king and has been offered by him. But David knows himself and is confident to be himself. He trusts his own judgment and will stand or fall fighting in the way that is familiar to him, with the weapons he is used to using. David is not refusing to go into battle armed. He is not demonstrating a greater trust in the Living God than he would have shown had he retained Saul's armour. It is rather that he is going into battle as himself: with the weapons he knows. He is a shepherd boy, not a soldier. It is as a shepherd boy, not a soldier, that he has previously overcome lions and bears and has experienced the deliverance of God, and he is confident that that experience can be replicated here. He is not confident of what will happen if he enters the battle in alien dress.

This is an important lesson. Borrowed armour is seldom an asset. Almost always, it is a liability. It is clutter. But when it is offered by someone senior, someone in authority, someone older and more experienced, it can be hard to refuse. Yet each of us is called to be ourselves before God and not the imitators of another. Our calling is not to emulate others, or to please them by adopting their practices; it is to be fully and truly our own selves before God: true to our own identity, true to our own experience and especially our own experience of God. This can be a hard lesson to learn, and one that is often only learned slowly. Rather than dressing up in a borrowed piety, we are each called to be fully and truly ourselves before God.

There is also, however, an implied rebuke of Saul by David here. When David rejects Saul's armour, he is also rejecting Saul and his whole approach to battle and to kingship. David's way is not Saul's way, and the open, public rejection of the king's offer must have been awkward for all involved.

So David takes his staff (for use only as a decoy?), his five smooth stones from the stream, his shepherd's pouch and his sling, and advances towards Goliath. And the Philistine advances towards David, his shield-bearer leading the way. When he sees David, fresh-faced, he laughs in scorn. 'Do you take me for a dog,' he shouts, 'that you come to fight me armed only with sticks?' It is only the staff that Goliath has seen. 'Come any closer, and the birds and animals will feast on your flesh.' Goliath is apparently unaware of the tradition in Israel of warriors skilled in the use of the sling (compare Jdgs. 20:16, 'there were seven hundred picked men who were left-handed: every one could sling a stone at a hair and not miss.' Perhaps David was also left-handed and Goliath had eyes only for the stick in his right hand).

But David does not regard his staff and his sling as his chief weapons. His power for the battle is derived not from these, but from the Lord God. So he makes his famous confession of faith. It is Goliath and his Philistine colleagues who will be fed to the birds and the animals, and not David: 'You come to me with sword and spear and javelin' – David is not naïve; he has seen the weapons at Goliath's disposal and he understands their threat – 'but I come to you in the name of the Lord of hosts, the God of the armies of Israel, whom you have defied. This very day the Lord will deliver you into my hand . . . so that all the earth may know that there is a God in Israel, and that all this assembly' – that is, not only the defiant Philistines, but the faltering Israelites, including his own brothers – 'may know that the Lord does not save by sword and spear; for the battle is the Lord's and he will give you into our hand.'

There are some bloodthirsty declarations made by David here. Such is his confidence that he sets out with precision what he intends to do to Goliath: first 'I will strike you down' and then I will 'cut off your head' – and so it will prove. More than that, 'I will give the dead bodies of the Philistine army this very day to the birds of the air and to the wild animals of the earth'. But these declarations of intent, almost promises, are founded on David's sense of what the Lord will do. First and last he says, 'the Lord will deliver/give you into my/our hand'. David is coming at Goliath not in his own name, but in the name of Israel's God, the one who over centuries has repeatedly delivered Israel against the odds. Perhaps Goliath was aware of this reputation and experienced his first doubts about the outcome of the forthcoming combat. David is also clear what the outcome will be: not just Goliath's death – that is almost incidental. The outcome will be that the earth will know that there is a God in Israel.

So exploiting his own mobility on the one hand and the Philistine's lack of it on the other (he is a huge man, and he is weighed down with pounds and pounds of iron and bronze), and with minimum fuss, David runs at Goliath and strikes him dead with a single stone from his sling. He was never close enough to his opponent for the latter's might to be any great threat. Goliath all along supposed any battle would be fought hand to hand, and under those circumstances he could not envisage defeat. But David refused to fight or even think on those terms.

Having felled the Philistine, David beheads him, just as he had said he would. There is a small ambiguity about the point at which Goliath was killed. Did he die when he was hit by the pebble from David's sling (which seems to be the implication of verse 50: 'so David prevailed over the Philistine with a sling and a stone, striking down the Philistine and killing him; there was no sword in David's hand') or did he die only when he was struck by his own sword immediately before he was decapitated (as verse 51 seems to imply: 'then David ran and stood over the Philistine; he grasped his sword, drew it out of its sheath, and killed him; then he cut off his head with it')?

Scene Three (verses 51b–58): Whose son is he?

51b *When the Philistines saw that their champion was dead, they fled. 52 The troops of Israel and Judah rose up with a shout and pursued the Philistines as far as Gath and the gates of Ekron, so that the wounded Philistines fell on the way from Shaaraim as far as Gath and Ekron. 53 The Israelites came back from chasing the Philistines, and they plundered their camp. 54 David took the head of the Philistine and brought it to Jerusalem; but he put his armour in his tent.*

55 When Saul saw David go out against the Philistine, he said to Abner, the commander of the army, 'Abner, whose son is this young man?' Abner said, 'As your soul lives, O king, I do not know.' 56 The king said, 'Inquire whose son the stripling is.' 57 On David's return from killing the Philistine, Abner took him and brought him before Saul, with the head of the Philistine in his hand. 58 Saul said to him, 'Whose son are you, young man?' And David answered, 'I am the son of your servant Jesse the Bethlehemite.'

There are three puzzles in this final scene. The first relates to the fate of the Philistines. Goliath's great challenge had been that he and an Israelite should fight one against one to decide the destinies of their respective armies. The losing side was to be enslaved by the winning one. But this seems to have been forgotten in the aftermath of Goliath's death. Instead, the Philistines flee and the Israelites pursue and plunder them. Had they taken to heart David's words in verse 46?

The second puzzle relates to Jerusalem. Jerusalem will, at the very end of this story, become 'the city of David', Zion. At this point however it has played barely any part, and it is not clear why David should have taken Goliath's head (surely the greatest trophy of the day) there, when he was content to keep the rest of the spoils in his tent (what tent?). It may be an anachronistic reference, referring to a later time.

The final puzzle relates to the dialogue at the very end of the passage, between Saul and his chief of staff, Abner. Again we are confronted by the confused pre-textual history of this narrative. As a written story, it is odd that after David has served for some time as Saul's remedial musician and armour bearer (and this after a formal request from Saul to David's father Jesse in 1 Sam. 16:22) neither Saul nor Abner should recognize him. The obvious explanation is that the stories now woven into a sequence in chapters 16 and 17 first existed independently, and that little effort has been made, in weaving them together, to harmonize them. Given the literary carefulness exhibited in many aspects of the text, it should not be supposed that these apparent inconsistencies went un-noticed by the editor whose hand has shaped the narrative as we know it. Rather, the editor was content to leave these tensions in the text, and the reader should not be too quick to smooth over them or to stumble at them. For the narrator, any incongruity in setting these stories side by side is more than outweighed by the advantage of having two windows onto David at the outset of his story. The narrator has chosen to introduce David as it were in stereo.

There is something important here, in terms of Saul's inability to grasp who David is, which is heightened by the reader's ready recollection of chapter 16. At the end of this episode, Saul is left asking three times over (in verses 55, 56 and 58), 'Whose son is this? In terms of the narrative this is a crucial question. But Saul can't get a satisfactory answer, except from David himself. And even then there is something of a mystery still. When in the closing words of the chapter David says to Saul, 'I am the son of Jesse the Bethlehemite', it is the fourth time he has been introduced to the reader in this way (1 Sam. 16:1, 18; 17:12), and at least the second time he has been introduced in these terms to Saul (1 Sam. 16:18). He does not say, 'I am David.' There is a subtle but sustained reticence about David's name in the presence of Saul. As often as not he is only 'the son of Jesse'. This is as much as Saul can cope with; 'David' is too much of a threat. The apparent conflict in the narrative over David's origins, in other words, reflects Saul's conflicted attitude to 'the son of Jesse'. Similarly, the lack of any editorial reconciliation of divergent narratives is appropriate, given Saul's inability to reconcile himself to David's identity and to all that the presence of 'the son of Jesse' means for the future of his kingdom.

Conclusion

For such a youth, David offers a refreshing example in this episode – not just of faith, but of holiness. His trust in God to deliver him is inspiring. But such faith is often given to the young. What is less common in a teenager is the combination of humility with self-assurance which David manifests. He not only has the courage to go into battle against Goliath, but the wisdom to do so on his own terms. That step involves confounding not only the expectations of his obvious foe, but also those of his apparent ally. To be true to oneself, when to do so means refusing to conform to the expectations of those who are on your side, is a mark of either of naivety or of exceptional maturity.

To combine faith with holiness, courage with wisdom, humility with self-assurance, so that it is possible not just to discern what battles to fight but also what weapons to use, and so to have that integrity which refuses to conform to the expectations of others – this is something to which institutions (the church included), as well as individuals, can aspire.

Chapter Three
(1 Samuel 18:1–30)

David and Saul

Introduction

Popular people attract enemies. Those who are loved by many will be resented by those of us who feel ourselves unloved. But it is not possible to control the way that others see us and react to us. In this third episode of the story, David finds what others have also experienced: that when we encounter the hostility of others, the love and merciful acceptance of God is a sure refuge.

The third episode in David's story falls into four scenes, although in fact the chapter break is not obviously the start of a new scene. At the start of this episode, David is still on the battlefield: Goliath's blood is barely dry and Saul's bewildered query to Abner about the identity of the Philistine's killer still hangs in the air. At the end of the very first episode in the story, Saul was said to have loved David greatly (1 Sam. 16:21). Now in the course of this third episode, first Saul's son Jonathan (verses 1, 3), then 'all Israel and Judah' (verse 16), then Saul's daughter Michal (verses 20, 28) and finally 'all Saul's servants' (verse 22) are also said to love him. Saul, meanwhile, declines from love to anger (verse 8) to jealousy (verse 9), to fear (verse 12), to awe (verse 15) to still greater fear (verse 29) and ultimately to outright, implacable enmity (verse 29). David meanwhile simply grew in popularity (verses 5) and success (verses 5, 14, 15, 30) – because the Lord was with him (verses 12, 14, 28).

Scene One (verses 1–5): Jonathan loved David as his own soul

1 When David had finished speaking to Saul, the soul of Jonathan was bound to the soul of David, and Jonathan loved him as his own soul. 2 Saul took him that day and would not let him return to his father's house. 3 Then Jonathan made a covenant with David, because he loved him as his own soul. 4 Jonathan stripped himself of the robe that he was wearing, and gave it to David, and his armour, and even his sword and his bow and his belt. 5 David went out and was successful wherever Saul sent him; as a result, Saul set him over the army. And all the people, even the servants of Saul, approved.

There has been no reference to Jonathan since the start of the David story. If he was present in episode one, when David became Saul's armour bearer (1 Sam. 16:21) and when he played his lyre to soothe Saul's dark moods, it was as a silent bystander. Clearly he was present in episode two (1 Sam. 17), to see David slay Goliath – but again, as a silent onlooker. But he has seen enough to ensure that his relationship with David will be the most precious of his life.

Two things are clear from the moment Jonathan is introduced. The first is that he is an exceptionally sensitive man. The second is that his relationship with David was not fully mutual.

In relation to the first point, the language in verse 1 is striking: Jonathan is a profoundly spiritual man, emotionally literate and with a special capacity for loving friendship. He may not have known David long and he may not know him well, but his soul is bound to David. Twice we are told, presumably for emphasis, that Jonathan loved David 'as his own soul'. The language of binding and of 'soul' (better, 'innermost self' or 'whole person' – this is a Hebrew word, after all, and not a technical term from Greek philosophy) is unusual in Scripture, especially as a way of describing the feelings of one man for another. In a culture like ours, where notions of friendship are so impoverished, there is a lot to learn from Jonathan's example: from the extreme commitment implied, from the utter identification of one's own interests with those of another, and from the sense of connection and belonging. (On the relevance of the friendship between Jonathan and David to the contemporary debate in the church over homosexuality, see chapter 5, page 59.) Yet for much of the story the relationship between Jonathan and David is not reciprocal. It is Jonathan who loves David 'as his own soul', not vice versa. Indeed at this point in the story, many people are said to love David; but he is not said to love anyone. At this point in the story for all his courage and wisdom, humility and self-awareness, David has not learnt to love.

Jonathan was himself a brave warrior (1 Sam. 14:6–15). He had himself trusted in God for deliverance (1 Sam. 14:6, compare 17:37) and had used the same term of contempt for the Philistines (1 Sam. 14:6, compare 17:36) as David had recently done. Presumably it had occurred to him that he himself might go into battle against Goliath. Yet he had not gone. It is also worth noting that Jonathan's relationship with his father was already strained, before David ever appeared on the scene. In 1 Samuel 14 Jonathan had defied Saul and had publicly criticized him (verse 28). It may be then that in the opening verses of this chapter, Jonathan is in reaction against his father. His feelings are certainly feelings for David; but they may also feelings against Saul. Perhaps this is why Saul's immediate reaction is to take David that day and not to 'let him return to his father's house'. Here is the first hint that, out of jealousy, Saul wants David where he can see him and at least attempt to control him.

But Jonathan goes further. The first verse of the chapter merely relates Jonathan's private, inner feelings for David. In verse 3 he acts. Jonathan makes a covenant with David. Usually in Scripture, the initiative in covenant-making is significant. It is not a mutual act: a more powerful, senior partner makes a covenant with another. The covenant between God and Israel is made by God with Israel. It is not made by God and Israel. Here it is Jonathan who makes a covenant with David, not the other way around. He may be older; he certainly has the greater social status.

Throughout 1 Samuel Jonathan is portrayed as an impetuous risk taker. Unlike David he is not a person given to calculation, but is wholeheartedly spontaneous. The gesture described in verse 4 is typically extravagant: he strips off his clothes and his weapons and gives them to David – presumably leaving himself at least partially bare and vulnerable. For Christian readers there is something equivalent here to the action of the woman who anointed Jesus with her tears and dried them with her hair (Lk. 7:36–50) and to Jesus himself, stripping off his clothing to wash the feet of his disciples (Jn. 13:1–5).

What Jonathan gave David was in fact his armour. In the previous chapter David had rejected Saul's. Whether physically, spiritually or emotionally, Jonathan's armour is apparently a better fit. Some political concession might be symbolized here: it is possible that what Jonathan divested and handed to David was his right and aspiration to succeed his father as king. He certainly divests himself of his cloak and hands it to David – and Saul's cloak is apparently a symbol of his kingship (1 Sam. 24:5). It may be that the covenant established here was a political one as well as a personal one

Thus when David goes out in battle in verse 5, the implication seems to be that he does so armed with all that Jonathan (as well as Saul) has given him. Saul has given him credibility and authority. Jonathan has given him a robe, a belt, armour, a sword and a bow – and love. The result is that David is empowered, and even Saul's servants approve.

Scene Two (verses 6–9): Saul eyed David from that day on

6 As they were coming home, when David returned from killing the Philistine, the women came out of all the towns of Israel, singing and dancing, to meet King Saul, with tambourines, with songs of joy, and with musical instruments. 7 And the women sang to one another as they made merry,
> *'Saul has killed his thousands,*
> *and David his tens of thousands.'*
8 Saul was very angry, for this saying displeased him. He said, 'They have ascribed to David tens of thousands, and to me they have ascribed thousands; what more can he have but the kingdom?' 9 So Saul eyed David from that day on.

There are not many leaders who cope easily with being compared directly and to their relative disadvantage with a member of their own team. Most of us are at our least secure, and are least able to cope with competition and with rivals (especially those who are younger, newer or junior), when we have lost our spiritual bearings and have come adrift in relation to God. Conversely, most of us are at our most secure and are most able to cope with the success of others (even when it eclipses our own), when our relationship with God is strong.

As David returns from killing Philistines (or 'killing the Philistine': he may have been out on other successful mission by now, but it is still the slaying of Goliath that has captured the popular imagination), the women come out in force. They come out to meet King Saul; but when they come out, while their song is a celebration of the king, it is even more a celebration of David. Saul latches at once not just onto the comparison, but onto the implication: 'They have ascribed to David tens of thousands, and to me they have ascribed thousands; what more can he have but the kingdom?' At some deep level Saul seems to intuit what God's purpose for the future of Israel might be. If he had heard any hint of what happened at Bethlehem, how Samuel had anointed a son of Jesse there, there is no suggestion of it in the text. The reader understands that Saul is right – not because David is an ambitious, determined rival to Saul, but because of the will of God. It will be a long time (1 Sam. 24:20, 30:31) before Saul acknowledges what he now suspects – but the suspicion is now there, and informs the way in which Saul relates to David from this point onwards: David is a rival, destined to inherit Saul's throne. Saul now perceives David as a threat, not an ally; and his black moods are now provoked by David, not soothed by him. He 'eyes' David, watching him jealously.

Scene Three (verses 10–16): David had success

10 The next day an evil spirit from God rushed upon Saul, and he raved within his house, while David was playing the lyre, as he did day by day. Saul had his spear in his hand; 11 and Saul threw the spear, for he thought, 'I will pin David to the wall.' But David eluded him twice.
12 Saul was afraid of David, because the Lord was with him but had departed from Saul. 13 So Saul removed him from his presence, and made him a commander of a thousand; and David marched out and came in,

leading the army. 14 David had success in all his undertakings; for the
Lord was with him. 15 When Saul saw that he had great success, he stood
in awe of him. 16 But all Israel and Judah loved David; for it was he who
marched out and came in leading them.

The following scene unfolds 'on the next day'. On the assumption that verse 5 is proleptic (i.e., it refers to campaigns fought and won by David in the weeks, months and possibly years after he was given Jonathan's armour), it is now only the day after the slaying of Goliath. David has apparently reverted from his role as warrior to his role as musician. As usual David is playing his lyre. But to no avail. An evil spirit from God has rushed on Saul and has provoked him to rave (the same word as the one used to describe Saul's frenzy among the prophets in 1 Sam. 10:11, 12; 19:24).

But now there is a new departure. Such is Saul's sense of insecurity and vulnerability to David that he flings the spear which he holds habitually in his hand, in an attempt to pin David to the wall. This is the first of six attempts that Saul will make on David's life, before David flees from Saul's presence. Three times he throws a spear at him (1 Sam. 18:11 twice; 19:10); twice he makes battle plans which he hopes will result in David's death (1 Sam. 18:17, 21); and once he sends a killing squad to assassinate his rival (1 Sam. 19:11). At first (verse 11) Saul's attempts to kill David are impetuous and impulsive. Soon however he begins to plot. It is clear that, by verse 21, Saul has resorted to deceit. But it may be that the first sign of Machiavellian art comes in verse 13, when Saul removes him from his presence and makes him 'the commander of a thousand'. By doing so, Saul was presumably hoping, or at least not caring, that David might fall on the field of battle.

Given the direction in which the spears are flying, one might have thought that it would be David who is afraid of Saul. But no: Saul is afraid of David. Saul's escalating fear (verse 12) is a recurring theme in this narrative. There is a good reason for it, of course: Saul has discerned that the Lord is with David and has departed from himself. This means that Saul's attempts at killing David are doomed. For as long as the Lord is with David, there is no possible outcome but David's success. Now that the

Lord has departed from Saul, his ultimate failure is equally inevitable.

Saul's reaction is shocking partly because it is provoked not by David's sin, but by his goodness. David has benefited Saul professionally by killing Goliath, and personally by providing a balm (if not quite a healing) for his black depression and insane rages. But this also is a fact of life: goodness will sometimes provoke evil. Opposition is at its most disconcerting when we are doing good. In fact, however, it isn't quite David's acts which have provoked Saul. It is other people's response to David's acts. Saul is jealous not just of David's success, but of his popularity (verse 16). It is often the reaction of a third party which provokes jealousy.

Scene Four (verses 17–30): David and Saul's daughters

17 Then Saul said to David, 'Here is my elder daughter Merab; I will give her to you as a wife; only be valiant for me and fight the Lord's battles.' For Saul thought, 'I will not raise a hand against him; let the Philistines deal with him.' 18 David said to Saul, 'Who am I and who are my kinsfolk, my father's family in Israel, that I should be son-in-law to the king?' 19 But at the time when Saul's daughter Merab should have been given to David, she was given to Adriel the Meholathite as a wife.

20 Now Saul's daughter Michal loved David. Saul was told, and the thing pleased him. 21 Saul thought, 'Let me give her to him that she may be a snare for him and that the hand of the Philistines may be against him.' Therefore Saul said to David a second time, 'You shall now be my son-in-law.' 22 Saul commanded his servants, 'Speak to David in private and say, "See, the king is delighted with you, and all his servants love you; now then, become the king's son-in-law."' 23 So Saul's servants reported these words to David in private. And David said, 'Does it seem to you a little thing to become the king's son-in-law, seeing that I am a poor man and of no repute?' 24 The servants of Saul told him, 'This is what David said.' 25 Then Saul said, 'Thus shall you say to David, "The king desires no marriage present except a hundred foreskins of the Philistines, that he may be avenged on the king's enemies."' Now Saul planned to make David fall by the hand of the Philistines. 26 When his servants told David these words, David was well pleased to be the king's son-in-law. Before the time had expired, 27 David rose and went, along with his men, and killed two hundred of the Philistines; and David brought their foreskins, which were given in full number to the king, that he might become the king's son-in-law. Saul gave him his daughter Michal as a wife. 28 But when Saul realized that the Lord was with David, and that Saul's daughter Michal loved him, 29 Saul was still more afraid of David. So Saul was David's enemy from that time forward.

30 Then the commanders of the Philistines came out to battle; and as often as they came out, David had more success than all the servants of Saul, so that his fame became very great.

By the opening verse of this final scene in this episode, Saul's impetuosity in relation to David has given way to something more calculating. Where his hostility to David was previously impulsive and sporadic, it has now hardened into something more scheming and settled.

Given that 'all Israel and Judah' loves David, Saul is in a quandary. On the one hand he wants David eliminated. On the other hand he wants to appear generous and well-disposed towards him. In order to curry favour with his people, who see David as their saviour (verse 16), Saul offers David the hand of his eldest daughter Merab in marriage. Publicly, the only condition is that David will continue in Saul's service: 'Be valiant for me,' the king pleads, 'and fight the Lord's battles.' But privately, Saul has conceived a sinister purpose. His hope is that in his valour, in his fighting of the Lord's battles, David will die at the hand of the Philistines (while Saul himself will apparently be innocent of any harmful intent: 'I will not raise a hand against him', verse 17). Later in the narrative, the tables are turned: in 1 Samuel 24:6 and 26:9 it will be David who is anxious not to raise his hand against Saul. But whereas David seems genuinely concerned that no harm should come to Saul, here Saul's concern seems somehow to be a technicality only. He wants David dead: he just doesn't wish to be implicated. The name of the Lord may be on Saul's lips, but the Lord's ways are not in his heart. He has no real interest in the Lord's will.

As it turns out, Saul's offer of his daughter's hand is not made in good faith. When it is made, David responds with appropriate modesty. There is nothing in his response to offend Saul, unless it is his unrelenting rightness: 'Who am I?,' David asks, 'and who are my relatives and what is my father's family, that I should become the king's son in law?' (verse 18). But when the time comes (verse 19), Merab is given to another.

To what extent this was a disappointment to David, or even a humiliation, the reader is not told. It may be that Saul was the humiliated one, at having to renege on a public promise. Perhaps the speed with which the narrative moves on to the sequel in verse 20, suggests that Saul was sufficiently embarrassed at the course of events to be relieved when it transpires that his younger daughter Michal loves David. The king takes David for a son-in-law after all.

But again Saul's motives are dubious. It may have pleased him to know that his daughter is in love with David. But it is not her happiness that pleases him, or the opportunity to honour David. It is the opportunity to engineer David's death. He uses his daughter, in the hope that she 'will be a snare for him and that the hand of the Philistines may be against him'. Saul wants David dead and he hopes that the Philistines will do the dirty work for him. In the light of much later events, the reader is bound to wonder if David recognized and subsequently adopted the strategy: when he wanted Uriah the Hittite killed, in 2 Samuel 11:14, he sought to effect his death on the battlefield in a very similar way. The only difference would be that in this respect, as in every other, David would succeed where Saul was doomed to fail.

When Michal is said to love David in verses 20 and 28, it is the only time in the entire Bible that a woman is explicitly said to love a man (as Jacob, for example, is said to have loved Rachel in Gen. 29:20, or Samson Delilah in Jdgs. 16; though compare Song 5:8). The statement is remarkable, given the lack of status enjoyed by women at this time. But Michal is not alone. All Saul's servants love David. Saul evidently does not love him any longer – but he is prepared to exploit the fact others do.

If there was an element of false modesty when David responded to the prospect of marrying Merab in verse 18, there is less when he responds to the prospect of marrying Michal in verse 23. This time David protests not generally and formally – but quite specifically about his poverty. His protestation is relayed to the king, who therefore stipulates a bride-price to be paid in kind, not in cash. David is assured that the king desires no dowry 'except a hundred foreskins of the Philistines'. But Saul's intention – that David should die in the attempt – is mocked: David voluntarily doubles the requirement (though compare 2 Sam. 3:14), and presents the king with not one hundred but two hundred Philistine foreskins 'before the time had expired'.

This is too much for Saul to bear. Not only is the Lord with David, but his own daughter is besotted with him. David's success (everything he touches is apparently turning to gold) provokes Saul's fear, and his enmity from that time forward. If, at the start of the chapter, there was something lopsided about Jonathan's love for David, there is something equally uneven about Saul's fear of him and hatred for him. If the narrator was careful to state that it was Jonathan who loved David, rather than David who loved Jonathan or David and Jonathan who loved each other, so here the narrator is careful to state that it is Saul who is the enemy of David. The relationship is not mutual.

Conclusion

By the end of the chapter, it is clear what it means for David, that the Lord is with him. Where Saul intended to rid himself of David, he has only succeeded in promoting him into his own household. David, as the son in law of the king, is a credible future sovereign in a way that, as an interloper-shepherdboy (albeit also a popular warrior too) he was not. Because the Lord is with David, his star is rising inexorably. And because the Lord has departed from Saul, all his actions are rebounding on him. He cannot win, just as David cannot lose. He must shrink, as David grows in stature; but whereas John the Baptist would later embrace a similar relationship nobly as his vocation (Jn. 3.30), for Saul it represents an insurmountable challenge.

Chapter Four
(1 Samuel 19:1–2)

David leaves Saul

Introduction

It is distressing to watch a human life unravel, as the reader of this episode must. Saul has found something about David (his potential? his faith? his sheer youthfulness?) impossible to cope with and has fallen into a terminal decline. One of the signs of this is his murderous intent towards David. Even in the previous episode, there was some development: his first attempts to kill David (when he twice threw a spear at him) were apparently impulsive; his later attempts (when he first sent him out into battle as the commander of a thousand, then urged him to 'fight the Lord's battles', and finally demanded a dowry for Michal which involved an almost suicidal risk on David's part) were more calculating. But they were nevertheless private. There was no conspiracy, no public policy. In this episode (which falls into four scenes), that changes. He is still capable of acting impulsively, and of flinging his spear at his enemy; but he is now also capable of drawing others into his murderous schemes. But David inevitably escapes, and in the fourth and final scene of this episode, the extent of Saul's decline is made clear.

In one sense Saul's kingship had ended before David ever arrived on the scene. The Lord's rejection of him is explicit in 1 Samuel 15; and David doesn't enter the story until chapter 16. In another sense, Saul's kingship will only end with his death in chapter 31. But in a significant literary sense, this episode marks an end: the end of Saul's moral authority as king, the end of his spiritual capacity. For as a young man, before he became king, Saul had once fallen into a prophetic frenzy, such that people had asked, in a tone full of wonder at future possibilities, 'Is Saul also among the prophets?' (1 Sam. 10:12). Now, in scene four, he again falls into a prophetic frenzy. The same question is again asked, but there was surely a note of cynicism and disillusion among those who were asking on this occasion, 'Is Saul also among the prophets?' (verse 24, the final verse of this episode).

Scene One (verses 1–7): Jonathan mediates for David with Saul

1 Saul spoke to his son Jonathan and to all his servants about killing David. But Saul's son Jonathan took great delight in David. 2 Jonathan told David, 'My father Saul is trying to kill you; therefore be on guard tomorrow morning; stay in a secret place and hide yourself. 3 I will go out and stand beside my father in the field where you are, and I will speak to my father about you; if I learn anything I will tell you.' 4 Jonathan spoke well of David to his father Saul, saying to him, 'The king should not sin against his servant David, because he has not sinned against you, and because his deeds have been of good service to you; 5 for he took his life in his hand when he attacked the Philistine, and the Lord brought about a great victory for all Israel. You saw it, and rejoiced; why then will you sin against an innocent person by killing David without cause?' 6 Saul heeded the voice of Jonathan; Saul swore, 'As the Lord lives, he shall not be put to death.' 7 So Jonathan called David and related all these things to him. Jonathan then brought David to Saul, and he was in his presence as before.

Towards the end of the previous episode, what had initially been a sporadic hostility towards David on Saul's part had become a settled enmity. Here for the first time Saul speaks openly about his intention to kill David. He speaks about it to 'all his servants', but also to Jonathan. In taking his son into his confidence in this way, Saul is presumably either oblivious to the fact that Jonathan 'took great delight in David' (verse 1; is there anyone who loves David more at this point?); or he is fully aware of it, and is hoping to force Jonathan to take sides and to choose kinship above any emotional tie.

Either way it was a miscalculation on Saul's part. Jonathan remains committed to his friend and takes two courses of action.

First he speaks to David: he warns him of the danger in which he stands, advises him to escape at least for a time, and promises to speak on his behalf to Saul and to report back. The fact that Jonathan speaks first to David and only then to his father is an indication of his priorities. But secondly, he does speak to Saul. He not only seeks to establish Saul's intentions (although in the light of verse 1 these must have been pretty clear); he seeks to dissuade him from the course on which he is bent. True, he speaks with deference, addressing his father as 'the king'. But he dares to challenge him all the same. Jonathan speaks of sin. He stresses that David has not wronged Saul; more positively, he argues that that David's actions have been a real help to Saul. Jonathan reminds his father that David had risked his life in attacking Goliath, and that Saul himself had seen it and rejoiced. He further asserts that in David's defeat of the Philistine champion, 'the Lord brought about a great victory for all Israel'. In terms of Jonathan's appeal to his father, this is a crucial step: he confronts Saul with a theological interpretation of events with which Saul cannot possibly agree and remain committed to harming David. (There is an allusion here to Saul's own magnanimous words in 1 Sam. 11:13, following his own victory against the Ammonites. Jonathan – and the reader – knows that David is 'the new Saul'.)

When Jonathan has made his case, Saul (temporarily open to reason) is persuaded. Hearing his son invoke the name of the Lord, Saul follows suit: 'As the Lord lives', he swears, '[David] shall not be put to death.'

It had been Jonathan's stated aim to have this conversation with his father, 'in the field where you are', presumably so that David can overhear it. Perhaps that was not possible, for Jonathan now summons his friend 'and relates all these things to him', and then acts as an escort to ensure David's safe restoration to court, where David was in Saul's presence 'as before' (verse 7). But the reference to the field in verse 3 hints at what is to come (1 Sam. 20:11).

Scene Two (verses 8–10): David flees from Saul

> *8 Again there was war, and David went out to fight the Philistines. He launched a heavy attack on them, so that they fled before him. 9 Then an*

evil spirit from the Lord came upon Saul, as he sat in his house with his spear in his hand, while David was playing music. 10 Saul sought to pin David to the wall with the spear; but he eluded Saul, so that he struck the spear into the wall. David fled and escaped that night.

In chapter 16, David is introduced first as shepherd boy (verses 6–13), then as a musician (verses 14–23). In chapter 17, he is still a shepherd boy (verses 15 and 28), but is now also a warrior (especially verses 50–54). In chapter 18, his shepherd role (already in fact expressed in the past tense in 1 Samuel 17:34) falls away, and his identity is consolidated as a musician (verse 10) and a warrior (verses 6–9, 13–16, 30). When David is here said in verse 9 to be playing music, it is the last such reference in the narrative. From now on, David's identity is not as a shepherd or as a musician, but exclusively as a warrior and a future king.

Scene two is essentially a pair of attackings and fleeings. First David attacks the Philistines heavily, and they flee before him. But this apparently inflames Saul's jealousy once again, so that he attacks David, who flees. There is an ambiguity here: on the one hand, an external threat to Saul's throne is reduced; on the other hand, an internal threat is increased. So the word 'then' at the beginning of verse 9 has psychological as well as chronological force: it wasn't just after David had routed the Philistines that Saul made this further desperate attempt on his life, but because he had done so. Once again, an evil spirit from the Lord (compare 1 Sam. 16:14) came upon Saul, who for the last time, impulsively flings his spear at David to kill him.

As in the previous chapter, Saul has a spear in his hand; David is playing music with his hand. Such repetitions are significant to the narrative. True, they may hint at an editorial process underlying the text: they may be 'doublets' which betray the prior existence of two, once independent, sources for the story. But dramatically, the repetitions allow the narrator to highlight the nature of Saul's illness: his mood swings come and go, like much mental illness or the kind of compulsive behaviour typified by domestic violence. Now Saul is ready to deal peaceably with David (verse 6), now he is overwhelmed with violent impulses he cannot control (verse 10). Dramatically, the repetitions also allow the narrator to stress development: thus in this case David once again eludes danger; but whereas previously he had stayed at court (1 Sam. 18:11), now he flees. The variation moves the story forward.

Scene Three (verses 11–17): David escapes from Saul

11 Saul sent messengers to David's house to keep watch over him, planning to kill him in the morning. David's wife Michal told him, 'If you do not save your life tonight, tomorrow you will be killed.' 12 So Michal let David down through the window; he fled away and escaped. 13 Michal took an idol and laid it on the bed; she put a net of goats' hair on its head, and covered it with the clothes. 14 When Saul sent messengers to take David, she said, 'He is sick.' 15 Then Saul sent the messengers to see David for themselves. He said, 'Bring him up to me in the bed, that I may kill him.' 16 When the messengers came in, the idol was in the bed, with the covering of goats' hair on its head. 17 Saul said to Michal, 'Why have you deceived me like this, and let my enemy go, so that he has escaped?' Michal answered Saul, 'He said to me, "Let me go; why should I kill you?" '

Just as David's actions provide evidence of development, so do the actions of Saul and his family. In the previous episode, there is escalation in Saul's attitude towards David, which moves from anger and jealousy, to fear and enmity. At the start of this episode, Saul speaks about his intention to kill David with his son and his servants – but his son intervenes. Now Saul goes a step further: he enlists the active collaboration of others in his plan to kill David – but his daughter intervenes. But where Jonathan confronted Saul directly, Michal is more devious and circumvents her father. When, in verse 12, the text states that David 'fled away and escaped', there is a repetition of verse 10.

In verse 11 Michal is for the first time defined as 'David's wife'. In 1 Samuel 18:28, though the text has just reported her marriage to David, she remains 'Saul's daughter'. Even then her allegiance to David was being emphasized: she 'loved him'. Here that allegiance is demonstrated: Michal takes David's side against her father. First she warns him that his life is in danger (verse 11); then she helps him escape (verse 12); and finally she covers for him in both deed (verse 13) and word (verse 14). Interestingly David is silent throughout this scene. He remains a surprisingly passive and acquiescent figure. David's inner motivations and emotions are mostly hidden. There is a reticence here about David's feelings for Michal, as there has been about his feelings for Jonathan.

It is not clear how Michal came by the knowledge that Saul was intending to make an attempt on David's life that very night. But she was right. When his henchmen arrive, Michal is able to deflect them with a report (which they take back to Saul) that he is sick. But Saul suspects a ruse and sends his servants to establish David's condition for themselves. In fact he orders them to bring David, sickbed and all. 'Bring him up to me in the bed, that I may kill him' (verse 15). When David's flight is discovered, Saul accuses Michal of deceiving him and of letting his 'enemy' go. That is now David's fixed position: he is Saul's enemy. But Michal lies a second time. She had already said, 'He is sick'. Now she says that she only let him go, because her husband threatened her. Surprisingly often in this story, the providence of God is furthered by (or at least, works with) deception.

Scene Four (verses 18–24): David flees to Samuel

18 Now David fled and escaped; he came to Samuel at Ramah, and told him all that Saul had done to him. He and Samuel went and settled at Naioth. 19 Saul was told, 'David is at Naioth in Ramah.' 20 Then Saul sent messengers to take David. When they saw the company of the prophets in a frenzy, with Samuel standing in charge of them, the spirit of God came upon the messengers of Saul, and they also fell into a prophetic frenzy. 21 When Saul was told, he sent other messengers, and they also fell into a frenzy. Saul sent messengers again the third time, and they also fell into a frenzy. 22 Then he himself went to Ramah. He came to the great well that is in Secu; he asked, 'Where are Samuel and David?' And someone said, 'They are at Naioth in Ramah.' 23 He went there, towards Naioth in Ramah; and the spirit of God came upon him. As he was going, he fell into a prophetic frenzy, until he came to Naioth in Ramah. 24 He too stripped off his clothes, and he too fell into a frenzy before Samuel. He lay naked all that day and all that night. Therefore it is said, 'Is Saul also among the prophets?'

For the third time in just a few verses, the narrative states that David fled and escaped (verse 18; compare verses 10, 12). This time his flight takes him away from Saul's court for good. He flees to Samuel in Ramah. This is the first time that Samuel has entered the story since he anointed David in 1 Samuel 16. David pours out his heart to Samuel and tells him his predicament – perhaps he was confused about his calling. Then the two decamp to Naioth.

Verse 19 is a new development, but one which will become routine. David has fled from the court of King Saul for good, and until Saul's death he will lead the life of a fugitive and an outlaw. But Saul will consistently receive intelligence about David's whereabouts. In this case, he is told that 'David is at Naioth in Ramah'.

When he discovers David's whereabouts, Saul at once sends messengers to seize David. But then the narrative takes an unexpected turn. When the messengers find Samuel and David, 'the company of prophets' was mid-frenzy. Suddenly the Spirit of God comes upon Saul's messengers, and they fall into a frenzy too (verse 20). Reports of this swiftly reach Saul, who sends out a further band of messengers. The same thing happens again (verse 21). So Saul himself goes to Naioth in Ramah. When he arrives, before he is able to threaten David in any way or even engage Samuel or David in conversation, the Spirit of God falls upon Saul. Given the finality with which, in 1 Samuel 16, the Spirit was said to have departed from Saul, this is a startling turn of events. Yet the reader senses that it may not augur well. The manifestation of the Spirit, usually a sign of the gracious salvation of God, can occasionally be a mark of judgment instead.

So it proves in Saul's case. When the Spirit came upon him, 'he fell into a frenzy' (verses 23, 24), stripped off his clothes and lay naked. The passage harks back to 1 Samuel 10:9–23. However, to suggest (as some commentators do) that this incident is merely a doublet, a vestige of the confused literary origins of the text, is to miss its narrative weight. The two accounts of his prophetic frenzy act as boundary markers in the account of Saul's relationship with Samuel. They serve as narrative 'bookends': in the first case, the experience comes early in Saul's career as the anointed king of Israel – indeed, it comes directly after his anointing; in the latter case, it comes towards the end. The question 'Is Saul also among the prophets' perhaps assumes the answer 'Yes!' in the former episode, and 'No!' in the latter. In the first passage, Saul is effectively invested with the kingship, here he is divested of it (this is the last time Saul will be in the living presence of Samuel, who anointed him). His nakedness is metaphorical as much as literal. Saul, prostrate before Samuel, is stripped not only of his robes, but also of his majesty. Saul's act echoes that of his son in 1 Samuel 18:4. In this light, Jonathan's act seems prophetic.

Conclusion

The curtain falls on this episode, with Saul still lying prostrate and naked. There is no word of his return to Gibeah, where he is found in 1 Samuel 20:24. As a result, it is easy to miss the fact that the end of this episode marks the end of Act One of the drama, in which David has served in the court of King Saul. In Act Two, which is destined to last as long as Saul lives, David will be an exile.

Three times in this episode David is said to have 'fled and escaped' (verses 10, 12, 18). It is something of a surprise to find the warrior who so bravely fought with Goliath, now fleeing for his life. But his 'fleeing' is what defines David's life in the central section of the story (1 Sam. 20:1; 21:10; 22:17; 27:4). He is a fugitive.

It is often right to fight, to stand one's ground, to remain in a situation of difficulty, to battle through, or at least to struggle to persevere. Sometimes, however, within the will and purpose of God it is right to flee. Although the call to faithful endurance and potential martyrdom has always to be weighed, it is often right to flee when, as it was for David, one's life is literally at stake. There are also times, for example in a ministry or even a relationship, when it is right to flee not because of the risk of literal death, but because the cost of faithful endurance has become spiritually or emotionally too great to sustain. Sometimes, within the providence of God, escape (humiliating and distressing as it might be) is the least worst option. The only alternative open to David is to kill Saul, and that's an option he has renounced.

The church has a fuller theology of martyrdom than it does of flight. But it is not only the church which prizes perseverance and stigmatizes quitters. The five-times Tour de France winner Lance Armstrong used to say, 'Pain is temporary. Quitting lasts forever.' Such voices can make it hard for those pondering the right choice in difficult circumstances to see it, when the moment has come to flee. For those seeking to discern whether to stand fast or to flee, particular attention is to be paid to those voices (like those of Jonathan and Michal in David's case) which might have been expected to urge steadfastness, but are in fact urging escape.

David's act was open to misunderstanding. It could be construed as an act of treason or even of cowardice. For those who flee, part of the cost of doing so is the knowledge that the act is not likely to be perceived as a noble one.

ACT TWO

David flees from the presence of Saul

1 Samuel 20 – 31

Chapter Five
(1 Samuel 20:1–42)

David and Jonathan

Introduction

In the first four chapters of the David story (Act One), he and Saul keep company together; however precariously, David is in Saul's service and lives at court. In the last five chapters of the story (Act Three), Saul is dead and David is free to assume the kingship. In the middle section of the story (Act Two, which begins here), David is an exile fleeing for his life from Saul.

The friendship between David and Jonathan is often celebrated as epitomizing an intimacy which is in short supply in the contemporary West, and in particular as modelling an important way for men to relate to one another. It is also often cited in contemporary debates about homosexuality in the church. True intimacy is rare in our culture and we urgently need to recover ways in which friendship can blossom – and that need may well be most urgent where male friendships are concerned. But if the hallmark of a close and healthy friendship is real mutuality, then there are grounds to doubt that the relationship between David and Jonathan is such a fine example after all. Jonathan definitely models something noble and heroic. His capacity for selfless love – and for expressing it – is extraordinary and wonderful; but the narrative leaves some doubt whether it was fully reciprocated.

David starts this new episode where he finished the previous chapter: in Naioth at Ramah. But he flees from there, back to the heartland of Saul's kingdom at Gibeah (assuming that is that Saul retained his birthplace as his residence throughout his reign: 1 Samuel 11:4; 13:15; 15:34; 22:6; 23:19; 26:1). David returns there in order to seek out Jonathan (who had already once successfully

mediated for David with Saul, in 1 Samuel 19:1–7). Finding him,
David explains his predicament. Jonathan agrees to a plan, which
unfolds in four scenes.

Scene One (verses 1–11): Jonathan's sacred covenant with David

*1 David fled from Naioth in Ramah. He came before Jonathan and said,
'What have I done? What is my guilt? And what is my sin against your
father that he is trying to take my life?' 2 He said to him, 'Perish the
thought! You shall not die. My father does nothing either great or small
without disclosing it to me; and why should my father hide this from me?
Never!' 3 But David also swore, 'Your father knows well that you like me;
and he thinks, "Do not let Jonathan know this, or he will be grieved." But
truly, as the Lord lives and as you yourself live, there is but a step
between me and death.' 4 Then Jonathan said to David, 'Whatever you
say, I will do for you.' 5 David said to Jonathan, 'Tomorrow is the new
moon, and I should not fail to sit with the king at the meal; but let me go,
so that I may hide in the field until the third evening. 6 If your father
misses me at all, then say, "David earnestly asked leave of me to run to
Bethlehem his city; for there is a yearly sacrifice there for all the family."
7 If he says, "Good!" it will be well with your servant; but if he is angry,
then know that evil has been determined by him. 8 Therefore deal kindly
with your servant, for you have brought your servant into a sacred
covenant with you. But if there is guilt in me, kill me yourself; why
should you bring me to your father?' 9 Jonathan said, 'Far be it from you!
If I knew that it was decided by my father that evil should come upon you,
would I not tell you?' 10 Then David said to Jonathan, 'Who will tell me
if your father answers you harshly?' 11 Jonathan replied to David,
'Come, let us go out into the field.' So they both went out into the field.*

Two things are striking about David's opening words. For one
thing, this is in fact the first recorded speech of David to Jonathan
in the narrative (and the first time he initiates conversation with
anyone). In the previous episode Jonathan spoke to David, but
David remained silent – reinforcing the impression he creates of
someone extremely self-contained, keeping his cards close to his
chest. The second thing is that the note of outraged innocence is

a recurring one for David. He uses the very same words 'What
have I done?' both earlier in the story in speaking to his brother
Eliab in 1 Samuel 17:29, and later too in speaking to the Philistine
King Achish in 1 Samuel 29:8. 'What have I done to provoke such
hostility?', David asks, 'Why is Saul set on my destruction?'
Jonathan's immediate and instinctive reply is odd. 'Far be it!'
he says (the same expression recurs in verse 9). 'My father is not
out to kill you. If he were, I would be sure to know'. But Jonathan
is not ignorant of Saul's intentions. His father had confided in
him (1 Sam. 19:1). He must surely also have known that, since he
had negotiated David's return to Saul's presence in 1 Samuel
19:7, his father had made two further attempts on his life (one
with a spear and the other with a hit-squad) and that it was these
further assassination attempts which had forced David to flee to
Naioth. Yet, however naïve he may be, Jonathan seems to be sincere. He can't see that his father might hide the truth from him –
despite the fact that in the previous episode it was Jonathan who
urged David to hide himself in the field (1 Sam. 19:2) – something
David will shortly volunteer to do again in verse 5. There is a
great deal of hiding in David's story.

When David speaks again he refers directly to his relationship
with Jonathan and to the way it is viewed by Saul. David's language is noticeably more guarded and low-key than the language
of the narrator. He says merely, 'Your father knows well that you
like me.' But the word 'like' is hugely inadequate to describe
Jonathan's feelings for David. Jonathan loved him; his soul was
bound to David; he loved him as his own soul (1 Sam. 18:1–3).
This reticence on David's part probably reflects his social inferi-
ority relative to Jonathan; but it also reflects his more guarded
personality. 'As the Lord lives,' David concludes (taking on his
lips the same oath that Saul had used in 1 Samuel 19:6), 'there is
but a step between me and death.'

This time Jonathan's response acknowledges that David has a
case. He promises to do whatever is necessary to help him. David
asks Jonathan to collude with him in a deceit. He intends to be
absent from a feast in Saul's presence to mark the new moon.
(There is a further inconsistency in the narrative here, that this
should be treat as an unexpected development, when Saul knows
that David has fled). He asks Jonathan, if he (David) should be

missed, to explain that he has had to go urgently to Bethlehem, to attend an annual sacrifice there with his family. If Saul's response to such an explanation is mild it will indicate that David is not in such danger after all; if Saul's reaction is hostile it will prove the seriousness of David's predicament. There is some shrewd psychology on David's part here: those in favour are frequently forgiven for minor discourtesies and misdemeanours by those in authority over them; those under suspicion are not. This is, of course, the second time in the story that a feast in Bethlehem has been used as a ruse to deceive Saul (1 Sam. 16:1–13). If, in the interim, the story of David's anointing at a feast with his family in Bethlehem has become known to Saul, it is understandable that he should feel threatened by David's return there.

Perhaps fearing that Jonathan may yet side with his father, David then reminds Jonathan (verse 8) of the covenant between them. But the language David uses only serves to emphasize the inequality in this relationship. David stresses that it was Jonathan who drew him into a covenant of love and not the other way around. Now he calls on Jonathan to show true to covenant kindness. And when David posits his own guilt, Jonathan repeats his words earlier in the chapter: 'God forbid!' If Saul intends to harm David, Jonathan will surely say so. 'But how?', David asks. 'How will you communicate the fact, if it emerges that Saul is intent on killing me?' The scene ends with the two men going out into the field, to put their strategy into effect.

Scene Two (verses 12–23): Jonathan's covenant with the house of David

> 12 *Jonathan said to David, 'By the Lord, the God of Israel! When I have sounded out my father, about this time tomorrow, or on the third day, if he is well disposed towards David, shall I not then send and disclose it to you? 13 But if my father intends to do you harm, the Lord do so to Jonathan, and more also, if I do not disclose it to you, and send you away, so that you may go in safety. May the Lord be with you, as he has been with my father. 14 If I am still alive, show me the faithful love of the Lord; but if I die, 15 never cut off your faithful love from my house, even if the Lord were to cut off every one of the enemies of David from the face of the*

earth.' 16 Thus Jonathan made a covenant with the house of David, saying, 'May the Lord seek out the enemies of David.' 17 Jonathan made
David swear again by his love for him; for he loved him as he loved his
own life.

18 Jonathan said to him, 'Tomorrow is the new moon; you will be missed,
because your place will be empty. 19 On the day after tomorrow, you
shall go a long way down; go to the place where you hid yourself earlier,
and remain beside the stone there. 20 I will shoot three arrows to the side
of it, as though I shot at a mark. 21 Then I will send the boy, saying, "Go,
find the arrows." If I say to the boy, "Look, the arrows are on this side of
you, collect them", then you are to come, for, as the Lord lives, it is safe
for you and there is no danger. 22 But if I say to the young man, "Look,
the arrows are beyond you", then go; for the Lord has sent you away. 23
As for the matter about which you and I have spoken, the Lord is witness
between you and me for ever.'

The second scene is set in the field where David will await news
from Jonathan. Jonathan is the protagonist throughout. The scene
comprises two speeches, both made by him (in verses 12 to 15,
and then in verses 18 to 23). In between come two single-verse
summaries of the utmost significance; in both Jonathan is the
emphatic subject of the sentence, the one who acts; David is acted
upon.

Jonathan's first speech is typical of his heroism and godliness
all through the narrative. He prefaces his remarks with an invo-
cation of 'the Lord the God of Israel' and proceeds to speak of the
Lord four more times in the next three verses. The burden of his
promise is that, for good or ill, he will disclose to David the outcome of his conversation with Saul: if Saul is disposed to accept
David back, Jonathan will say so; if Saul proves hostile to David,
then at whatever cost to himself, Jonathan will say so. But
Jonathan asks for something in return: whatever the future holds,
he asks David to show 'faithful love' (i.e. covenant love) to him
and to his descendants. Along the way Jonathan acknowledges
that David has supplanted his father: 'May the Lord be with you,'
he says, 'as he has been with my father.' When in verse 16 he adds
the hope that 'the Lord will seek out the enemies of David', he is
aware that his father numbers himself among them.

If the covenant Jonathan made with David in 1 Samuel 18:3 was something purely personal, there is a development here. In verse 16 when he renews the covenant, it is not just with David, but with all David's house – just as he asks David to show faithful love not only to him (the distinction is explicit in verses 14 and 15), but to his house. Once more, as in 1 Samuel 18:3, it is Jonathan who makes the covenant with David, not the other way around.

Verse 17 is difficult: commentators agree that the sense of the Hebrew is literally, 'Jonathan made David swear again by his [Jonathan's] love for him [David].' But how can David swear by Jonathan's love? The Greek Old Testament resorts to switching around the subject and object of the sentence: 'Jonathan again swore to David by his love for him.' But perhaps Jonathan means, 'Swear, and so honour my love for you.' In any case, when the verse concludes: 'for he loved him as he loved his own life', the phrase is an echo of 1 Samuel 18:1–3: it is Jonathan who loves David as himself. It is repeatedly affirmed just how dear David was to Jonathan. The reverse is not made explicit.

There are repeated references to the Lord in Jonathan's second speech also. He accepts David's proposal to make his absence from a 'new moon feast' a test of Saul's disposition, and now devises a plan to let David know what Saul's reaction to his absence might be. The plan involves more hiding on David's part.

The elaborate scheme involving the shooting of arrows is peculiar. There seems to be no need for subterfuge, given the freedom with which out in the fields these plans are made. In the event the shooting of arrows will indeed take place – but afterwards the two men will speak as openly face-to-face as they do here, apparently with impunity.

The speech makes clear Jonathan's trust in the providence of God. He is ready to take his father's reaction to David's absence from the feast as a sure indication of the will of God. If his father is favourable to David and it is safe for David to return to court, it will be because that is the will of the Lord. And if not, if it is necessary for David to flee, it will be because 'the Lord has sent you away'.

The scene concludes with a final solemn reference to the Lord, and a reminder to David of what had been spoken between them.

Jonathan couches the reminder in more mutual terms than the narrative itself justifies.

Scene Three (verses 24–34): Saul's anger towards Jonathan

24 So David hid himself in the field. When the new moon came, the king sat at the feast to eat. 25 The king sat upon his seat, as at other times, upon the seat by the wall. Jonathan stood, while Abner sat by Saul's side; but David's place was empty.

26 Saul did not say anything that day; for he thought, 'Something has befallen him; he is not clean, surely he is not clean.' 27 But on the second day, the day after the new moon, David's place was empty. And Saul said to his son Jonathan, 'Why has the son of Jesse not come to the feast, either yesterday or today?' 28 Jonathan answered Saul, 'David earnestly asked leave of me to go to Bethlehem; 29 he said, "Let me go; for our family is holding a sacrifice in the city, and my brother has commanded me to be there. So now, if I have found favour in your sight, let me get away, and see my brothers." For this reason he has not come to the king's table.'

30 Then Saul's anger was kindled against Jonathan. He said to him, 'You son of a perverse, rebellious woman! Do I not know that you have chosen the son of Jesse to your own shame, and to the shame of your mother's nakedness? 31 For as long as the son of Jesse lives upon the earth, neither you nor your kingdom shall be established. Now send and bring him to me, for he shall surely die.' 32 Then Jonathan answered his father Saul, 'Why should he be put to death? What has he done?' 33 But Saul threw his spear at him to strike him; so Jonathan knew that it was the decision of his father to put David to death. 34 Jonathan rose from the table in fierce anger and ate no food on the second day of the month, for he was grieved for David, and because his father had disgraced him.

Scene three takes place not in the fields, but at Saul's palace in Gibeah. The feast table is set. The king and his courtiers are assembled but David's place is empty. On the first night of the feast, Saul notes his enemy's absence but makes nothing of it. He assumes David is somehow ritually unclean and so unable to participate in the feast. But on the second day his suspicions are aroused. 'Why is the son of Jesse not here?', he asks. The question is addressed directly to Jonathan and not to Abner, say, or to the assembled company in general. Saul is fully aware of the closeness of David to Jonathan: if anyone present knows David's whereabouts it will be his own son. But as usual in this narrative, Saul cannot bring himself to speak of his enemy by name. He is 'the son of Jesse'. There may be a note of defiance therefore in the first word of Jonathan's reply: 'David'.

Jonathan's reply redefines the web of relationships between himself, his father and David. In not only taking up David's suggested ruse ('David earnestly asked leave of me to run to Bethlehem his city, for there is a yearly sacrifice there for all the family', verse 6), but elaborating upon it ('My brother had commanded me to be there. So now if I have found favour in your sight, let me get away, and see my brothers'), Jonathan is deliberately deceiving his father.

When, right at the start of the David story, the Lord invites Samuel to cloak the real purpose of his visit to Bethlehem by letting it be known he is there for a feast, there is dissimulation but no outright lie: a feast is held. Here the lie is outright. David has not gone to Bethlehem, not even as a ruse. He is in the field, the place of his rendezvous with Jonathan. When he does flee it is first to Nob (1 Sam. 21:1) and then to the cave of Adullam (1 Sam. 22:1). True, he does meet up there with is brothers, so perhaps that part of Jonathan's improvisation (like the words 'let me get away') revealed more of the truth than he intended.

But the lie makes it clear to the reader just how far Jonathan is prepared to prefer his friend to his father; and Saul evidently sensed it too: he is furious with his son. That is a new development too. Perhaps it is the precise phrase 'Let me get away' which so incenses Saul. A safe 'getaway' is indeed exactly what David has engineered. Saul's understands this and now also understands that his son, as well as his daughter, has facilitated it.

In his fury Saul first speaks and then acts. Both word and deed are revealing. 'You son of a perverse and rebellious woman!', he exclaims. Then he goes on, 'I know that you have chosen the son of Jesse to your own shame and to the shame of your mother's nakedness.'

The nature of the relationship between David and Jonathan has been the subject of considerable scholarly attention. Clearly, at least on Jonathan's side, it is an intimate relationship, involving a wholehearted commitment. But is it a homosexual relationship? If the text implies such a thing anywhere, it is not in 1 Samuel 18:1–3, where Jonathan's soul is said to have been 'bound to the soul of David'; nor in verse 17 of this chapter, where Jonathan is said to have loved David 'as he loved his own life'; nor even in 2 Samuel 1:26, where in his grief at the news of Jonathan's death, David says, 'Your love to me was wonderful, passing the love of women.' Rather it is here, where the language Saul uses is the language of shame and nakedness. But the implication is not to be relied upon. In his fury Saul is setting out to insult his son. It is not even certain that his words amount to an accusation that Jonathan's relationship with David is a homosexual one. But even if they do, the accusation is no more accurate a reflection of the character of Jonathan's relationship with David than the phrase 'a perverse and rebellious woman' is an accurate reflection of the character of Jonathan's mother. It is, however, shocking language.

On the other hand, in verse 31, there is no denying that Saul's fury has enabled him to see clearly. His discernment is profound: he knows, as Jonathan himself had also discerned as early as 1 Samuel 18:4, that David is a threat to Jonathan's inheritance of Saul's kingdom. Saul may not be able to bring himself to name David but at this point the true nature and identity of 'the son of Jesse' has become all too clear to him. In the next moment Saul's implacable hostility to David becomes all too clear to Jonathan: his father states openly and unambiguously, 'He shall surely die.'

Jonathan makes a brief attempt to mediate but after such an onslaught his heart cannot have been in it. His two questions take up just four words in Hebrew: 'Why die, what done?' The second question echoes that of David in verse 1.

Then Saul acts: he throws his spear at his own son. The extent of Saul's madness is clear. He has just urged Jonathan to beware that 'as long as the son of Jesse lives upon the earth, neither you nor your kingdom shall be established'. Now he attempts to kill Jonathan himself, apparently prepared to cut off that kingdom once and for all. Unsurprisingly the act convinces Jonathan that there is no hope for David in Saul's court. In a fury of his own (a rare thing in this most mild of men), Jonathan leaves the feast-table: he is angry with his father both for exiling David and for insulting himself.

Scene Four (verses 35–42): Jonathan dismisses David in peace

> 35 *In the morning Jonathan went out into the field to the appointment with David, and with him was a little boy. 36 He said to the boy, 'Run and find the arrows that I shoot.' As the boy ran, he shot an arrow beyond him. 37 When the boy came to the place where Jonathan's arrow had fallen, Jonathan called after the boy and said, 'Is the arrow not beyond you?' 38 Jonathan called after the boy, 'Hurry, be quick, do not linger.' So Jonathan's boy gathered up the arrows and came to his master. 39 But the boy knew nothing; only Jonathan and David knew the arrangement. 40 Jonathan gave his weapons to the boy and said to him, 'Go and carry them to the city.' 41 As soon as the boy had gone, David rose from beside the stone heap and prostrated himself with his face to the ground. He bowed three times, and they kissed each other, and wept with each other; David wept the more. 42 Then Jonathan said to David, 'Go in peace, since both of us have sworn in the name of the Lord, saying, "The Lord shall be between me and you, and between my descendants and your descendants, for ever." ' He got up and left; and Jonathan went into the city.*

The following morning, his mind now made up, Jonathan returns to the field – ostensibly for archery practice. His bow is to Jonathan what Saul's spear is to him (1 Sam. 18:4; 2 Samuel 1:18, 22). He performs something of a charade: in keeping with the plan set out in verses 19–22, Jonathan duly shoots an arrow beyond David and then shouts to the boy whose task is to retrieve the it, 'Is the arrow not beyond you?' – the sign that David's life is in danger and that he must flee at once.

For good measure – what was not in the plan – Jonathan adds, 'Hurry, be quick, do not linger.' But David does linger. Jonathan sends the boy back to the city with his bow and arrows, so that he and David can speak face to face. The fact that the two men are able to meet and speak in this way makes the performance with the arrows confusing. It is not clear why it was not possible (and would not have been preferable) for them to do so from the outset. It may be that Jonathan needed a pretext to leave his father's court and the 'shooting practice' provided it.

In what follows there is finally a glimpse of genuine mutuality in the relationship between Jonathan and David. David prostrates himself on the ground before his friend. Getting up, he bows to Jonathan three times. Then 'they kissed each other and wept with each other' (the mutuality is emphatic here) – but David wept the more. Yet once again it is Jonathan alone who speaks about the covenant between them and when he states in verse 42 that 'both of us have sworn in the name of the Lord, saying "The Lord shall be between you and "', the reader is reminded that the narrative has only ever in fact shown Jonathan doing so. Typically it is Jonathan who, at the end of the episode, dismisses David in peace and not the other way around. David is still the commoner and Jonathan the crown prince.

When the two friends part – David going on his way and Jonathan returning to the city – it is for the penultimate time. They will meet only once more (1 Sam. 23:16–18).

Conclusion

Many of us hate conflict and would prefer not to make hard choices, where our relationships are concerned. In particular most of us would prefer not to have to choose between friendships and family ties. But that is Jonathan's dilemma in this passage. The time has come for him to choose between the friend (to whom his soul is tied) and his father (to whom he owes every obligation of loyalty and service).

It is part of the heart-rendingly noble portrait of Jonathan in this story, that he finds a costly middle way. He chooses the way of truth and love (and faithfulness to the providence of God) in committing himself to David's security and peace. He will do whatever is necessary to protect David, for the destiny to which he knows the Lord has called him. But he will not leave his father, to be with the one he loves as his own soul. He remains *at* the side (if no longer quite *on* the side) of the father who has tried to kill him, and will show him, as the Lord's anointed, as much loyal service as his prior commitment to David allows.

Most hard choices seem to us to admit of only two possible alternatives. It is surprising how often the Lord's will opens up a third way – and unsurprising that it should often be the most costly path of all.

Chapter Six
(1 Samuel 21:1–15)

David and Ahimelech

Introduction

David is at his most vulnerable in this episode. Through the ensuing ten chapters, his position – while precarious – grows in strength. He has a growing entourage, a growing harem and a growing stature. But at this early stage in his exile, he is reduced to begging bread and borrowing weapons. His dependency on others for food and arms is never again quite so acute but it remains a fact of life for David right through this middle part of his story.

The present episode falls into two scenes: the first is set at the shrine of God at Nob, where it is the priest Ahimelech who (somewhat reluctantly) functions as David's provider and protector; the second is astonishingly set at the court of King Achish of Gath, where the king himself does so, if only briefly.

Scene One (verses 1–9): David flees to the priest at Nob

1 David came to Nob to the priest Ahimelech. Ahimelech came trembling to meet David, and said to him, 'Why are you alone, and no one with you?' 2 David said to the priest Ahimelech, 'The king has charged me with a matter, and said to me, "No one must know anything of the matter about which I send you, and with which I have charged you." I have made an appointment with the young men for such and such a place. 3 Now then, what have you at hand? Give me five loaves of bread, or whatever is here.' 4 The priest answered David, 'I have no ordinary bread at hand, only holy bread — provided that the young men have kept themselves from women.'

5 David answered the priest, 'Indeed, women have been kept from us as always when I go on an expedition; the vessels of the young men are holy even when it is a common journey; how much more today will their vessels be holy?' 6 So the priest gave him the holy bread; for there was no bread there except the bread of the Presence, which is removed from before the Lord to be replaced by hot bread on the day it is taken away.

7 Now a certain man of the servants of Saul was there that day, detained before the Lord; his name was Doeg the Edomite, the chief of Saul's shepherds.

8 David said to Ahimelech, 'Is there no spear or sword here with you? I did not bring my sword or my weapons with me, because the king's business required haste.' 9 The priest said, 'The sword of Goliath the Philistine, whom you killed in the valley of Elah, is here wrapped in a cloth behind the ephod; if you will take that, take it, for there is none here except that one.' David said, 'There is none like it; give it to me.'

David hasn't travelled far from the place from which it can be assumed he left Jonathan: Nob is only three miles from Gibeah. If the action in this episode follows swiftly on the close of the previous one, it would account both for the nervous reaction of the priest Ahimelech and for the credibility of David's response.

When David turns up, Ahimelech 'comes trembling' to meet him. Perhaps rumours abound that there has been a breakdown of relationship between David and the king and Ahimelech (like the elders of Bethlehem in 1 Sam. 16) is afraid of finding himself caught up in the conflict and at risk of incurring Saul's wrath. Ahimelech is also surprised to find David arriving alone. But firm news that Saul is seeking to kill David and that David has fled for his life is clearly not out. David's escape is sufficiently recent for it to be possible for him to pass himself off as still in the king's service. Where in the previous episode David was only encouraging Jonathan to lie on his behalf, here he is lying for himself: 'The king has entrusted me with a secret mission', he says, 'and I can't tell anyone what it is. I'm due to meet up with the men in such-and-such a place. But I need food. What can you give me?' (He asks specifically for 'five loaves' as in Mt. 14:17.) Ahimelech apparently accepts David's story at face value, but explains that the only food he has (at hand) is holy bread, which he is only prepared to give David on the assurance that his men 'have kept themselves from women'.

It is a moot point whether at this point in the story David has any men. The text later states that he has acquired some (1 Sam. 22:1–2); and it is likely that he had already begun to attract a following. He certainly does not however have the sort of men Ahimelech is assuming: a company of soldiers and servants sent by Saul to support David's mission. But David keeps up the pretence: 'Indeed, the men have kept themselves from women', he says. The deceit comes easily to him. It is hard to see how David's cavalier attitude to ritual here is less serious than the transgressions of Saul in 1 Samuel 13 and 15, but he incurs no equivalent penalty.

So Ahimelech is tricked into providing David with food – and not just any food: the Bread of the Presence, symbolic somehow of the Lord's blessing upon David even in these compromised circumstances. This is the only part of the narrative of David taken up by Jesus (in Mt. 12:1–5), and it is taken up in such a way as to exonerate him (and indeed in such a way as to confirm that David had companions).

Verse 7 is an aside but one with severe repercussions. There is one servant and soldier of Saul's present at Nob: Doeg the Edomite, 'the chief of Saul's shepherds'. For ritual reasons he is 'detained before the Lord'. Presumably he is obliged to spend time at the holy place in penance or at least in cleansing. Here his presence is simply noted in passing – and although it is not stated, the reader understands that he has overheard the conversation between David and Ahimelech.

Having secured food David seeks to make good his other deficit: arms. 'Is there no sword here or spear you could let me have?', he asks, adding the further deceit: 'I was in such a hurry to do the king's business that I didn't have time to collect my own weapons.' Ahimelech's reply in verse 9 is garbled and repetitious, as if in renewed nervousness his words came spilling out. Instead of a succinct: 'The only sword we have is the sword of Goliath, whom you killed. You can have that if you need it', he adds details about where David slew Goliath, where the sword is now laid, and how it is wrapped. 'If you will take it, take it', he concludes, 'for there is none here except that one'. David's reply could not be more of a contrast. In Hebrew it is just four words: 'No other! Give me!' There's a directness and urgency in David which contrasts with a garrulousness and hesitancy in Ahimelech. The narrative glosses over the question of whether David will be able to use Goliath's great sword. Perhaps David, the mild and inexperienced youth, has grown into a mature and battle-hardened man, capable of wielding a weapon of prodigious size. This is the third time he has been borne someone else's arms (first Saul's in 1 Sam. 17:38; then Jonathan's in 1 Sam. 18:4), but the first time he has chosen to do so. David's circumstances have hardly prospered since he last held this sword in a moment of great triumph.

So David leaves the sanctuary supplied with bread and a sword: the two resources he most needs. But 'bread' and 'sword' are so symbolic of spiritual strength (so that the Word of God is likened to both in the Bible) that the reader wonders if David did not also leave the sanctuary renewed in his sense of 'the Presence'. Doeg, on the other hand, though 'detained before the Lord', may in due course have left spiritually unrefreshed.

Scene Two (verses 10–14): David is very much afraid

> 10 *David rose and fled that day from Saul; he went to King Achish of Gath. 11 The servants of Achish said to him, 'Is this not David the king of the land? Did they not sing to one another of him in dances,*
> *"Saul has killed his thousands,*
> *and David his tens of thousands"?'*
> 12 *David took these words to heart and was very much afraid of King Achish of Gath. 13 So he changed his behaviour before them; he preten-ded to be mad when in their presence. He scratched marks on the doors of the gate, and let his spittle run down his beard. 14 Achish said to his ser-vants, 'Look, you see the man is mad; why then have you brought him to me? 15 Do I lack madmen, that you have brought this fellow to play the madman in my presence? Shall this fellow come into my house?'*

Scene two begins oddly when the text states that 'David rose and fled that day from Saul'. It sounds as if this follows directly from 1 Samuel 20:42. This may mean 'David rose and fled that day from Saul's kingdom – out of the area of Saul's jurisdiction, to King Achish of Gath'. This is at any rate a most unexpected development: how ironic that the first thing David does, on being reunited with Goliath's sword, is to flee not just to the Philistines but to Gath itself, Goliath's home town (1 Sam. 27:2–4; 2 Sam. 1:20).

In Gath he is recognized. The king's servants, presumably in some anxiety, ask Achish, 'Is this not David?' Quite how they knew him is not clear. Interestingly, they call him 'the king of the land'. They do not call him 'the king of Israel': Saul's status as such is not in question for now at least. But plainly Saul's sense of being under threat by David, and his warning to Jonathan about the future of the kingdom, was not without substance. David's repeated military victories (1 Sam. 18:13–16, 27, 30; 19:8) have acquired for him a considerable reputation: he is a king *de facto* if not yet *de jure*. The servants of Achish know what the women first sang at the time of Goliath's death (and have continued to sing ever since) and they can see, as no one in Israel can see, where matters are destined to lead. This is the first time in the narrative that David has been called a king and the title is bestowed upon him by those who first encountered his extraordinary giftedness.

But once recognized, David is vulnerable. Indeed, he is terrified. If this is the first time that the narrative has named David as king, it is also the first time it has named his fear. Earlier in the story others have been very afraid, including (especially) Saul – but not David. He has not been afraid of lions or bears, of Goliath (unlike the Israelite army) or Saul (unlike Samuel, Ahimelech or the elders of Bethlehem); but he is now afraid of Achish. Perhaps he feels that the Lord has forsaken him.

Fear is always the enemy of faith. One wonders why David does not respond before this Philistine the way he responded before Goliath: full of trust in the power of the Lord to deliver him. Instead, he resorts to pretence. He feigns mental illness, presumably acting much as Saul must have acted in his prophetic frenzy. But Saul was not pretending: where symptoms of madness took control of Saul, David exercises control of the symptoms of madness. He claws at doorways and lets spittle run down his beard. The ploy works. Achish has quite enough Philistine madmen: the last thing he needs in Gath is a mad Israelite. So he makes no attempt to confine or even kill David, but rather commands his servants to remove him from his house (and presumably also city).

Conclusion

David is presented in both this and the previous episode as showing more initiative than previously. He is more assertive in this episode than he was particularly in episodes 3, 4 and 5. He is prepared to take surprising, even shocking, courses of action: prepared to defy convention in taking resources from a sacred place and in seeking refuge with the enemy. He will make use of both sacred bread and pagan sword. This may reflect nothing more than the extremity of his circumstances; or it may reflect a developing character trait; or, most likely, it may reflect precisely the way his character was bound to develop in the extremity of his circumstances.

Those individuals and institutions that are most in tune with the will and purpose of God are often those most capable of breaking with convention – of imagining a future that looks unlike the past. The bold options chosen by David shape both his own character and the future around him. Those who serve God boldly will often find that their faithful adherence to the will and purpose of God brings about change and development for themselves as much as for the circumstances they face.

Chapter Seven
(1 Samuel 22:1–23)

David at Adullam

Introduction

To face hostility alone can be a desperate thing. It can create a sense of profound isolation. When you are under attack or even feel that you are, there is nothing so welcome as allies. In this next episode of the story, David is coming to terms with his predicament: he is an outlaw. But he is not alone.

This episode unfolds in five scenes over the course of which the narrative develops significantly. In the third and fourth scenes of the episode (which are the two longest central scenes and which take up more than half of the verses in this chapter), David is off-stage. The first two scenes emphasize the solidarity David enjoyed with both his family and various fellow-fugitives as well as with a prophet of God. Together, his brothers and a motley crew of malcontents formed an entourage around David when he returned to Judah from Philistia. The final scene relates how David was also joined by a priest of Nob, who brought with him the means which enabled David to inquire of the Lord. In scenes three and four however it is Saul who is centre stage. He believes himself to the subject of a conspiracy and challenges his closest advisers about their loyalty to his cause. As a result Saul's murderous hostility, compounded presumably by a sense of frustration and helplessness in his attempts to kill David, is unleashed against innocent bystanders.

Counter to Saul's intention however (although his opponent is still vulnerable, and will remain in danger and in hiding to the end of his life) David is better supplied and better resourced at the end of the episode than he was at the beginning. He has more allies and Saul has fewer. David also has ready access to God; Saul has none.

Scene One (verses 1–2): David becomes the captain of a company

1 David left there and escaped to the cave of Adullam; when his brothers and all his father's house heard of it, they went down there to him. 2 Everyone who was in distress, and everyone who was in debt, and everyone who was discontented gathered to him; and he became captain over them. Those who were with him numbered about four hundred.

In the previous episode there was the first hint that in fleeing from Saul, David did not go alone. He appears to have had with him a small band of men – a small enough number to have been fed with the bread of the Presence. But when David escapes from Philistia back into Judah to the cave of Adullam, a new phase begins: he draws to himself a considerable community.

News reaches Bethlehem that David has escaped to relative safety. At once 'his brothers and all his father's house . . . went down to him there'. (Most Bible readers, confronted with that phrase out of context, might suppose it was part of the Joseph story in Genesis 37–50; there are many such loose parallels and points of connection between the two narratives.) The fact that his brothers were apparently keen to join him at the cave of Adullam implies a change in their relationship with David since they last featured in the story in 1 Samuel 17. There Eliab at least was contemptuous of his kid-brother. Here there is loyalty and respect. The excuse Jonathan gave Saul in 1 Samuel 20 to explain David's absence from the feast (that he had been called away to a family festival) had some basis in fact: it seems David did make such visits from time to time. Perhaps Saul's angry response had some basis too: perhaps he was right to fear that David's continued contact with his brothers constituted a threat, and had a political as well as a purely personal dimension to it.

Such is David's reputation as a military leader, however, that it is not just members of his family (including servants presumably) who are drawn to his side. Their ranks are swelled by others, so that the company seeking his captaincy numbers about four hundred. The circumstances of these others is significant enough for the narrator to emphasize that they represented '*everyone* who was in distress, *everyone* who was in debt and *everyone* who was discontented'. At a stroke the conflict between Saul and David is redefined. It is no longer something personal or even tribal. It has become sociological and ideological. David's men are a community of the dispossessed, united by a shared marginalization in Saul's kingdom – the have-nots seeking protection and possible redress against the haves (compare Jdgs. 11:3, where Jephthah is joined by a group of 'outlaws'). In terms of the underlying exploration of power in the narrative this is a key moment.

The destitute nature of David's band is underlined by their headquarters: Saul dwells in a city, David in a cave. The location is apparently in the wilderness area of Judea, south west of Jerusalem, close to Philistine territory – that is, as one might expect, between Gibeah (the centre of Saul's kingdom) and Gath (the centre of Achish's). Over time David's men not only grew in size but in military discipline and skill. It was presumably from among the members of this outlaw mob that David found 'mighty and experienced warriors, expert with shield and spear, whose faces were like the faces of lions, and who were as swift as the gazelles on the mountains' (1 Chron. 12:8).

Scene Two (verses 3–5): David seeks refuge in Moab

> *3 David went from there to Mizpeh of Moab. He said to the king of Moab,*
> *'Please let my father and mother come to you, until I know what God will*
> *do for me.' 4 He left them with the king of Moab, and they stayed with*
> *him all the time that David was in the stronghold. 5 Then the prophet*
> *Gad said to David, 'Do not remain in the stronghold; leave, and go into*
> *the land of Judah.' So David left, and went into the forest of Hereth.*

It is a mark of David's status that he has such easy access to neighbouring kings. Having already made a first brief visit to the court of King Achish in Gath (to which he will return), he now pays a more fruitful visit to the king of Moab. His mission is on the face of it a remarkable one: he is seeking a place of refuge for his parents. Jesse 'was already old and advanced in years' by the time David fought Goliath (1 Sam. 17:12) and is now certainly too old to play any active part in David's band of fighting men – though among his brothers are some experienced soldiers, who might well have a valuable contribution to make. But to seek refuge amongst those against whom Saul had led the armies of Israel into battle (1 Sam. 14:47) was a risky strategy. The request is granted, however, and David leaves his parents with the king of Moab and 'they stayed there all the time David was in the stronghold'. As far as the king of Moab is concerned, any enemy of Saul's is a welcome ally; but there may also be a small corroboration here of the witness of the book of Ruth, that David's family had Moabite ancestry (Ruth 1:1–4; 4:13–22).

This is a time of uncertainty for David. Beyond the fact of his anointing, with its promise that he will one day become Israel's king, he has no idea what the future holds. But he is confident that it is in God's hands. He tells the king of Moab that he needs help only 'until I know what God will do for me'. He does not know how long the uncertainty will last, or precisely what the outcome of the waiting will be. But he is confident that whatever the future brings, it will be what God has in store for him. The whole of Act Two of his drama (that is to say, the period between his departure from Saul's court and his ultimate accession to the kingship, this period of flight in the wilderness) is for David a time of discovery, when he waits to find out what God will do for him. It is by far the longest of the three Acts in the story of David's rise: much of the life of faith is about waiting.

David's continued faith and his looking to God is further emphasized by the introduction of the prophet Gad. This is the first reference to Gad in the story. Nothing is said about where he has come from or how he has joined David's circle. But at the start of this episode the allies of David gathering: they include not just his family, a promising band of fighting men, and even a foreign king – but a prophet of God, who brings David direct access to the will of God. In the succeeding episodes it is a recurring theme that David has this access and Saul does not. David's obedience to God's will is also emphasized: Gad tells him that it is not safe for him to remain in the cave stronghold and instructs him to leave. So David leaves and goes instead to the forest of Hereth.

Scene Three (verses 6–10): Saul fears a conspiracy

> *6 Saul heard that David and those who were with him had been located. Saul was sitting at Gibeah, under the tamarisk tree on the height, with his spear in his hand, and all his servants were standing around him. 7 Saul said to his servants who stood around him, 'Hear now, you Benjaminites; will the son of Jesse give every one of you fields and vineyards, will he make you all commanders of thousands and commanders of hundreds? 8 Is that why all of you have conspired against me? No one discloses to me when my son makes a league with the son of Jesse, none of you is sorry for me or discloses to me that my son has stirred up my servant against me, to lie in wait, as he is doing today.'*

> *9 Doeg the Edomite, who was in charge of Saul's servants, answered, 'I saw the son of Jesse coming to Nob, to Ahimelech son of Ahitub; 10 he inquired of the Lord for him, gave him provisions, and gave him the sword of Goliath the Philistine.'*

There is a sudden change of scene in verse 6: the spotlight reverts to Saul's court at Gibeah. The king has received word about where David 'and those who were with him' are located.

As usual (compare 1 Sam. 18:10; 19:9) Saul is sitting, spear in hand. It is the spear he has thrown at David and at his own son Jonathan, over whose disloyalty he is again about to lament. Where the previous scene closes with David facing the future with confidence and trust in God, the present one opens with Saul facing the future with fear – to the point of paranoia. He himself is a Benjaminite (1 Sam. 9:1) and his fellow tribesmen are his core support. But he suspects them of conspiring against him – or at least of failing to help him as much as they might. In a long outburst (which in Hebrew is a single sentence), he first challenges his servants whether they can expect 'the son of Jesse' to provide 'fields and vineyards' for them as generously as he himself has done, and whether he will prefer them, as Saul has done, in choosing officers for his army. (Samuel had warned the Israelites specifically that a king would appropriate field and vineyards to shore up his own power. This is what kings do: 1 Sam. 8:11–16.) Presumably in drawing attention to the property and positions of influence that his followers have, Saul intends to remind them where their interests lie. In the process however he reminds the reader of the contrast between these followers and those of David, who are the dispossessed and the powerless (and yet who live in hope).

When Saul goes on to accuse his servants of conspiring against him, there are two grounds for his complaint. The first is that no one has disclosed to him his own son's betrayal: 'no one tells me', he says, 'that my own son makes a league with the son of Jesse'. (Was Jonathan standing by, as he was being spoken of in these terms?) But Saul has come to learn of it anyway – and not just to learn that the relationship between Jonathan and David is a covenant one, but apparently even that the covenant was made at Jonathan's initiative. Such is Saul's sense of betrayal that his words suggest that the real baddie now is Jonathan, rather than David: it is his own son who is 'stirring up my servant against him'. Saul cuts a pathetic figure when he complains, secondly (presumably feeling thoroughly sorry for himself), that 'none of you feels sorry for me'.

Saul's outburst prompts one of his servants to disclose something that had until now apparently remained secret. Doeg the Edomite (introduced here as 'in charge of Saul's servants', as opposed to 'the chief of Saul's shepherds' in 1 Sam. 21:7) tells Saul not anything new about David's dealings with Jonathan, but all that he knows about David's visit to Nob and his dealings with the priest Ahimelech. According to Doeg, Ahimelech did three things for David (though Doeg carefully adopts Saul's preferred designation for David and speaks only of 'the son of Jesse'): he inquired of the Lord for him, gave him provisions, and gave him Goliath's sword.

The food and the sword the reader knows about already. But the text of chapter 21 does not in fact state that Ahimelech inquired of the Lord for David. So it comes as something of a surprise to find that this was so – and Ahimelech will freely admit as much in the next scene. The newness of the disclosure and the fact that Doeg puts it first in his report combine to underline this part of what Ahimelech did for David – and it becomes clear in what follows that this was the part that enraged Saul most. He knows that he is no longer is a position to inquire of the Lord himself, as he was once able to do (1 Sam. 14:37).

Scene Four (verses 11–19): Saul and the slaughter of the priests of Nob

11 The king sent for the priest Ahimelech son of Ahitub and for all his father's house, the priests who were at Nob; and all of them came to the king. 12 Saul said, 'Listen now, son of Ahitub.' He answered, 'Here I am, my lord.' 13 Saul said to him, 'Why have you conspired against me, you and the son of Jesse, by giving him bread and a sword, and by inquiring of God for him, so that he has risen against me, to lie in wait, as he is doing today?'

14 Then Ahimelech answered the king, 'Who among all your servants is so faithful as David? He is the king's son-in-law, and is quick to do your bidding, and is honoured in your house. 15 Is today the first time that I have inquired of God for him? By no means! Do not let the king impute anything to his servant or to any member of my father's house; for your servant has known nothing of all this, much or little.' 16 The king said, 'You shall surely die, Ahimelech, you and all your father's house.' 17 The king said to the guard who stood around him, 'Turn and kill the priests of the Lord, because their hand also is with David; they knew that he fled, and did not disclose it to me.' But the servants of the king would not raise their hand to attack the priests of the Lord. 18 Then the king said to Doeg, 'You, Doeg, turn and attack the priests.' Doeg the Edomite turned and attacked the priests; on that day he killed eighty-five who wore the linen ephod. 19 Nob, the city of the priests, he put to the sword; men and women, children and infants, oxen, donkeys, and sheep, he put to the sword.

Ahimelech is summoned; but not just he himself – 'all his father's house' (compare verse 1) are summoned too; and all of them came before the king. When Saul addresses him, it is already clear that he is extremely angry indeed and that Ahimelech is in extreme danger: Saul says to him, 'Listen now, son of Ahitub.' There is a hint that Ahimelech is now lumped together with David in the failure to call him by name. A rebuke is already implied. But Ahimelech's reply could not be more courteous and appropriate: 'Here I am, my lord', he says. (On this response, see for example, Gen. 22:1; 46:2; Ex. 3:4, but also Is. 58:9 and 65:1.)

Saul's allegations are a combination of elements from verses 8–10: he accuses Ahimelech of conspiracy (compare verse 8), of supplying David with bread and a sword and (this element is now reported last) of inquiring of the Lord for him (compare verse 10), so that he has risen up against Saul 'to lie in wait as he does today' (compare verse 8).

Ahimelech's response suggests that he knows it is not the bread or indeed the sword that troubles Saul but the inquiring of the Lord. In his defence he notes three things: first that David is a faithful servant of Saul (indeed, he is kin to the king and quick to do his bidding); second that this is by no means the first time he has inquired of the Lord for David – implying that the act has never created any difficulty for Saul before; and thirdly that if there is any falling out between Saul and David, he knows nothing about it.

Effectively Ahimelech signs his own death warrant; for he only defends himself by defending David and in the process provokes Saul still further. In verse 16 Saul pronounces sentence against Ahimelech and all his father's house and then calls on the guards who stand in his presence to carry out the execution. But he shifts the grounds for his judgment and so undermines its validity. 'Turn and kill the priests of the Lord', he says (underlining the priests' status and so perhaps inhibiting the guards), 'because their hand also is with David (more hands): 'they knew that he fled and did not disclose it to me.' The priests are to be killed not for any of the three things that in innocence they did do but because of the one thing that in innocence they failed to do: 'they knew that he fled' (they almost certainly didn't) 'and failed to disclose it to me'.

The guards refuse. They know that Ahimelech is innocent; and in any case they hesitate to strike the Lord's priest. So Saul turns to Doeg and commands him to kill the priests. When in verse 18 Doeg is referred to as 'the Edomite', this is the second of three times in this chapter when his ethnic origins are emphasized (compare verses 9 and 22). It is presumably somehow less shocking, and more credible, that a non-Israelite should be responsible for the atrocity that follows.

Doeg not only does as Saul commands ('You, Doeg, turn and attack the priests') but goes beyond the command: he not only slaughters eighty-five priests (verse 18), but puts the whole city of Nob to the sword (verse 19): the women, infants and toddlers, and animals too. There is a sobering verbal correspondence between 1 Samuel 22:19 and 1 Samuel 15:3. Where Saul had failed to comply with the command of Samuel, to slaughter the Amalekites 'both man and woman, child and infant, ox and sheep, camel and donkey', Doeg here goes beyond the command of Saul and kills, 'men and women, children and infants, oxen, donkeys, and sheep'. Were there no camels in Nob?

Scene Five (verses 20–23): A priest flees to David

> 20 But one of the sons of Ahimelech son of Ahitub, named Abiathar, escaped and fled after David. 21 Abiathar told David that Saul had killed the priests of the Lord. 22 David said to Abiathar, 'I knew on that day, when Doeg the Edomite was there, that he would surely tell Saul. I am responsible for the lives of all your father's house. 23 Stay with me, and do not be afraid; for the one who seeks my life seeks your life; you will be safe with me.'

Eighty-five priests are killed; but one survives: Abiathar (whose name, appropriately enough, means 'my father remains'). He escapes and flees to David and reports what has happened. Again Saul's best efforts have backfired. By eradicating the whole Israelite priesthood he has only succeeded in eradicating his own access to Yahweh. The one priest who has survived the slaughter has run hot-foot to David, so that David now has what he did not have before: a priest (as well as in Gad, a prophet) among his entourage. David offers him refuge and (another good sign this, and a consistent attribute in him) accepts responsibility for what has happened. Apparently he knew that Doeg was there on that day when he begged bread from Ahimelech, and guessed what the consequences might be. So he holds himself responsible for the slaughter that followed. He senses that it was his lie in 1 Samuel 21:2 that set the whole disastrous course of events in motion.

It has been said that 'sin is expensive'. It is a rare thing to 'get away with it'. True, by grace, sinners may not always face the full consequences of their failure or folly. But by and large there is a reckoning. Deliberate and calculated deceit has consequences. But to the extent that David acted badly before Ahimelech, he now acts well; to the extent that he acted foolishly, he now acts wisely. He urges Abiathar, presumably traumatized by the wholesale slaughter of his family, not to be afraid and offers him sanctuary.

Conclusion

David is in exile. Exile is never a comfortable place to be: it is by definition not home. Exile involves a loss of power and control, an exclusion and marginalization. It is inevitably a hard place to be, whether for an individual or for an institution. In David's case part of the hardship arises from a knowledge of the sufferings that others have experienced and that he has at least escaped and possibly caused.

But exile can be a good place too. It is a good place to find out who one's friends are. They are likely, themselves, to be the excluded and the marginalized – there is solidarity among outcasts. But it is also a good place to discern the will and purpose of God. Such discernment is sometimes only possible for the exile. After David slew Goliath, throughout the time he remained at Saul's court, he never spoke of God. Jonathan spoke of the Lord; even Saul did – but David did not. It is no coincidence that he began to do so just as soon as he had fled (see 1 Sam. 20:3). In exile, discerning the will and purpose of God becomes a priority for David (verse 3). Not only does a sense of need propel him – the exile also provides the space (the time and the quietness) that a deliberate seeking of God's face usually requires.

Chapter Eight
(1 Samuel 23:1–29)

David eludes Saul

Introduction

There are few clues in this story as to the passage of time. The reader has little help in gauging how long David was on the run from Saul. He fled from Saul's court in 1 Samuel 19 – first to his mentor at Naioth (19:18), then to Jonathan (1 Sam. 20:1; back in Gibeah?), then to Ahimelech in Nob (1 Sam. 21:1), then to Achish in Gath (1 Sam. 21:10), then to the cave of Adullam (1 Sam. 22:1) and on to Mizpeh in Moab (1 Sam. 22:3) and finally to the forest of Hereth (1 Sam. 22:5). In this episode he begins in the Wilderness of Ziph (verse 15) and goes via the Wilderness of Maon (verse 24b) to the strongholds of En-gedi (verse 29). The impression is that these movements followed swiftly, one after another, during a period to be measured in days and weeks, rather than months and years. Yet by the end of 1 Samuel the impression is also that David's flight from Saul has lasted years – such that David the youth has become a man.

The present episode, which unfolds in five scenes, opens with David fighting the Philistines and in the process giving away his location to Saul. It closes with Saul fighting the Philistines and in the process giving David a means of escape. The first four scenes are linked by their references to hands (verses 4, 6, 7, 12, 14, 16, 17, 20).

Scene One (verses 1–5): David delivers Keilah

1 Now they told David, 'The Philistines are fighting against Keilah, and are robbing the threshing-floors.' 2 David inquired of the Lord, 'Shall I go and

attack these Philistines?' The Lord said to David, 'Go and attack the
Philistines and save Keilah.' 3 But David's men said to him, 'Look, we are
afraid here in Judah; how much more then if we go to Keilah against the
armies of the Philistines?' 4 Then David inquired of the Lord again. The
Lord answered him, 'Yes, go down to Keilah; for I will give the Philistines
into your hand.' 5 So David and his men went to Keilah, fought with the
Philistines, brought away their livestock, and dealt them a heavy defeat.
Thus David rescued the inhabitants of Keilah. 6 When Abiathar son of
Ahimelech fled to David at Keilah, he came down with an ephod in his hand.

Where is Keilah? Is it in Judah or not? The fact that David is concerned about Philistine attacks there and raids on its threshing
floor suggests that it is. It is at least in the Judean sphere of influence. But the fact that his men regard it as a dangerous area into
which to venture, a place even more vulnerable to the Philistines
than 'here in Judah' suggests it isn't quite. It is borderland.

There is an important departure in the narrative here in two
respects. For one thing this is the first time that in his own right
(without authorization from Saul) David has done battle with the
Philistines and 'dealt them a heavy defeat'. In terms of establishing his credentials to rule over Israel this is a huge step: David
delivers a city from Philistine oppression.

Secondly, David undertakes the attack only after twice
'enquiring of the Lord'. First in verse 2, when he hears what the
Philistines are doing to Keilah, David asks the Lord, 'Shall I go
and attack these Philistines?'; and is told, 'Yes, go and attack
them and save Keilah'. But his men are not sure: the proposal
strikes them as risky. They are having a hard enough time
defending themselves against the threat of Saul without going
looking for trouble by picking a fight against the Philistines too.
So David seeks a second opinion – albeit from the same source.
He is again assured of victory: the Lord will give the Philistines
into his hand. So he attacks and duly inflicts on them a heavy
defeat – strengthening his own position in the process through
the acquisition of their cattle. David not only does right in seeking guidance from the Lord before embarking on an attack
against the Philistines: the Lord also answers David both immediately and positively. David receives not only the guidance he
seeks but blessing also.

Although the scene concludes by stating that 'Abiathar, son of Ahimelech fled to David at Keilah' (as if David had already concluded the victory there when Abiathar arrived) 'with an ephod in his hand', it is in fact clear from the end of the previous episode (1 Sam. 22:20–23),that Abiathar joined David while he was still at the cave of Adullam. The emphasis this scene places on David's enquiring of the Lord underlines Abiathar's value as a recruit to David's cause.

Scene Two (verses 7–14): Saul pursues David

> *7 Now it was told Saul that David had come to Keilah. And Saul said, 'God has given him into my hand; for he has shut himself in by entering a town that has gates and bars.' 8 Saul summoned all the people to war, to go down to Keilah, to besiege David and his men. 9 When David learned that Saul was plotting evil against him, he said to the priest Abiathar, 'Bring the ephod here.' 10 David said, 'O Lord, the God of Israel, your servant has heard that Saul seeks to come to Keilah, to destroy the city on my account. 11 And now, will Saul come down as your servant has heard? O Lord, the God of Israel, I beseech you, tell your servant.' The Lord said, 'He will come down.' 12 Then David said, 'Will the men of Keilah surrender me and my men into the hand of Saul?' The Lord said, 'They will surrender you.' 13 Then David and his men, who were about six hundred, set out and left Keilah; they wandered wherever they could go. When Saul was told that David had escaped from Keilah, he gave up the expedition. 14 David remained in the strongholds in the wilderness, in the hill country of the Wilderness of Ziph. Saul sought him every day, but the Lord did not give him into his hand.*

The spotlight shifts back and forth in this episode from David to Saul and back to David again. The previous scene ended with Abiathar arriving in David's presence 'ephod in hand'; this one opens with Saul discovering David's whereabouts and becoming certain not just that he is about to capture his enemy, but that 'God has given him into his hand.' Saul is not quite reconciled yet to the fact that God has rejected him: he still believes that God is acting with him and for him. But he is deluding himself. The conclusion of this scene will be that 'the Lord did not give [David] into [Saul's] hand'.

In attacking Keilah David has let his whereabouts be known. In the cave of Adullam he had been as hard to find as Al Qaeda in the caves of Afghanistan. So Saul makes ready and mobilizes his forces to besiege Keilah. But David also has access to intelligence and learns of Saul's intentions. To discover the Lord's intentions, however, he summons Abiathar and his ephod. The ephod was apparently a linen garment, from which the 'urim' and 'thummim' were drawn as lots, so indicating the will of God (Ex. 28:6–30; 1 Sam. 14:36–42).

David addresses himself deliberately and solemnly to 'the Lord, the God of Israel' (verses 10, 11). First (for the ephod is capable only of mediating answers 'Yes' or 'No') he asks whether the intelligence he has received is true: 'Will Saul come down?' The answer is 'Yes.' David then asks a supplementary question, which is less than obvious: 'Will the men Keilah betray me and my forces?' Again the answer is 'Yes.' (There is a similar two-stage query of the ephod in 1 Sam. 30:8.)

So David abandons Keilah before its residents can abandon him. He leaves with his six hundred men (the company has grown). But David has no definite destination: he and his men 'wander wherever they could go'. He stays in the hill country of Ziph in the strongholds of the wilderness. And although Saul gives up the specific expedition against Keilah, he does not give up his pursuit of David: 'Saul sought him every day, but the Lord did not give him into his hand.'

In the previous episode, Saul was complaining that he was everywhere surrounded by treachery. In fact, here and in the sequel below, it is David who is betrayed. Yet he survives because of the Lord.

Scene Three (verses 15–18): Jonathan strengthens David's hand through the Lord

> *15 David was in the Wilderness of Ziph at Horesh when he learned that Saul had come out to seek his life. 16 Saul's son Jonathan set out and came to David at Horesh; there he strengthened his hand through the Lord. 17 He said to him, 'Do not be afraid; for the hand of my father Saul shall not find you; you shall be king over Israel, and I shall be second to*

you; my father Saul also knows that this is so.' 18 Then the two of them made a covenant before the Lord; David remained at Horesh, and Jonathan went home.

Saul and David are not the only ones with access to secret intelligence. Jonathan has it too. David is only temporarily at Horesh. Yet Jonathan finds him with an ease his father lacks. In his case lines of communication are presumably still open.

Again it is Jonathan who takes the initiative in his relationship with David. He comes to David at Horesh and 'strengthens his hand through the Lord'. This is the last time the two friends will ever meet. Of all the references to hands in this episode, this one in the middle scene is the most vital. The expression is unique in the Old Testament. Presumably – although this is not explicit in verse 17 – it means that Jonathan encouraged David by reminding him of the Lord's promises. 'Do not be afraid', he says. In Scripture these are usually the words of an angel, usually spoken to people who have good grounds to fear.

'You shall be king over Israel,' he goes on, 'I shall be second to you.' This too is a new departure. No one in Israel has yet stated so clearly the expectation that David will be king. Moreover Jonathan adds (what the reader has not yet heard directly from Saul) that his father knows this to be true. It is right that the first to do so should be the very one who might have harboured hopes of assuming the kingship himself. But when he says, 'I shall be second to you', he is only half right. Jonathan rightly discerns that his own future destiny is now secondary relative to David's. But he is wrong if he thought that one day he would himself enjoy prominence in a kingdom ruled by David. Again Christian readers are reminded of the words of John the Baptist in relation to Jesus 'he must increase and I must decrease' (Jn. 3:30).

Characteristically it is Jonathan, not David, who speaks in verse 17 and who discloses his heart and mind. David does not respond.

When, in verse 18, the text states that 'the two of them made a covenant before the Lord', this is the third time their relationship has been described in these terms (compare 1 Sam. 18:3, 20:16). Here, for the first time however, the act is described mutually.

Previously it could not have been clearer that it was Jonathan who made a covenant with David. Here the two of them make a covenant with one another. The irony is that their relationship achieves a degree of mutuality only at their last meeting. There is something utterly final about it when the text states that David then 'remained at Horeb and Jonathan went home'.

Scene Four (verses 19–24a): The Ziphites betray David's hiding place to Saul

19 Then some Ziphites went up to Saul at Gibeah and said, 'David is hiding among us in the strongholds of Horesh, on the hill of Hachilah, which is south of Jeshimon. 20 Now, O king, whenever you wish to come down, do so; and our part will be to surrender him into the king's hand.' 21 Saul said, 'May you be blessed by the Lord for showing me compassion! 22 Go and make sure once more; find out exactly where he is, and who has seen him there; for I am told that he is very cunning. 23 Look around and learn all the hiding-places where he lurks, and come back to me with sure information. Then I will go with you; and if he is in the land, I will search him out among all the thousands of Judah.' 24 So they set out and went to Ziph ahead of Saul.

Now it emerges how Saul came by his information about David's whereabouts, at least some of the time. Local people tell him. On this occasion some Ziphites – David is in the hill country of Ziph (verse 14) – tell Saul in considerable detail where he can find David: 'in the strongholds of Horesh, on the hill of Hachilah south of Jeshimon'. Moreover they promise that they will betray David 'into the king's hand'. Perhaps the slaughter at Nob had persuaded some communities that their best hope of security was to seek Saul's favour.

Saul is immensely grateful to the Ziphites. 'May you be blessed by the Lord for showing me compassion', he says. It is striking that Saul is still invoking the Lord; and it is striking that he regards the Ziphites' gesture as one not just of loyalty but of compassion. It is usually the weak who evoke compassion. There is some acknowledgment here on Saul's part that despite political appearances in his struggle against David he is up against a power beyond his own.

There is something obsessive about Saul's need for further detail and for proof. 'Go and make sure once more,' he demands, 'find out exactly where he is, and who has seen him there; for I am told that he is very cunning.' Saul's second appeal reflects David's at the start of the chapter, except that David inquires twice of the Lord, and Saul of the Ziphites. He wants to know 'all the hiding-places where he lurks', and to be supplied with 'sure information'. Only then will Saul go with them. But then he asserts that he will search David out 'among all the thousands of Judah'.

Scene Five (verses 24b–29): Saul and his men close in on David

> *24b David and his men were in the wilderness of Maon, in the Arabah to the south of Jeshimon. 25 Saul and his men went to search for him. When David was told, he went down to the rock and stayed in the wilderness of Maon. When Saul heard that, he pursued David into the wilderness of Maon. 26 Saul went on one side of the mountain, and David and his men on the other side of the mountain. David was hurrying to get away from Saul, while Saul and his men were closing in on David and his men to capture them. 27 Then a messenger came to Saul, saying, 'Hurry and come; for the Philistines have made a raid on the land.' 28 So Saul stopped pursuing David, and went against the Philistines; therefore that place was called the Rock of Escape. 29 David then went up from there, and lived in the strongholds of En-gedi.*

The Ziphites are apparently able to provide more precise intelligence: David and his men are in the wilderness of Maon 'in the Arabah, south of Jeshimon'. So Saul and his men go searching for him. But David's intelligence is also good. When he hears that Saul is searching for him, David moves on, going 'down to the rock'. Saul again hears of it and pursues him: the king and his men on one side of the mountain and David and his men on the other. David hurries to escape but Saul closes in. Just as it seems certain that Saul must capture David, a messenger arrives with news that the Philistines have attacked Israelite territory. Saul is forced to abandon his pursuit of David, the fugitive is gifted an unexpected reprieve and the rock acquires a new name: it becomes 'the Rock of escape'. It's hardly surprising to find God so often likened to a rock of refuge in the Psalms of David. In the providence of God, David is effectively rescued – by the Philistines. What appears at one level to be an extraordinary stroke of good fortune on David's part in fact illustrates Saul's folly: it is the Philistines, not David, who represent a real threat to his kingdom – and yet he is expending precious time and energy pursuing the latter not the former.

Conclusion

The issue of divine providence reaches something of a resolution in this episode in the repeated references to human hands.

On the one side are Saul and his allies. The hand of Saul reaches for David and towards the end of the episode seems almost certain to take him. The men of Keilah (verse 12) and the men of Ziph (verse 20) are ready to betrayal David into Saul's hand. And Saul is confident not just of taking David, but that it is the will and purpose of God for him to do so. When in verse 7, he rejoices that 'God has given [David] into my hand', it is the last moment in the story when it is possible for Saul to deceive himself in this way. It is often the way that those boasting most loudly that the Lord is on their side are deluding themselves.

On the other side are David and his allies. David makes no equivalent claim about the will of God. But there is no need. Events demonstrate that the Lord is with him. David can rely on the help of God in both attack and defence. Thus the episode opens with David's providential victory over the Philistines ('for I will give [them] into your hand'), and ends with his providential escape by their intervention (for 'the Lord did not give him into [Saul's] hand').

Crucial to David's deliverance was his capacity to inquire of the Lord – something he owed to the presence of Abiathar and 'the ephod in his hand'. Equally crucial was the encouragement of Jonathan, who 'strengthened David's hand in the Lord'. The parts played of Abiathar and Jonathan are not to be underestimated.

They provide the context for David's experiences of divine favour. It is no coincidence that the events which most clearly show that David is the personal beneficiary of providence come in the episode which also offers the greatest evidence both of his own deepening relationship with the Lord, and of his solidarity with others in faith.

Chapter Nine
(1 Samuel 24:1–22)

David and Saul's cloak

Introduction

Throughout this narrative David's character as well as his destiny is defined in relation to Saul. In that regard the story of 'David in the wilderness' has a carefully crafted shape. It pivots on the next episode, in chapter 25 – a lengthy story about David's encounter with Abigail, wife of Nabal. Either side of that story (in this chapter and in 1 Samuel 26) are a pair of related episodes in which (for the only occasions between David's flight from Gibeah and Saul's death) the two men come face to face. The rest of the account of David's wilderness years is distributed fairly evenly either side of those episodes: four chapters comprising 109 verses of the biblical text in 1 Samuel 20 – 23 and five chapters comprising 114 verses in 1 Samuel 27 – 31.

The present episode picks up the story as Saul again resumes his pursuit of David, having 'returned from following the Philistines'. The narrative does not say what the outcome was of any skirmish Saul might have had with them, but events had presumably gone sufficiently well from his point of view for him to feel he could now afford to turn his attention to the internal threat once more. The episode unfolds in two scenes, in both of which the hand motif is again prominent.

Scene One (verses 1–7): Saul resumes his pursuit of David

1 When Saul returned from following the Philistines, he was told, 'David is in the wilderness of En-gedi.' 2 Then Saul took three thousand chosen men out of all Israel, and went to look for David and his men in the direction of the Rocks of the Wild Goats. 3 He came to the sheepfolds beside the road, where there was a cave; and Saul went in to relieve himself. Now David and his men were sitting in the innermost parts of the cave. 4 The men of David said to him, 'Here is the day of which the Lord said to you, "I will give your enemy into your hand, and you shall do to him as it seems good to you." ' Then David went and stealthily cut off a corner of Saul's cloak. 5 Afterwards David was stricken to the heart because he had cut off a corner of Saul's cloak. 6 He said to his men, 'The Lord forbid that I should do this thing to my lord, the Lord's anointed, to raise my hand against him; for he is the Lord's anointed.' 7 So David scolded his men severely and did not permit them to attack Saul. Then Saul got up and left the cave, and went on his way.

David may consistently elude Saul, but Saul is not short of good intelligence concerning David's whereabouts. The fact that Saul receives regular tip-offs, which consistently prove to be reliable, only serves to underline the extent to which David is protected by divine providence: Saul can get near his opponent but he cannot harm him.

On this occasion Saul receives reports that David is – as the reader was told in 1 Samuel 23:29 – in the wilderness of En-Gedi. So he takes three thousand men 'out of all Israel' and hunts for David and his men once again.

Passing a cave, Saul enters it – alone presumably – in order 'to relieve himself'. (The Hebrew idiom is, 'to cover his feet'. This is the verse infamously translated by Kenneth Naylor in his 1971 publication, *The Living Bible*: 'Saul went into a cave to go to the bathroom.') Now 'David and his men' were hiding in the depths of the cave. (Are we to imagine this means all six hundred of them or more probably just a contingent?)

To them it is obvious that this is David's moment. They tell him, 'Today is the day the Lord promised, when he would give your enemy into your hand, so fully that you'd be able to do with him whatever you want'. If David was ever given such a promise (as an oracle?) the reader wasn't told. In just the previous episode, it's true, the Lord had promised to give the Philistines into his hand (1 Sam. 23:6). But that enemy and Saul are two entirely different opponents.

Saul is defenceless. He squats, unarmed and alone. A more vulnerable position is hard to imagine. If David wants to kill Saul (and that is what his men mean, even if they cannot bring themselves to say it in so many words), he will never have a better chance. David does not reply; but as they watched him creep stealthily forward, knife in hand, towards Saul, his men must surely have thought that they had persuaded him to their own way of thinking. Yet David cuts off not Saul's head from his shoulders, but merely a corner from his cloak. Admittedly the gesture had some symbolic significance in the light of Samuel's words to Saul in chapter 15, after Saul had grabbed and torn the prophet's robe ('the Lord has torn the kingdom of Israel from you', verse 28). The language of 'cutting off' also recalls the promises extracted from David by Jonathan in chapter 20:14–16. David's men were nevertheless presumably both incredulous and frustrated that their leader should pass up such an apparently God-sent opportunity.

David however is conscience-stricken. This moment marks an important development in the narrative. When in verse 4 his men urge him to kill Saul and David decides not to, the narrator establishes a distinction between David's perspective and that of his men – and the reader easily relates to David's point of view. But in verses 5 and 6, the narrator also establishes a distinction between David's perspective and that of most readers. To most readers, the way David has acted towards Saul in sparing his life and contriving a way to demonstrate his innocent intentions is extremely magnanimous. But to David himself, while his act may not have harmed Saul physically, it has nevertheless amounted to a 'raising of [his] hand' against him. The repetition of the words 'the Lord's anointed' is emphatic: 'The Lord forbid that I should do this thing to my lord, the Lord's anointed – for he **is** the Lord's anointed.' The narrative presents David here not just as loyal to Saul, but as scrupulously – almost laughably – loyal to him.

David has not just to restrain himself, however: he has to restrain his men. So he scolds them and will not permit them to attack Saul, who is therefore able to leave the cave unharmed.

Scene Two (verses 8–22): David appeals to Saul

8 Afterwards David also rose up and went out of the cave and called after Saul, 'My lord the king!' When Saul looked behind him, David bowed with his face to the ground, and did obeisance. 9 David said to Saul, 'Why do you listen to the words of those who say, "David seeks to do you harm"? 10 This very day your eyes have seen how the Lord gave you into my hand in the cave; and some urged me to kill you, but I spared you. I said, "I will not raise my hand against my lord; for he is the Lord's anointed." 11 See, my father, see the corner of your cloak in my hand; for by the fact that I cut off the corner of your cloak, and did not kill you, you may know for certain that there is no wrong or treason in my hands. I have not sinned against you, though you are hunting me to take my life. 12 May the Lord judge between me and you! May the Lord avenge me on you; but my hand shall not be against you. 13 As the ancient proverb says, "Out of the wicked comes forth wickedness"; but my hand shall not be against you. 14 Against whom has the king of Israel come out? Whom do you pursue? A dead dog? A single flea? 15 May the Lord therefore be judge, and give sentence between me and you. May he see to it, and plead my cause, and vindicate me against you.'

16 When David had finished speaking these words to Saul, Saul said, 'Is that your voice, my son David?' Saul lifted up his voice and wept. 17 He said to David, 'You are more righteous than I; for you have repaid me good, whereas I have repaid you evil. 18 Today you have explained how you have dealt well with me, in that you did not kill me when the Lord put me into your hands. 19 For who has ever found an enemy, and sent the enemy safely away? So may the Lord reward you with good for what you have done to me this day. 20 Now I know that you shall surely be king, and that the kingdom of Israel shall be established in your hand. 21 Swear to me therefore by the Lord that you will not cut off my descendants after me, and that you will not wipe out my name from my father's house.' 22 So David swore this to Saul. Then Saul went home; but David and his men went up to the stronghold.

To what extent is David prepared to put himself and his men at risk? At the end of the previous scene Saul left the cave; now 'David also rose up and went out of the cave and called after Saul'. Presumably he waits until Saul is only just within calling distance – with a ravine, or at least an uphill climb, between them. But the moment David shouts, he surely takes a chance: for the first time since David fled from the court, Saul knows not just roughly but exactly where he is. And he is near enough to hold a conversation

– albeit shouted. David and his men are at most minutes from Saul and his men – and are outnumbered five to one. But by bowing and declaring his loyalty, and showing off the piece of Saul's cloak which he has cut off, David is confident of securing a hearing. Whatever remorse he was feeling, it is not enough to prevent him from exploiting the moral high ground now that he has spared Saul's life and has the evidence to prove it.

The impassioned speech he makes in verses 9–15 is by far the longest David has made in the story to this point. It refers repeatedly, once again, to hands (twice in verse 10, twice in verse 11, and again in verses 12, 13 and 16).

First, David demands Saul's attention: 'My lord the king', he shouts (verse 8). Then he does obeisance, bowing to the ground. He challenges the charge that he has been seeking to do Saul harm on the grounds that just now, presented with the perfect opportunity to kill him, he has spared Saul's life (verse 10) precisely because he is the Lord's anointed. As proof David shows off the corner of Saul's robe in his hand. The text may not say so, but at that point Saul surely looked down at his cloak and saw the hole left by David's cut. The argument is conclusive: what more compelling proof could Saul ask? If David were seeking to harm Saul, what better opportunity could he have? If he did not take it, surely his loyalty cannot be in question.

At the climax of the first part of the speech he seeks to re-establish a relationship with Saul: he calls him 'my father' (verse 11).

In the second half of the speech, having proved his innocence, he appeals to God for vindication. Three times he calls upon the Lord: 'May the Lord judge . . . may the Lord avenge . . . may the Lord be judge' (verses 12, 15). Twice he promises that his 'hand shall not be against you'. When in verse 13, he quotes a proverb ('Out of the wicked comes forth wickedness'), the implication is that it is Saul, not David, who is wicked. It is after all 'the king of Israel' who has 'come out' (verse 14).

When David has finished speaking, Saul replies. It is a moving response and fleetingly hopeful to the reader. First he calls David by name. It is the first time Saul has done so to his face in the whole story. Moreover he calls him 'David my son'. Then Saul 'lifted up his voice and wept'. His tears are both for what might have been and for what he now accepts must be. They are tears on the one hand of penitence; but also on the other hand of resignation. When he speaks again it is first to express repentance: in words reminiscent of those uttered by Judah to Tamar in Genesis 38:26 (from whose line David was born), he acknowledges David to be more righteous than himself (verse 17). There is nowhere in the story where the reader has more sympathy for Saul than when he recognizes that, quite unjustifiably, he has done evil to David. The reader understands that Saul himself is a victim in this story as well as a villain: the Lord has after all sent an evil spirit upon him. In 'repaying' David evil for good, he has to some extent been subject to forces beyond his control.

Indeed, Saul exonerates David so fulsomely that it is hard to avoid the impression that it is the narrator's voice, rather than his own that is heard: 'Today you have explained how you dealt well with me in that you did not kill me when the Lord put me into your hands. For who has ever found an enemy and sent the enemy safely away?' But his tears are also for what is to come, as Saul states for the first time here what the reader has known since chapter 16, that David will be king. 'Now I know,' he says, 'that you will surely be king and that the kingdom of Israel will be established in your hand.'

In fact Saul's behaviour almost since the first day he encountered David has suggested that at some intuitive level he has recognized this destiny. He has even hinted previously that 'the son of Jesse', rather than his own son Jonathan, will succeed him (1 Sam. 20:31; 22:7). But this is the first time he has stated the matter in so many words and certainly the first time he has done so to David. But if, in his tears, Saul is here acting and seeing truly and even speaking the truth, it is a short-lived moment, from which he will soon once again descend into deceit and denial.

In this moment, however, he is farsighted enough to appeal to David not to act cruelly towards his house. Just as Jonathan had done previously (1 Sam. 20:15) he asks David (in verse 23) not to 'cut off' [his] descendants after [him]. There is an allusion here to the language used by David in verse 11 (compare verses 4–5), with reference to Saul's cloak.

The episode ends with David promising what Saul has requested. He is as magnanimous in the openness of the valley as he had been in the privacy of the cave. But he can afford to be:

Saul has given him more than he asked for. David had asked only for vindication and for deliverance from Saul's murderous intent; he has been given public legitimization in relation to the crown.

Conclusion

There is a significant shift in the balance of power in this episode, which is reflected in its closing words. Saul just 'went home'; but David and his men 'went up to the stronghold'. Their position is less precarious than before.

The shift in the balance of power is reflected in the fact that it is only David's 'hand' (or 'hands') that are mentioned in this chapter. When his men speak in verse 4; when David himself is speaking in verses 6, 10 (twice), 11 (twice), 12 and 13; and when Saul speaks 18 and 20 – in every case the reference is to David's hands.

Yet the shift in the balance of power is negotiated nobly by both men. Both seek to honour the other. Both seek also to honour the Lord. Both accept that there is a reckoning for what is past; and both accept that the future belongs to the Lord.

Chapter Ten
(1 Samuel 25:1–44)

David and Nabal

Introduction

This tenth chapter of the (not quite) twenty-one chapters in the story of David's rise is the centre-piece. Before it come several episodes relating to David's flight from Saul in the wilderness, as well as the few opening stories about David's life in Saul's court. After it come several more episodes relating to the flight, as well as the few stories about David's life after Saul's death. Given its central placement, its emphasis on 'evil' (verses 3, 17, 21, 26, 28, 39) may have significance for the whole story. Up to this point in the story, evil has only reared its ugly head in relation to Saul (culminating in the acknowledgement by Saul in the previous episode that he has repaid David only evil for good). In this episode, what is at stake is David's relationship to evil. Evil threatens David – and if he does not capitulate to it, this has less to do with his own goodness than to the goodness of a woman, Abigail.

In the episodes either side of this one, David is presented as the model of self-restraint. With Saul twice at his mercy, he refuses to lift his hand against the Lord's anointed. He refuses to heed his men, who urge him to violence. The same themes are present in this episode too but in reverse. Sorely provoked, David is ready to lift his hand against Nabal. He is kept from bloodshed only because he does heed Nabal's wife. David comes over as an impetuous and potentially violent man, altogether less calm and composed than he has appeared in earlier episodes; and yet also as wise and open to reason, capable of changing his mind and taking advice. The episode unfolds in six scenes.

Scene One (verse 1): The death of Samuel reported

1 Now Samuel died; and all Israel assembled and mourned for him. They buried him at his home in Ramah.
Then David got up and went down to the wilderness of Paran.

The report of Samuel's death is as sudden as it is brief. It comes without warning and without elaboration. There is no explanation of how Samuel died (although the very brevity of the opening three words invite the reader to assume that it was an entirely natural and predictable thing, not so unexpected as far as his contemporaries were concerned and certainly not violent). There is also no account of how Israel assembled and mourned for its great prophet or of any ceremony associated with the burial, although the text does relate that his final resting place was at his home in Ramah. Presumably Saul attended the funeral. The final sentence in the opening verse may imply that David did also.

But the timing of the announcement is entirely appropriate in the context of the narrative as a whole. In the previous episode a significant turning point was reached when Saul recognized the inevitability of David's kingship. This inevitability was first known to Samuel. It was then a private matter, barely spelt out even to those who were present at the anointing in Bethlehem. Now the inevitability of David's accession to the throne of Israel is publicly recognized, acknowledged and accepted by even the person most threatened by it. Samuel's king-making work in Israel is done.

Scene Two (verses 2–13): David's request of Nabal

2 There was a man in Maon, whose property was in Carmel. The man was very rich; he had three thousand sheep and a thousand goats. He was shearing his sheep in Carmel. 3 Now the name of the man was Nabal, and the name of his wife Abigail. The woman was clever and beautiful, but the man was surly and mean; he was a Calebite. 4 David heard in the wilderness that Nabal was shearing his sheep. 5 So David sent ten young men; and David said to the young men, 'Go up to Carmel, and go to Nabal, and greet him in my name. 6 Thus you shall salute him: "Peace

be to you, and peace be to your house, and peace be to all that you have.
7 I hear that you have shearers; now your shepherds have been with us,
and we did them no harm, and they missed nothing, all the time they
were in Carmel. 8 Ask your young men, and they will tell you. Therefore
let my young men find favour in your sight; for we have come on a feast
day. Please give whatever you have at hand to your servants and to your
son David." '

9 When David's young men came, they said all this to Nabal in the name
of David; and then they waited. 10 But Nabal answered David's servants,
'Who is David? Who is the son of Jesse? There are many servants today
who are breaking away from their masters. 11 Shall I take my bread and
my water and the meat that I have butchered for my shearers, and give it
to men who come from I do not know where?' 12 So David's young men
turned away, and came back and told him all this. 13 David said to his
men, 'Every man strap on his sword!' And every one of them strapped on
his sword; David also strapped on his sword; and about four hundred
men went up after David, while two hundred remained with the baggage.

The way a story begins in Scripture is often informative. The line,
'There was a man' is entirely conventional. It is repeated many
times in the Bible and is analogous to the English 'Once upon a
time'. But what usually follows is the man's name (in Jdgs. 17:1;
1 Sam. 1:1; 9:1; Job.1:1; Lk. 2:25 and Jn. 1:6). Here it does not. (The
only other time the formula is used and is not at once followed by
the man's name is in Lk. 15:11 in Jesus' parable – when the man
in question was fictional.) What follows here is a series of statements that spell out the man's great wealth: his property, it is
said, was in Carmel; the man was very rich; he had three thousand sheep and a thousand goats; and he was shearing his sheep
in Carmel. This man is not just rich – he is defined by his wealth.
It is even more definitive for him than his name. His name is also
significant however. He is called 'Nabal' – which means 'Fool', or
'Oaf'. But he is not just an idiot and a surly man: he is mean (the
word in verse 3 is equally well translated 'evil').

The other definitive thing about Nabal is his wife. As soon as
the text discloses his name, it shifts to his wife – and the statement of her character precedes the statement of his. Abigail is as
clever (verse 3, literally 'good of understanding') as her husband

was stupid; and as beautiful (the same word is used to describe David in 1 Sam. 16:12) as he was mean. These attributes are vital: her intelligence will enable her to negotiate the impending crisis; and her beauty will ensure that she captivates David.

Now David has heard in the wilderness that Nabal is shearing his sheep and sends his men to request a voluntary, but in the circumstances apparently appropriate, gift. From David's point of view Nabal is in his debt; but any such debt is not recognized by mean Nabal. From the brief commission David gives to his men in verse 7 it is not quite clear whether David is saying that his men positively helped Nabal's men or just that they have refrained from harming him: 'You shepherds have been with us and we did them no harm and they missed nothing all the time they were in Carmel.' This may mean that David's men have been offering protection to Nabal's men preventing others from stealing from their flocks (if the emphasis is on the final clause of the sentence). Or it may just mean that despite constant opportunity, they have refrained from stealing anything themselves (if the emphasis is on the first clause). Commentators suggest that David is in fact racketeering (this is certainly what Nabal thought), and that this overture is a piece of classic intimidation, as if 'they missed nothing all the time' implies, 'and you will want to keep it that way'. But the narrative does not encourage that reading. In previous episodes (for example, in the sanctuary he has offered to Abiatar and to debtors, the discontented and the dispossessed), David has been presented as a liberator, not an oppressor; a defender of rights not a violator of them. And later in the story (in verses 15 and 16), Nabal's men report to Abigail how good David's men have been to them. It makes better sense to take David's words at face value: he is simply expecting an acknowledgment of his genuine neighbourliness.

So David sends his men to Nabal and instructs them to greet him warmly with a three-fold greeting of peace. 'Peace to you, peace to your house, peace to all that you have.' They are to present their request on the basis of kinship: 'Please give whatever you have to your son David for we have come on a feast day' (literally, verse 7, a 'good' day). The imprecise request diplomatically allows Nabal some room for manoeuvre; and the timing of the request is emphasized. Sheep-shearing time was party time in

Old Testament Israel (compare Gen. 38:12–16; 2 Sam. 13:23–29). If Nabal is not generous now, at a time of feasting, when will he be?

Yet Nabal rejects not just the request but the relationship too. He answers 'Who is David and who is the son of Jesse?' Both David's presentation of himself and the response it elicits are reminiscent of his dialogues with Saul: David says he is Nabal's son; Nabal dismisses him as 'the son of Jesse'. His opening words imply, 'I have heard of David of course. But he is nothing to me.' But then he goes on: 'There are many servants breaking away from their masters'. What he has heard about David, he does not care for. He has presumably heard that David has fled from Saul's house; and probably shares Saul's perspective that David is conspiring against the king. Doubtless David is known to be the captain of an outlaw band (1 Sam. 22:2). 'Why should I take my hard earned bread, water and meat,' Nabal asks, 'and give them to men I know nothing about?'

Nabal speaks as a landowner, a successful man, with an interest in preserving the status quo and with understandable reservations about anyone who might threaten the establishment. In another context this might be read as the entirely appropriate response of a person whose property is under attack by someone who has no right to it. But 'folly' in Old Testament thought is not just political, but moral misjudgment; and Nabal is a fool. He is shirking a social obligation. It is he rather than David whose greed is leading him astray. Even in English there are six first-person singular personal pronouns in verse 11 ('I', 'my'); in the original Hebrew there are eight. Like the rich fool in Jesus' parable (Lk. 12:13–21), Nabal is a man whose empire is defined to the north, south, east and west by himself.

His men return to David and report this reception to him. His band still numbers six hundred. All of them immediately arm themselves at David's command and two-thirds set off with him to exact revenge, while two hundred stay to defend the camp. There is development in the narrative here. David has frequently been fighting in the story to date; but until now his battles have been against the Philistines in the national interest. This battle, even if it in pursuit of a legitimate goal, is a more partisan confrontation.

Scene Three (verses 14–35): Abigail's response to David

14 But one of the young men told Abigail, Nabal's wife, 'David sent messengers out of the wilderness to salute our master; and he shouted insults at them. 15 Yet the men were very good to us, and we suffered no harm, and we never missed anything when we were in the fields, as long as we were with them; 16 they were a wall to us both by night and by day, all the while we were with them keeping the sheep. 17 Now therefore know this and consider what you should do; for evil has been decided against our master and against all his house; he is so ill-natured that no one can speak to him.'

18 Then Abigail hurried and took two hundred loaves, two skins of wine, five sheep ready dressed, five measures of parched grain, one hundred clusters of raisins, and two hundred cakes of figs. She loaded them on donkeys 19 and said to her young men, 'Go on ahead of me; I am coming after you.' But she did not tell her husband Nabal. 20 As she rode on the donkey and came down under cover of the mountain, David and his men came down towards her; and she met them. 21 Now David had said, 'Surely it was in vain that I protected all that this fellow has in the wilderness, so that nothing was missed of all that belonged to him; but he has returned me evil for good. 22 God do so to David and more also, if by morning I leave as much as one male of all who belong to him.'

23 When Abigail saw David, she hurried and alighted from the donkey, and fell before David on her face, bowing to the ground. 24 She fell at his feet and said, 'Upon me alone, my lord, be the guilt; please let your servant speak in your ears, and hear the words of your servant. 25 My lord, do not take seriously this ill-natured fellow Nabal; for as his name is, so is he; Nabal is his name, and folly is with him; but I, your servant, did not see the young men of my lord, whom you sent.

26 'Now then, my lord, as the Lord lives, and as you yourself live, since the Lord has restrained you from blood-guilt and from taking vengeance with your own hand, now let your enemies and those who seek to do evil to my lord be like Nabal. 27 And now let this present that your servant has brought to my lord be given to the young men who follow my lord. 28 Please forgive the trespass of your servant; for the LORD will certainly make my lord a sure house, because my lord is fighting the battles of the Lord; and evil shall not be found in you as long as you live. 29 If

anyone should rise up to pursue you and to seek your life, the life of my
lord shall be bound in the bundle of the living under the care of the Lord
your God; but the lives of your enemies he shall sling out as from the
hollow of a sling. 30 When the Lord has done to my lord according to
all the good that he has spoken concerning you, and has appointed you
prince over Israel, 31 my lord shall have no cause of grief, or pangs of
conscience, for having shed blood without cause or for having saved
himself. And when the Lord has dealt well with my lord, then remem-
ber your servant.'

32 David said to Abigail, 'Blessed be the Lord, the God of Israel, who sent
you to meet me today! 33 Blessed be your good sense, and blessed be you,
who have kept me today from blood-guilt and from avenging myself by
my own hand! 34 For as surely as the Lord the God of Israel lives, who
has restrained me from hurting you, unless you had hurried and come to
meet me, truly by morning there would not have been left to Nabal as
much as one male.' 35 Then David received from her hand what she had
brought him; he said to her, 'Go up to your house in peace; see, I have
heeded your voice, and I have granted your petition.'

If there is any ambiguity in verses 7–8 about the nature of David's
report to Nabal and request from him, or any hint that he is only
seeking to bully Nabal, it is surely removed in verses 15–16 and
21.

One of Nabal's servants (one of the shepherds who had been
with David's men: 'us . . . we . . . we' in verse 15), appalled at the
way in which his master has acted and foreseeing the outcome,
appeals to Abigail. David had sent men to 'salute' ('Peace, peace,
peace') Nabal, but he had – the reader is now told – not only
spurned David's servants, but had hurled abuse at them (verse
14). This despite the fact that David's men had been good to the
shepherds. When the servant says, 'They were like a wall to us by
night and by day, all the while we were with them keeping the
sheep', it is clear that David's men had performed some service
for the shepherds, protecting them from attack by both wild animals and marauders. David was genuinely on the side of shepherds. The servant's words not only reinforce the impression of
David's goodness but of Nabal's badness: 'he is so ill-natured
('such a son of Belial') no one can speak to him'. It is a mark of

Nabal's extreme bad character that a servant can describe him in such terms to his mistress with impunity. Abigail herself will repeat the word 'ill-natured' to describe her husband to David in verse 25.

Abigail's response is immediate, decisive and generous. She accepts the servant's account completely, not contesting his blunt judgment of her husband's manners. She knows that what the servant has said is true: Nabal 'is so ill-natured no one can speak to him'. So she does not try. Instead, without reference to him, she takes 'two hundred loaves, two skins of wine, five sheep ready dressed, five measures of parched grain, one hundred clusters of raisins, and two hundred cakes of figs' and sends them on ahead of herself to David. Her action is reminiscent of Jacob in Genesis 32:13–15, who sent gifts before him when he set out to meet his brother Esau. Like David, Esau was approaching with four hundred men (Gen. 33:1).

Meanwhile, David and his men are on the way. David is angry. It is in vain, he thinks, that he has offered Nabal protection 'so that nothing was missed of all that belonged to him' (this is the third time in the story that this point has been made, compare verses 7, 15). He is furious because ['this fellow'] 'has returned me evil for good'. In only the previous chapter, Saul acknowledged that whereas David had repaid him 'good', he himself had repaid David 'evil'. A link is implied here between Nabal and Saul – almost as if Nabal is the 'Saul' David feels free to attack, where he does not feel able to assault the Lord's anointed. Indeed he promises himself before God to destroy Nabal's household. The Hebrew in verse 22 contains a vulgarity entirely in keeping with David's fury. Where the NRSV has simply 'one male', the Authorised Version translated literally, 'one pisser against the wall'. The phrase occurs several times in the Old Testament, but only ever in a pejorative sense, when a curse or a threat is implied (1 Kgs. 14:10; 16:11–12; 21:21; 2 Kgs. 9:8). David is planning an act of savage ferocity – on a par with Saul's act against the priests of Nob.

Abigail's intervention is urgently necessary. In verse 23 the narrator is at pains to emphasize the extent of Abigail's humility: she quickly alights from her donkey and falls before David, on her face, bowing to the ground, falling at his feet. When she speaks, she takes full responsibility for what has gone wrong ('Upon me alone, my lord, be the guilt', verse 24), even if she also goes on to blame her husband ('as his name is, so is he: Nabal is his name and folly is with him', verse 25) and to protest her own innocence ('But I, your servant, did not see the young men of my lord, whom you sent', verse 25).

Nabal affected to know little about 'David, the son of Jesse' (verse 10). Abigail by contrast knows the whole story. She knows the place that the Lord has in David's life and she knows the place that David has in the Lord's purpose; in her speech she plays on both. She refers to the Lord seven times in six verses, boldly setting her situation in the context of the David's God-given destiny. Indeed the speech is almost excessive, almost so flattering that it is difficult to take at face value. She offers her gift to David and his men (verse 27) and pleads for forgiveness (verse 28); but most of the speech is intended to remind David of his high calling and to suggest to him that to shed blood here would be unworthy of it. It is the Lord who has restrained David from blood-guilt thus far (verse 26) – presumably a reference to just the previous episode, in which David was kept from harming Saul. It is the Lord who will make David a sure house (verse 28, anticipating the language of 2 Sam. 7), for David is fighting the Lord's battles (compare 1 Sam. 18:17). David's life is 'bound in the bundle of the living in the care of the Lord', who will 'sling out as from the hollow of a sling' the lives of David's enemies (an allusion to the death of Goliath). When Abigail (here and in verse 26) utters a curse on David's enemies, she is not the first. Jonathan has led the way (1 Sam. 20:15, 16). The Lord has promised David, in fact, that he will be prince over Israel – and Abigail urges David to be merciful in this situation, so that he is not troubled by pangs of guilt over any unnecessary bloodshed when those promises are fulfilled. He can afford to leave the taking of vengeance to the Lord, in accordance with Deuteronomy 32:35.

At the last Abigail shows herself to be an opportunist: 'When the Lord has dealt with my lord,' she says, 'remember your servant.' This final plea seems disconcertingly prescient. It is not of course a proposal of marriage; in that culture it could not be. But it does sow the thought in David's mind that once Nabal is out of the way, Abigail might make a suitable match for him.

Whatever he made of those words, David is entirely won over by the speech as a whole. In a triple prayer of blessing, he first blesses the Lord, for sending Abigail to him. Then he blesses Abigail's 'good sense' (in contrast to her husband's folly); and finally he blesses Abigail herself – for keeping him from blood-guilt and from taking vengeance into his own hands. (He repeats in verse 34 the same vulgarity he had used in verse 22 – acknowledging that his intention to slaughter every male in Nabal's house would have hurt Abigail herself.).

The scene ends with David accepting her gift and granting her request and sending her on her way to her house in the peace he had originally extended to Nabal.

Scene Four (verses 36–38): The Lord strikes Nabal

> 36 Abigail came to Nabal; he was holding a feast in his house, like the feast of a king. Nabal's heart was merry within him, for he was very drunk; so she told him nothing at all until the morning light. 37 In the morning, when the wine had gone out of Nabal, his wife told him these things, and his heart died within him; he became like a stone. 38 About ten days later the Lord struck Nabal, and he died.

Abigail returns home, having averted disaster. When she arrives her husband is still playing the fool, oblivious to the danger in which he had placed himself and all his household; apparently oblivious indeed to his wife's absence and her errand. He is drunk and enjoying not just a feast, but a feast fit for a king – for a man like David in fact. Again showing wisdom, Abigail says nothing until he has sobered up in the morning. When she then tells him the whole story, the shock is so great that he suffers some kind of heart-attack or stroke. It is not clear whether he is more shocked by the reality of the threat posed by David or by the fact that his wife has taken matters into her own hands. Either way, 'his heart died within him'. Ten days later he died. The narrator leaves no doubt that his demise was the Lord's doing: the Lord struck Nabal and he died.

Scene Five (verses 39–42): David makes Abigail his wife

39 When David heard that Nabal was dead, he said, 'Blessed be the Lord who has judged the case of Nabal's insult to me, and has kept back his servant from evil; the Lord has returned the evildoing of Nabal upon his own head.' Then David sent and wooed Abigail, to make her his wife. 40 When David's servants came to Abigail at Carmel, they said to her, 'David has sent us to you to take you to him as his wife.' 41 She rose and bowed down, with her face to the ground, and said, 'Your servant is a slave to wash the feet of the servants of my lord.' 42 Abigail got up hurriedly and rode away on a donkey; her five maids attended her. She went after the messengers of David and became his wife.

Abigail's request that David should remember her 'when the Lord has dealt well with my lord' bears fruit presumably more quickly than she had imagined. When he hears the news that Nabal is dead, David rejoices that the Lord himself has avenged the insult he had suffered. What the narrator stated, David instinctively believed: Nabal's death was the Lord's doing – for which David again blesses the Lord.

At once David sent for Abigail and took her as his wife. 'Woo' in verse 39 is wishful. 'Summoned' would be better. Verse 40 is more realistic: when David's servants return to Nabal's estate, requesting what once belonged to him, they do not leave empty-handed this time. They tell Abigail, 'David has sent us to you to take you to him as his wife.' On this occasion he himself has not brought about the death of a woman's husband before marrying her; in future he will do so (2 Sam. 11).

Abigail acquiesces in the same humility she had shown in his presence and leaves, hurriedly, to take up her new role. 'Your servant is a slave to wash the feet of the servants of my Lord.' (The 'Authorised' and 'Revised' versions have 'Behold your handmaid is a servant . . . of my lord', which is reminiscent of Mary's words in Lk. 1:38.)

The marriage is doubtless politically helpful to David: presumably the land in Carmel to which reference is made in verse 2, and the flocks and servants of Nabal, as well as his wife, came to David. He ends the episode a still more powerful man than he began it. It is a mark of Abigail's status that she comes to David with five maids to attend her. The fact that (in verse 42) she 'got up hurriedly' and went after the messengers of David and became his wife suggests that she was not dragged kicking and screaming into the match.

Scene Six (verses 43–44): David's other wives

43 David also married Ahinoam of Jezreel; both of them became his wives. 44 Saul had given his daughter Michal, David's wife, to Palti son of Laish, who was from Gallim.

The episode ends on a jarring note. The reader learns first that Abigail was not the only new wife David took at that time: he also married Ahinoam of Jezreel (about whom nothing else is said); and second, that David's other wife, Michal (who loved him so, chapter 18:20) had been given by Saul to another man, Palti son of Laish. When (in verse 44) the text says, 'Michal, David's wife', this is emphatic and begs questions about what Michal thought about her father's act of giving her (though married) to another man. As it happens (2 Sam. 3:14–16) this man apparently grew to love her every bit as passionately as she loved David. But Saul's action nevertheless seems like a punishment for her act in betraying her father by colluding with, or even instigating, David's escape (1 Sam. 19:1–11). It is only in the very last verse of the chapter, and then incidentally, that Saul is mentioned at all.

Conclusion

The providence of God is thoroughly mysterious. It does not neatly favour the good and penalize the wicked.

Here in the central episode of the story of his rise, David comes over as thoroughly human. He has not been faultless in previous episodes, particularly in the ease with which he resorts to deceit. But he mostly acts well. He shows loyalty, bravery, humility, generosity, faith and patience. But in this episode, David is enraged and impetuous when he first hears of Nabal's slight and triumphant when he then hears of Nabal's demise. Evil lurks close at hand and he must resist it.

There are two points to be made about this: the first is that Scripture consistently presents 'faith heroes' presented in all their flawed-ness. In grace, God chooses and uses sinners. David is a case in point.

Yet it is also the case that 'much is required of those to whom much has been given'. David is a flawed human being and his flaws do not disqualify him from God's service; but those who are called to the knowledge and service of God, are called to holiness: their behaviour ought to reflect, as far as possible, the God who has called them. It is Abigail who reminds David of this – though she herself is not faultless. She shows herself to be intelligent and decisive but also thoroughly opportunistic. Yet she understands his high calling better than he does – she grasps both that 'the Lord has appointed you prince over Israel', and that it therefore matters that David 'shall have no cause of grief or pangs of conscience'.

Consistently in Scripture, the gracious calling of God – the election to glory – comes first; but equally consistently what follows is the summons to discipleship and holiness. It matters both that the former precedes the latter; and that the latter follows the former.

Chapter Eleven
(1 Samuel 26:1–25)

David and Saul's spear

Introduction

There are close similarities between this episode and 1 Samuel 24: in both chapters Saul hears a report that David is hiding in the wilderness and sets out to find him with three thousand 'chosen men of Israel'; in both it is David who finds Saul not the other way around; in both he does so at a moment of complete vulnerability on the part of the king; in both David refuses to do what seems obvious to his men to do, which is to lay hands on the Lord's anointed and kill him; in both David instead simply takes something that belongs to Saul; and in both there is afterwards a shouted conversation between the two men in which David protests – and Saul accepts – his innocence and in which Saul undertakes to stop seeking to harm him. There are even significant verbal parallels between the dialogues with which the two episodes conclude: in both Saul begins by crying out 'Is that your voice, my son David?'; in both David then speaks at some length, calling Saul 'the king of Israel' and himself 'a single flea'; and in both Saul answers with a confession that he is at fault.

The similarities have led some commentators to treat this episode as a doublet of chapter 24: it is suggested that in the evolution of the text, one incident might have been preserved in two ways and that both traditions might subsequently be incorporated into a single written account of the rise of David. But this is a very unsatisfactory reading of a carefully crafted literary text. For one thing, such a reading flattens out the differences between the two stories; for another, it fails to consider the significance of the repetitions within the overall structure of the narrative. Both are dramatically important.

In fact the similarities between the two stories serve to emphasize the subtle developments that take place between the earlier episode and the later one. It is not only the setting that has changed – though this too is part of the movement of the narrative: in 1 Samuel 24 the encounter between David and Saul takes place in a cave in the wilderness of En-gedi; in this chapter it takes place in a valley in the wilderness of Ziph. There are other significant differences too, which convey the shift in power between the two men which is underway at this stage in the narrative: in the earlier story it is Saul who inadvertently enters David's camp; here it is David who deliberately enters Saul's. If David's risk is greater in this episode, in that he actively seeks a confrontation (where previously he was its passive recipient), it is because he feels more confident of the strength of his position. In the dialogue too, in the final scene, the differences between the two episodes are as important as the parallels. In particular, the text of this chapter records two speeches each by David and Saul, where the earlier episode records only one. This is why the present episode is treated in three scenes, where chapter 24 was treated in only two. The second speech again reflects David's greater sense of his own independence and authority relative to Saul.

Scene One (verses 1–3a): The Ziphites again betray David's hiding place to Saul

> 1 Then the Ziphites came to Saul at Gibeah, saying, 'David is in hiding on the hill of Hachilah, which is opposite Jeshimon.' 2 So Saul rose and went down to the Wilderness of Ziph, with three thousand chosen men of Israel, to seek David in the Wilderness of Ziph. 3 Saul encamped on the hill of Hachilah, which is opposite Jeshimon beside the road. But David remained in the wilderness.

The statement that 'the Ziphites came to Saul at Gibeah, saying "David is hiding on the hill of Hachilah, which is opposite Jeshimon"' is itself a repetition. Almost exactly the same words are used in chapter 23:19. There, however, they led to a chase in the course of which David was at his most vulnerable: he was only saved from what seemed like his inevitable capture by a Philistine attack on Saul's kingdom. Here there is no stage at which David comes under real threat.

At the close of chapter 24, having acknowledged for the first time that David would one day be king of Israel, and having extracted from David certain assurances with regard to his house, Saul 'went home' resolved to leave David in peace. His good intentions did not last: his pursuit of David is compulsive. He is apparently overwhelmed by the urge to hurt the man he perceives as a rival and is powerless to control himself. If he is resigned to the inevitability of David's ultimate victory, it seems he is also resigned to his own continued – if futile – pursuit of him. So he rises once more and goes down to seek David in the wilderness (as before with three thousand 'chosen men of Israel', compare 1 Sam. 24:2). 'But David remained in the wilderness'.

Scene Two (verses 3b–12): David discovers Saul's camp and enters it

3b When he learned that Saul had come after him into the wilderness, 4 David sent out spies, and learned that Saul had indeed arrived. 5 Then David set out and came to the place where Saul had encamped; and David saw the place where Saul lay, with Abner son of Ner, the commander of his army. Saul was lying within the encampment, while the army was encamped around him.

6 Then David said to Ahimelech the Hittite, and to Joab's brother Abishai son of Zeruiah, 'Who will go down with me into the camp to Saul?' Abishai said, 'I will go down with you.' 7 So David and Abishai went to the army by night; there Saul lay sleeping within the encampment, with his spear stuck in the ground at his head; and Abner and the army lay around him. 8 Abishai said to David, 'God has given your enemy into your hand today; now therefore let me pin him to the ground with one stroke of the spear; I will not strike him twice.' 9 But David said to Abishai, 'Do not destroy him; for who can raise his hand against the Lord's anointed, and be guiltless?' 10 David said, 'As the Lord lives, the Lord will strike him down; or his day will come to die; or he will go down into battle and perish. 11 The Lord forbid that I should raise my hand against the Lord's anointed; but now take the spear that is at his head, and the water-jar, and let us go.' 12 So David took the spear that was at Saul's head and the water-jar, and they went away. No one saw it, or knew it, nor did anyone awake; for they were all asleep, because a deep sleep from the Lord had fallen upon them.

If Saul is the main protagonist in scene one, David is the main protagonist in scene two. Suddenly and unexpectedly the tables are turned: David, the hunted, turns hunter. There is no explanation of the change in the text: but in the context of the whole narrative, circumstances have changed for David since the end of chapter 24. His encounter with Nabal and Abigail has left him stronger and quite literally more resourceful. It is thus entirely appropriate that it is now David who sends out spies, not Saul; and David who locates Saul's camp, not the other way around.

It is night – and David can see Saul, lying beside Abner son of Ner, his deputy, in the middle of his camp. So David proposes an adventure. Turning to Ahimelech the Hittite and Abishai son of Zeruiah (whose first entrance into the narrative this is in both cases) David dares them to come with him into Saul's camp. Abishai accepts the challenge. (The incident calls to mind the night-visit made by Gideon and Purah to the camp of the Midianites in the book of Jdgs. 7:9–14.)

The two men creep into the camp under cover of darkness, right up to Saul and Abner. Abishai urges David to seize the moment: 'God has given your enemy into your hand' (compare 1 Sam. 24:5). Seeing the spear which is standing in the ground at Saul's head, Abishai asks David's permission to use it to despatch Saul. David had, after all, used Goliath's weapon against him. 'I will not need to strike twice', Abishai says.

But David maintains the stance he has consistently held: Saul is the Lord's anointed and he will not lift a finger against him (compare 1 Sam. 24:7). David speaks in verse 9; he speaks again, with a fresh introduction, in verse 10. The implied pause between his two statements allows the reader to imagine Abishai's bewilderment and incredulity at David's stance. When David speaks again, he goes further than anything he said in chapter 24, expressing more fully his sense of his own destiny relative to Saul within the providence of God. David understands that he has no need to take matters into his own hands: either the Lord will strike Saul down suddenly (as indeed the Lord struck down Nabal, apparently for crossing the Lord's other anointed, 1 Sam. 25:38); or he will die of naturally causes in due course; or – and this is the first hint of what is in fact to come – he will perish on the battlefield. Saul will die one day at a time and in a way determined by the Lord – but David will not hasten it.

Throughout the story important speeches are indicated by a proliferation of references to the Lord. This is a case in point: David speaks of the Lord five times in three verses. He concludes by commanding Abishai to take Saul's spear (a powerful symbol not only of Saul's presence, but of his hatred of David, 1 Sam. 18:10–11; 19:9–10; 20:33; 22:6) and a water jug from beside the sleeping king.

In the event it is apparently David who takes the spear – perhaps when it came to it, he did not trust Abishai to restrain himself, if he found himself standing over the sleeping king, with a spear in his hand. The two men are able to leave the camp safely and unnoticed. No one sees them, or even wakes up, because their sleep was 'a deep sleep from the Lord' (compare Gen. 2:21; 15:12). What might have seemed like a great risk on David's part, turns out to have been no such thing. He wasn't in any real danger because the Lord was with him. There is no level playing field in the struggle between David and Saul.

Scene Three (verses 13–25): David again appeals to Saul

13 Then David went over to the other side, and stood on top of a hill far away, with a great distance between them. 14 David called to the army and to Abner son of Ner, saying, 'Abner! Will you not answer?' Then Abner replied, 'Who are you that calls to the king?' 15 David said to Abner, 'Are you not a man? Who is like you in Israel? Why then have you not kept watch over your lord the king? For one of the people came in to destroy your lord the king. 16 This thing that you have done is not good. As the Lord lives, you deserve to die, because you have not kept watch over your lord, the LORD's anointed. See now, where is the king's spear, or the water-jar that was at his head?'

17 Saul recognized David's voice, and said, 'Is that your voice, my son David?' David said, 'It is my voice, my lord, O king.' 18 And he added, 'Why does my lord pursue his servant? For what have I done? What guilt is on my hands? 19 Now therefore let my lord the king hear the words of his servant. If it is the Lord who has stirred you up against me, may he accept an offering; but if it is mortals, may they be cursed before the Lord, for they have driven me out today from my share in the heritage of the Lord, saying, "Go, serve other gods." 20 Now, therefore, do not let my blood fall to the ground, away from the presence of the Lord; for the king of Israel has come out to seek a single flea, like one who hunts a partridge in the mountains.'

21 Then Saul said, 'I have done wrong; come back, my son David, for I will never harm you again, because my life was precious in your sight today; I have been a fool, and have made a great mistake.' 22 David replied, 'Here is the spear, O king! Let one of the young men come over and get it. 23 The Lord rewards everyone for his righteousness and his faithfulness; for the Lord gave you into my hand today, but I would not raise my hand against the Lord's anointed. 24 As your life was precious today in my sight, so may my life be precious in the sight of the Lord, and may he rescue me from all tribulation.' 25 Then Saul said to David, 'Blessed be you, my son David! You will do many things and will succeed in them.' So David went on his way, and Saul returned to his place.

Having left Saul's camp, David climbs a hill-top on 'the other side' of the valley, to find a position far enough away to mean that he is safe from attack by spear or arrow, but near enough to be heard when he calls. What follows is a series of brief shouted exchanges: first between David and Abner, and then between David and Saul.

First – in a manner reminiscent of Goliath's taunting of Israel in chapter 17 – David mocks Abner for his failure to protect Saul. In replying, 'Who is this that calls the king?', perhaps Abner was seeking to intimidate the stranger who was calling to him, by invoking the majesty of his master; or perhaps he was just making explicit what is implicit in David's shout: that ultimately any challenge to Abner is a challenge to the king. David accepts this, but accuses Abner of failing in his duty to protect 'your lord the king' (verse 15): 'As the Lord lives you deserve to die, because you have not kept watch over your lord, the Lord's anointed' (verse 16; but compare the respect David has for Abner in his death in 2 Sam. 3). David, Abishai and the reader know, as Abner and Saul do not, that Saul was indeed in real danger ('One of the people,' Abishai, 'came in to destroy your lord the king', verse 15) and that it was David who protected him where Abner failed to do. As proof of the threat, David asks Abner where the king's spear and water-jar have gone.

Then, before Abner can respond or attempt to justify himself, Saul interrupts. From this point the dialogue follows closely the shape of the conversation between David and Saul in 1 Samuel 24:8–22. Saul's opening question is word-for-word a repeat of 24:16 – the king recognizes the voice of David his son. But whereas in on that previous occasion, David had responded in kind to Saul's greeting, calling him 'my father', here he reverts to more formal categories: 'my lord, O king'. Twice more after verse 17 (in verses 21 and 25), Saul calls David 'my son'. But David maintains his formality throughout. This is an important dramatic development. What residual sense of close relationship David felt in the previous episode has now been destroyed by Saul's resumption, after an apparent resolution in 1 Samuel 24:22, of his pursuit.

As in the earlier encounter, David asserts his innocence and claims that he is no more a threat to Saul than would be 'a single flea' (verse 20; compare 1 Sam. 24:14). 'What guilt is on my hands?' is literally 'What evil is in my hand?' – the very hand, that is, which is now presumably holding Saul's spear. But there are elements in the dialogue which are not present in the earlier episode. Here David puts before Saul two possibilities. Is it the Lord himself who is stirring up Saul to pursue David? If so (though the reader understands that this option is not seriously considered, despite the evidence in the narrative that the Lord is indeed at work), David is prepared to offer a sacrifice to right any wrong. Or is it Saul's advisors who are stirring up this hatred? If so, David wishes Saul to understand how high the stakes have become: Saul's enmity has driven him out from his share 'in the heritage of the Lord'. Saul's allies are effectively forcing him to 'go serve other gods', so that he faces the prospect, which he can hardly bear, of dying 'away from the presence of the Lord'. The responsibility for this, it is implied, will lie with Saul. David anticipates that if Saul continues to persecute him, he will have to flee from Israel – as he does in the very next chapter. He is no longer 'a dead dog' (in 1 Sam. 24:14), but 'a partridge'.

Confronted for the second time with irrefutable evidence of David's loyalty, Saul makes a full confession of fault – much fuller than in the earlier episode. 'I have done wrong, I have been a fool' – a Nabal, in fact – 'I have made a great mistake'. Saul admits that his pursuit of David has not been the result of either the Lord's prompting or that of his advisers. It has been entirely his own doing. With the confession comes an appeal and an assurance: 'Come back,' Saul says, 'for I will never harm you again.'

Then David speaks again. This is a departure from the earlier episode and reflects David's greater assertiveness. His response is oblique: he doesn't directly acknowledge the confession, the appeal or the assurance that the king has made. David no longer trusts Saul enough to take his words at face value. What reason does he have to believe Saul's promise never to harm him again? Instead – in what is presumably a solemn and humiliating moment for Saul and his men – David cries out: 'Here is the spear, O king.' The spear, like Saul's cloak, has been a symbol of his sovereignty throughout the story. Now he has lost it to David, and although David offers to let him have it back, it will be as a concession, and one of Saul's young men will have to go and collect it. Thus, while there remains a civil, maybe even a conciliatory note in David's words, his distrust of Saul is clear. Making explicit what was already implicit in the speech to Abner, David presents the spear (and water jug) as proof that he had indeed been in a position to kill Saul and had not done so; and so as evidence that Saul should be able to trust David for the future.

David is not prepared to trust Saul. His trust is in the Lord alone. He trusts first that 'the Lord rewards everyone for his righteousness and faithfulness'. He trusts that his day will come and that his acts of righteousness and faithfulness today will bring their reward tomorrow. There is an unspoken corollary here and rebuke to Saul: the Lord who rewards righteousness and faithfulness also punishes wrongdoing and betrayal. He trusts secondly that his life is precious to the Lord. It is telling that when he says to Saul, 'As your life was precious today in my sight', he does not then go on to say, 'may my life be precious in your sight also', but rather, 'so may my life be precious in the sight of the Lord and may he rescue me from all tribulation'. Saul may have promised never to harm David again, but far from looking to him for protection, David suspects the king may yet be a source of further tribulation for him. Again references to the Lord proliferate in David's speeches, first to Abner (verse 16) and then to Saul (verses 23–24).

The last word belongs to Saul. 'Blessed are you, my son David', he says, recognizing in a few words both David's relation to the Lord and to himself. It is in effect the last word on Saul's relationship to David: to acknowledge that David is the one, blessed by the Lord, whose success is inevitable and whose achievements will therefore be many. There is something wistful and poignant about Saul's need, at the end, to use David's name in a way he was not able to do earlier in the narrative and to call him 'my son'. It is too little, too late.

When the episode concludes with the words 'Saul returned to his place', the words have metaphorical as well as literal force. His place is one of political failure and divine rejection.

Conclusion

One of the other differences between the episode in chapter 24 and this near repeat is the appeal Saul makes to David in verse 21 to come back. There is no equivalent in the earlier story. Again the desperation of the appeal and the fact that David doesn't even acknowledge it reflect the extent to which the dynamics of their relationship have changed. It may be similarly significant that in the earlier story, the final sentence states Saul's departure first, and then David's; where this one states David's departure first, and then Saul's.

In any case there is no reconciliation between the two men. David does not come back to Saul's court. They go their separate ways at the end of this episode and will not meet again. And yet they go in a sort of peace. David had already, in chapter 24, sworn to protect the members of Saul's house in future. To the end he has refused to raise his hand against Saul. Now Saul has promised –

and it is a promise he will keep – that he will never harm David again. And his last words to David are words of blessing.

There is some kind of template here for those who seek to do right even when relationships break down in politics – but also in business, church and family life. Reconciliation is not a realistic option for David and Saul. A parting of the ways is inevitable. But in parting, they commit themselves not to harm one another.

Chapter Twelve
(1 Samuel 27:1–12)

David and Achish

Introduction

When in verse 2 of this chapter it is stated that 'the length of time that David lived in the country of the Philistines was one year and four months', it is something of an exception. There are almost no clues elsewhere in the text to assist the reader in gauging the passage of time. So it is impossible to know how long David's wilderness years lasted – though since he was thirty when he eventually became king (2 Sam. 5:4), and since he was still a youth when he fought Goliath, the impression is that they occupied about a decade, corresponding roughly to David's twenties.

Similarly it is impossible to know how soon this present episode followed on from the previous one. On the one hand, since it brings upon David a situation he had predicted (his flight from Israelite territory, 1 Sam. 26:19), it might be thought to have followed quite swiftly. On the other hand, there has been sufficient passage of time for David's trust in the providence of God to be tested – for this chapter finds him despairing (where he was previously hopeful), and ruthless (where he was previously magnanimous). In view of this decline, it may be no coincidence that this the first chapter in the story in which the Lord is not mentioned. For all the shift in the balance of power in his relationship with Saul, and his growing resources through recent episodes, this chapter presents David at his lowest ebb, at the point at which the fulfilment of his destiny seems to him furthest from realization.

There are three scenes to the episode: in the first David flees to King Achish of Gath to seek refuge with him. It is an extreme irony that this is where David should feel safest. In the second David negotiates with Achish for the appropriation of Ziklag as a base for himself and his entourage; and in the third an account is given of the kind of raids he made on neighbouring cities from that base.

Scene One (verses 1–4): David flees to Gath

1 David said in his heart, 'I shall now perish one day by the hand of Saul; there is nothing better for me than to escape to the land of the Philistines; then Saul will despair of seeking me any longer within the borders of Israel, and I shall escape out of his hand.' 2 So David set out and went over, he and the six hundred men who were with him, to King Achish son of Maoch of Gath. 3 David stayed with Achish at Gath, he and his troops, every man with his household, and David with his two wives, Ahinoam of Jezreel, and Abigail of Carmel, Nabal's widow. 4 When Saul was told that David had fled to Gath, he no longer sought for him.

The opening verse of the new episode gives the reader a rare insight into David's thoughts and intentions, and it is not edifying. After the theologically rich and apparently sincere words with which David spoke of the Lord throughout the previous chapter, to Abishai (in 1 Sam. 26:9; 10–11), Abner (in 1 Sam. 26:16) and especially to Saul (in 1 Sam. 26:23–24), it is surprising at the start of this new episode to find him so full of fear and despair. Where before he had prayed that his life might be in precious to the Lord (1 Sam. 26:24) and where earlier Abigail has assured him that his life was indeed 'bound in the bundle of the living in the care of the Lord God' (1 Sam. 25:29), David has now convinced himself that he is destined to perish at Saul's hand. He is so desperate, that he is ready to contemplate an extreme measure: to flee for refuge to the Philistines. It is an episode which creates a difficulty for those who do not regard this narrative as a reliable historical source for the life of David, since it presents him in a deeply compromised – and even treacherous – light. One of the remarkable things about the Jewish and Christian Scriptures is their readiness to include such unflattering insights into the lives of their faith heroes.

But this is not the first time that David has resorted to such a step. Achish also provided him with refuge, briefly, in 1 Samuel 21:10. Then there was no advantage to Achish in harbouring David. Now circumstances have changed. David has become a powerful figure and any enemy of Saul's is a potential ally to Achish. But the challenge of offering refuge to David is also greater now. He has not come alone. He has not even come only with his six hundred men (verse 2), but with 'his troops, every man with his household, and David with his two wives, Ahinoam of Jezreel and Abigail of Carmel'. Nevertheless Achish offers David protection.

The outcome is just what David had hoped for: when Saul, who seems always to have a general idea of where David is and what he is doing, hears about this latest development, sure enough, he gives up hunting his rival down.

Scene Two (verses 5–7): David is granted the city of Ziklag

> *5 Then David said to Achish, 'If I have found favour in your sight, let a place be given me in one of the country towns, so that I may live there; for why should your servant live in the royal city with you?' 6 So that day Achish gave him Ziklag; therefore Ziklag has belonged to the kings of Judah to this day. 7 The length of time that David lived in the country of the Philistines was one year and four months.*

After some time in Gath, David approaches Achish with a request. By now he has convinced Achish of his loyalty. So he requests 'one of the country towns' as a place in which to live. 'For why should your servant live in the royal city with you?' he asks. For Achish to accommodate a company of six hundred men, plus wives and children is a considerable burden. On the face of it David is seeking to reduce the extent to which he is a liability to his host. But it becomes clear in what follows that he has military as well as economic ends in mind. He wants the freedom to operate independently in a way that was not possible under the close supervision of Achish in Gath.

Achish duly grants David the city of Ziklag. The text then says that 'Ziklag has therefore belonged to the kings of Judah to this day.' This is doubly important. For one thing it represents a further hint at David's destiny: one day he will be among 'the kings of Judah' (2 Sam. 2:4). For another it suggests that the whole narrative took shape (orally if not in written form) while the state of Judah was still in existence.

Scene Three (verses 8–12): David plunders the neighbours of Gath

8 Now David and his men went up and made raids on the Geshurites, the Girzites, and the Amalekites; for these were the landed settlements from Telam on the way to Shur and on to the land of Egypt. 9 David struck the land, leaving neither man nor woman alive, but took away the sheep, the oxen, the donkeys, the camels, and the clothing, and came back to Achish. 10 When Achish asked, 'Against whom have you made a raid today?' David would say, 'Against the Negeb of Judah', or 'Against the Negeb of the Jerahmeelites', or 'Against the Negeb of the Kenites.' 11 David left neither man nor woman alive to be brought back to Gath, thinking, 'They might tell about us, and say, "David has done so and so."' Such was his practice all the time he lived in the country of the Philistines. 12 Achish trusted David, thinking, 'He has made himself utterly abhorrent to his people Israel; therefore he shall always be my servant.'

During that time, David did not twiddle his thumbs in idleness. He began raiding the neighbouring settlements and doing so ruthlessly: capturing the livestock and even taking the clothing, and thus increasing his power and resources; but also killing the people, both men and women. The slaughter calls to mind the 'failure' of Saul to devote the Amalekites wholesale to destruction (1 Sam. 15:9, 15): like Saul, David has killed the humans and taken the cattle in spoil. But David's ruthlessness is not a response to any commandment of the Lord; and there is no sense in which the action was that extreme form of sacrifice known as a 'devotion to destruction'. David's motivations were political not devotional.

When Achish asks David against whom he has been raiding, it was not a hostile question. It was small talk between two powerful men – a regular conversational gambit, over drinks, as it were, on the palace balcony in the cool of the day. Routinely David would say, 'Against the Negeb of Judah', or 'Against the Negeb of the Kenites'. But this was not the case: David's raids were against 'the landed settlements from Telam on the way to Shur and on to the land of Egypt' (verse 8).

David is claiming to be raiding the borders of Judah and its natural allies, whereas he is in fact raiding the natural allies of Gath well to the south of Judah. His ruthlessness in killing those against whom his raids were directed now looks more sinister: it was motivated by his need to ensure that none were left alive to betray his deceit to Achish.

It may be that David was also attempting to create the impression that he has been engaged in battle against the Israelites, so that if at some future stage any conflict between Israel and Philistia should develop, David would be welcomed into the conflict on the Philistine side, and so be in a position to turn on Achish and deliver the battle to Saul. Either way his behaviour is treacherous: the Israelite who appears to be serving Philistine interests against Israel is actually still pursuing Israelite interests. In fact David had also deceived Achish on his one previous excursion to Gath (1 Sam. 21:10–15). Perhaps that experience emboldened him, so that deceiving Achish now comes easily to him: 'such was his practice all the time he lived in the country of the Philistines'.

The strategy was again apparently successful. The episode closes with Achish entirely taken in by David and trusting him. As far as Achish can see, both by seeking refuge in Gath and by mounting raids against the hinterlands of Saul's kingdom, 'David has made himself utterly abhorrent to his people Israel'. As far as Achish can see, David is his loyal servant. It seems it is not only Saul's children Jonathan and Michal, not only all Israel and Judah and all Saul's servants who are captivated by David: now even the king of the Philistines is drawn to him.

Conclusion

This scene is doubly troubling to a Christian reader. For one thing the violence involved in these raids is appalling and gratuitous.

For another David is double-crossing his host (who – for all that he is a despised Philistine – has been extraordinarily generous and trusting towards him) about the object of these raids. Against that background, the lack of any reference to God in this chapter seems meaningful. So much is directly attributed to the Lord in this narrative – from evil spirits to deep sleep – and so much theology is conveyed by the proliferation of namings of the Lord in speech, not least by David, that the non-naming of God is not to be regarded as neutral to the narrative. A theological question mark is placed over David's conduct here.

The problems begin with the opening words of the episode: where one might have hoped to read, 'David inquired of the Lord', the text says rather 'David said in his heart'. At the very least, the reader learns that David is not naïve. Driven by fear, he has become a shrewd politician, a schemer who is prepared to deceive in order to advance his cause. For the second episode in succession, the reader is aware of a shadow side (a self-serving impulse to violence) to the sunny disposition with which David was introduced in the first few chapters of the story. It is no coincidence that these negative aspects of his personality emerge at just the time when he is achieving something like parity with kings Saul and Achish. He is not immune to the corrupting effects of power.

Chapter Thirteen
(1 Samuel 28:1–25)

Saul and Samuel

Introduction

Uncertainty can be so difficult to live with that eventually even bad news is welcome, because of the resolution it brings. This is Saul's experience in the present episode. The storm clouds are gathering over him. Circumstances are conspiring against him. The Philistines are mustering for war. Samuel is dead. When he attempts to inquire of the Lord by conventional means, he receives no answer. Resorting to something he knows to be wrong, he consults a medium.

In this episode the pace quickens. Over the course of its three scenes, such new urgency is generated that by the end the narrative of 'the rise of king David' is hurtling towards its conclusion.

In the process there are hints that chronology has been sacrificed in the interests of dramatic tension in the placement of this episode. Geographical as well as temporal clues suggest that chronologically the sequence of episodes goes something like this: chapter 27, chapter 28:1–2 (scene 1), chapters 29 and 30, chapter 28:3–25 (scenes 2 and 3), chapter 31.

There are three reasons for supposing that this is the case. Firstly the final scene of this present episode is explicitly set on the eve of battle (1 Sam. 28:19) and so runs directly into the events described in chapter 31. Secondly the Philistine army, marching from Gath, is much more likely to have gone via Aphek (1 Sam. 29:1) to Shunem (1 Sam. 28:4), than vice versa – suggesting that chronologically chapter 29 belongs before 28:4–25, not after it. Thirdly if David was dismissed by Achish from Aphek, the events of chapter 30 (in which he fought the Amalekites) fit naturally into the interval during which the Philistine army moved from Aphek to Shunem.

What the present arrangement of the text gains, however, in this loss of chronological simplicity is heightened dramatic tension. The insertion of the story of Saul's visit to the witch at Endor creates a delay before David's dilemma, introduced at 1 Samuel 28:1–2, is resolved in chapter 29. And the insertion of the story of David's departure from the battlefield in chapter 29 and subsequent raid against the Amalekites in chapter 30 creates a delay before Saul's tragic fate, introduced at 1 Samuel 28:19, is resolved in chapter 31.

Scene One (verses 1–2): The Philistines muster to attack Israel

> *1 In those days the Philistines gathered their forces for war, to fight against Israel. Achish said to David, 'You know, of course, that you and your men are to go out with me in the army.' 2 David said to Achish, 'Very well, then you shall know what your servant can do.' Achish said to David, 'Very well, I will make you my bodyguard for life.'*

The first circumstance which precipitates Saul's final crisis is introduced in the opening verse. The Philistines are gathering their forces for war.

So calculating was David in the previous episode that he may well have foreseen the situation he now faces. Nevertheless his dilemma is a real one. He can't fight with Achish against Saul, because (as Achish's observation makes clear at the end of the previous episode) to do so would be to make himself utterly abhorrent to his people Israel. His whole strategy until now has been to remain scrupulously loyal to Saul and to refrain from attacking the Lord's anointed. On the other hand his alliance with Achish has been a useful one. It has given him a secure refuge in Ziklag, so that he and his entourage have not had to live as outlaws in the wilderness; and from there he has been able to enlarge his wealth by raiding neighbouring cities. If he sides against Achish he has something to lose – especially since there is no guarantee that his help will be welcome to Saul.

Achish does not so much invite David to join him in battle as inform him that an alliance is a consequence of the relationship that has grown up between them. David's reply is ambiguous. Does the phrase 'then you will know what your servant can do' mean 'then you will see what I am made of and why I have such a reputation as a warrior, for I will fight for you'; or does it mean 'then you will find out what I am really like, where my loyalties really lie, and what a fool you have been for trusting me'? There is equal ambiguity in Achish's reply. When he says, 'Very well, I will make you my bodyguard [literally, 'the keeper of my head'] for life', does he mean, 'I trust you so fully I am prepared to give you the closest possible access to me', or, 'I trust you so little I want you where I can see you'? There is a recognition here that the new situation creates sensitivities for both men.

The conversation between David and Achish is not developed until the next chapter; but the mustering of the Philistines is directly relevant to Saul's actions in this episode.

Scene Two (verses 3–7): In fear Saul inquires of the Lord

> 3 Now Samuel had died, and all Israel had mourned for him and buried him in Ramah, his own city. Saul had expelled the mediums and the wizards from the land. 4 The Philistines assembled, and came and encamped at Shunem. Saul gathered all Israel, and they encamped at Gilboa. 5 When Saul saw the army of the Philistines, he was afraid, and his heart trembled greatly. 6 When Saul inquired of the Lord, the Lord did not answer him, not by dreams, nor by Urim, nor by prophets. 7 Then Saul said to his servants, 'Seek out for me a woman who is a medium, so that I may go to her and inquire of her.' His servants said to him, 'There is a medium at Endor.'

On the face of it verse 3a is a repetition: Samuel has died, all Israel has mourned for him and he has been buried in his home city of Ramah. This says no more and no less than 1 Samuel 25:1a. But this is the second circumstance that sets in motion the train of events in this episode; and verse 3b refers to the third. It is to Samuel, for all the difficulties in their relationship, that Saul would have turned for help in the face of the Philistine threat; but that course is not open to him – at least not in the habitual way.

Nor is turning to the dead Samuel an easy option. For (verse 3b) Saul himself had expelled the mediums and wizards from the land. By all the standards of Scripture this was a right and godly thing for Saul to do: the sort of thing a king should do, if ruling as a faithful servant of the Lord (compare Dt. 18:9–14; Lev. 19:31; 20:27). But it is typical of Saul's predicament by the end of his life, that even his acts of righteousness seem somehow to backfire on him: when he wishes to find a medium the task is complicated by the fact that he himself has suppressed them.

By now the Philistines have not just assembled – they have invaded and are encamped on Israelite territory at Shunem. So Saul assembles the army of Israel and camps at Gilboa. When he sees the ranks of the Philistines, he is characteristically frightened (1 Sam. 17:11; 18:12–29). But his response is exactly what one would hope for in a king of Israel: he inquires of the Lord what he should do. Yet even Saul's apparently godly instincts are now futile. For the Lord does not answer: he is given no dreams, the lottery of the Urim fails him, and the prophets have no Word of the Lord to offer him. If Saul has no access to God by Urim, he is reaping what he sowed when he ordered the slaughter of the priests of Nob.

So in desperation Saul asks his servants to find him a medium. *In extremis*, he is prepared even to violate his own ban. It is hard not to sympathize with Saul a little. Things have gone badly wrong for him and he is no longer in any kind of control of his own destiny. He is oscillating violently between behaviour that is worthy of the Lord's anointed and behaviour that is anything but. Resorting to a medium in breach of his own edict seems like an acknowledgement of the failure of his reign.

Scene Three (verses 8–25): Saul visits the medium at Endor

> 8 So Saul disguised himself and put on other clothes and went there, he and two men with him. They came to the woman by night. And he said, 'Consult a spirit for me, and bring up for me the one whom I name to

you.' 9 *The woman said to him, 'Surely you know what Saul has done, how he has cut off the mediums and the wizards from the land. Why then are you laying a snare for my life to bring about my death?'* 10 *But Saul swore to her by the Lord, 'As the Lord lives, no punishment shall come upon you for this thing.'* 11 *Then the woman said, 'Whom shall I bring up for you?'* *He answered, 'Bring up Samuel for me.'* 12 *When the woman saw Samuel, she cried out with a loud voice; and the woman said to Saul, 'Why have you deceived me? You are Saul!'* 13 *The king said to her, 'Have no fear; what do you see?'* *The woman said to Saul, 'I see a divine being coming up out of the ground.'* 14 *He said to her, 'What is his appearance?'* *She said, 'An old man is coming up; he is wrapped in a robe.'* *So Saul knew that it was Samuel, and he bowed with his face to the ground, and did obeisance.*

15 *Then Samuel said to Saul, 'Why have you disturbed me by bringing me up?'* *Saul answered, 'I am in great distress, for the Philistines are warring against me, and God has turned away from me and answers me no more, either by prophets or by dreams; so I have summoned you to tell me what I should do.'* 16 *Samuel said, 'Why then do you ask me, since the Lord has turned from you and become your enemy?* 17 *The Lord has done to you just as he spoke by me; for the Lord has torn the kingdom out of your hand, and given it to your neighbour David.* 18 *Because you did not obey the voice of the Lord, and did not carry out his fierce wrath against Amalek, therefore the Lord has done this thing to you today.* 19 *Moreover, the Lord will give Israel along with you into the hands of the Philistines; and tomorrow you and your sons shall be with me; the Lord will also give the army of Israel into the hands of the Philistines.'*

20 *Immediately Saul fell full length on the ground, filled with fear because of the words of Samuel; and there was no strength in him, for he had eaten nothing all day and all night.* 21 *The woman came to Saul, and when she saw that he was terrified, she said to him, 'Your servant has listened to you; I have taken my life in my hand, and have listened to what you have said to me.* 22 *Now therefore, you also listen to your servant; let me set a morsel of bread before you. Eat, that you may have strength when you go on your way.'* 23 *He refused, and said, 'I will not eat.'* *But his servants, together with the woman, urged him; and he listened to their words. So he got up from the ground and sat on the bed.* 24 *Now the woman had a fatted calf in the house. She quickly slaughtered it, and she*

took flour, kneaded it, and baked unleavened cakes. 25 She put them before Saul and his servants, and they ate. Then they rose and went away that night.

Saul's edict has not been entirely effective. There is known to be a witch at Endor. So Saul disguises himself (presumably taking off either royal robes or military garb – in either case with symbolic significance) and goes in search of her with two men to accompany him.

When Saul finds her, he at once demands that she performs a consultation for him. 'Call up for me the one I shall name', he says. At first the woman denies she is a medium. This may be her usual opening gambit, whoever it is has come to consult her. Or she may have discerned that a denial is especially necessary in this case. Perhaps Saul's disguise fools no one. At any rate she tells her visitors, as if they don't already know, that King Saul has 'cut off' the mediums from the land, and accuses them of attempting to trap her. She fears a witch hunt and in his confused efforts to reassure her, Saul ironically ends up promising her 'as the Lord lives' that her help in this matter will not result in punishment – despite the fact that both her help and his assurance are plainly contrary to the Lord's will. Entirely in keeping with the inconsistency he has shown all through the narrative, Saul now authorizes what he had previously forbidden.

So the woman agrees to help and asks who it is she is to call up. 'Samuel', she is told. She does so and when he she sees him, the woman panics. She is apparently as surprised as anyone by the prophet's apparition; or perhaps, now that she now knows for certain that her visitor is Saul (did she sense that Samuel would deign to appear for no one less?), she fears for her life.

Saul is not concerned to punish the woman however. He just wants to know what she can see. 'I see a divine being', she tells him, 'coming up out of the ground'. 'What does he look like?', he asks. 'An old man, wrapped in a robe'. Now Saul knows it is Samuel. The robe convinces him. The last time Saul had seen Samuel alive, he had torn the prophet's robe, and Samuel had used the fact as a metaphor for Saul's kingdom, which was about to be torn from him by the Lord (1 Sam. 15:27).

Samuel is as displeased with Saul in death as he had been lat-
terly in life. He is abrupt and entirely unsympathetic. 'Why have
you disturbed me?' he asks. It is always a disturbance of the
proper order of things when the dead are 'called back' in this way
to assist the living and no good can come of it. Saul attempts to
justify what he has done. He explains that the Philistines are
attacking him and that God is refusing to answer him 'by
prophets or dreams'. Saul passes over the failure of the Urim –
presumably he does not wish to invite Samuel's scrutiny about
that. 'I have summoned you,' the king concludes, 'to tell me what
I should do.'

There is a pathetic note to Saul's plea; but there is no compassion in the prophet's reply. 'If the Lord has become your enemy,'
he replies, 'what on earth makes you think I am going to help
you?' 'Why do you ask me?' Samuel says, punning on Saul's
name (which means something like 'Asked'; compare 1 Samuel
12:13).

Here Saul's predicament is set out in full. It is not just that God
(in verse 15, Saul cannot bring himself to speak of 'the Lord' to
Samuel) has withdrawn from him. It is not just that the Lord will
no longer support or help him. It is not that the Lord is neutral
towards him. The Lord has become his enemy – as Saul had at a
definite point become David's (1 Sam. 18:29).

This is the moment for which, like Saul himself, readers have
been waiting. The critical act of Saul's reign took place in 1
Samuel 15. The story there is multifaceted and has to be read with
care. Saul was given a simple, if uncompromising, commission:
to 'go and attack Amalek and utterly destroy all that they have
. . . man and woman, child and infant, ox and sheep, camel and
donkey' (1 Sam. 15:3). This he failed to do. Although he did
attack and defeat the Amalekites, and although he 'utterly
destroyed all the people with the edge of the sword', he and the
people opted to spare King Agag and 'the best of the sheep and
of the cattle and of the fatlings, and the lambs and all that was
valuable'. In terms of spoil, they utterly destroyed only 'all that
was despised and worthless'.

But in two almost contradictory respects, it appears that this
course of action was merely a symptom of a deeper malaise. First
Saul had apparently become carried away with his own importance.

After securing victory in the battle against the Amalekites, he went to Carmel, 'where he set up a monument for himself' (1 Sam. 15:12). Saul's failure to observe the detail of the word of the Lord carries weight not because detailed observance of the law in itself matters to God, but because in Saul's case his failure reflects a deeper inner self-assertion which amounts to a rejection of God, a rebellion and stubbornness in relation to the Lord. Secondly it emerges that what Saul did in sparing the king and the best of the flocks of the Amalekites, he did against his better judgment, because it was what 'the people' wanted. He blames them repeatedly (1 Sam. 15:15, 21, 24) for what he has done.

All this history is reviewed when Samuel declares to Saul (in verse 18 of this episode), 'because you did not obey the voice of the Lord, and did not carry out his fierce wrath against Amalek, the Lord has done this thing to you today'. When in verse 17, Samuel pronounces that 'the Lord has torn your kingdom out of your hand and given it to your neighbour David', the phrase is a word for word repetition of 1 Samuel 15:28, with one vital addition: the 'neighbour' is now named.

Again the reader is alerted to the importance of the speech by the proliferation of references to Yahweh: seven in four verses. There are echoes also of Samuel's earlier speech in 1 Samuel 13, where he warns Saul that on account of his foolishness, his kingdom would not continue, but that instead, 'the Lord has sought out a man after his own heart' (1 Sam. 13:14; identified in the Acts 13:22 as David).

Then the narrative takes a decisive lurch towards a terrible denouement. Samuel's speech ends with a horrific prophecy to the effect that the Lord will give Israel, its army, Saul and his sons to the Philistines. Tomorrow Saul and his sons will be as dead as Samuel (compare Michal's provisional warning to David in 1 Sam. 19:11).

Saul has been waiting for this news for years. When it comes, it initially overwhelms him and he falls to the ground, full of fear and utterly exhausted. This is the last and climactic reference to Saul's terror. Where earlier there was an element of control in the gesture when he bowed to the ground before the apparition of Samuel, now he falls (or flings himself?) full length, out of control – just as he had done the last time they met (1 Sam. 19:24). But

Samuel says no more, and (presumably; although the text doesn't not record his disappearance in the way that it detailed his appearance) vanishes for good.

The episode ends intriguingly. The prophet may not have had compassion for the king but the woman has. She cannot bear to see him in such dire straits. When she sees his terror, she urges him to listen to her, as she has listened to him. She urges him to eat 'at least a morsel of bread' – minimizing her description of the meal, in the hope of making it easier for to accept. He refuses. It may be that, as on an earlier occasion (1 Sam. 14:24), Saul had imposed a fast on himself and his companions in the run up to a battle; and that to break it would be to invite defeat. However his men urge him and he changes his mind. He gets up and waits for the meal. At considerable cost to herself, the woman slaughters a fatted calf and baked cakes for Saul and his men. When the meal arrives it is no mere morsel. So Saul eats and recovers sufficient strength to leave that very night. Somehow in the act of eating, there seems to be a reconciliation for Saul to what has happened and what must follow. The medium has not only facilitated his encounter with Samuel and his appropriation of what he must do; she has also enabled him to come to terms with his destiny and to face it with dignity.

Conclusion

It is significant that almost the last act in the narrative on Saul's part is to listen and to do as he is told.

When the witch first invites Saul to eat, she begins by twice pointing out that, at some risk, she has listened to him (verse 21). 'Now therefore', she concludes (verse 22), 'you also listen to your servant'. Saul refuses. But when 'his servants, together with the woman, urged him', he 'listened to their words' (verse 23).

Saul had once before been urged to listen. Before he was charged with the slaughter of the Amalekites, Samuel solemnly urged him, 'Now therefore listen to the words of the Lord' (1 Sam. 15:1). On that occasion, however, Saul did not do as he was told. Instead of 'obeying the voice of the Lord', he 'feared the people and obeyed their voice' (1 Sam. 15:19, 24).

'Obedience' is not a word we usually associate with leadership. For many in contemporary culture, which prizes autonomy and independence, it has mostly negative connotations. But it is in fact an important leadership gift. The word has a noble etymology: it derives from the Latin for 'to hear'. Leaders more than anyone need to be those who listen carefully and hear well. The challenge facing those who exercise leadership (whether in politics, business, church life or even family life) is to discern when the voice of others is the word of the Lord to us, and when it amounts to a competing word. It was a challenge with which Saul never came to terms.

Chapter Fourteen
(1 Samuel 29:1–11)

David at Aphek

Introduction

It was Saul, not David, who was centre stage in the previous episode; but at its outset, David's dilemma was introduced. In the coming battle between Achish and Saul, between the Philistines and the Israelites, on which side will David and his men line up? Saul's visit to the witch at Endor has temporarily deflected attention away from that question – but the narrative now addresses it again.

Achish at least affects to believe that David is his loyal servant. But the reader knows otherwise. Twice before this episode David has refused to lift his hand against the Lord's anointed; and twice after this episode he will deal ruthlessly with those who do so. It is hard, then, to believe that he would enter the battlefield ranged against the king of Israel. The fact that David has consistently been deceiving Achish makes it more likely that, if he enters the battlefield at all, it will be to betray the king of Gath. It emerges over the course of the two scenes in this short episode, that if Achish has been taken in, the same is not true of his commanders, who simply do not trust 'these Hebrews'.

Scene One (verses 1–5): The commanders of the Philistines object to David

1 Now the Philistines gathered all their forces at Aphek, while the Israelites were encamped by the fountain that is in Jezreel. 2 As the lords of the Philistines were marching on by hundreds and by thousands, and

David and his men were marching in the rear with Achish, 3 the commanders of the Philistines said, 'What are these Hebrews doing here?' Achish said to the commanders of the Philistines, 'Is this not David, the servant of King Saul of Israel, who has been with me now for days and years? Since he deserted to me I have found no fault in him to this day.' 4 But the commanders of the Philistines were angry with him; and the commanders of the Philistines said to him, 'Send the man back, so that he may return to the place that you have assigned to him; he shall not go down with us to battle, or else he may become an adversary to us in the battle. For how could this fellow reconcile himself to his lord? Would it not be with the heads of the men here? 5 Is this not David, of whom they sing to one another in dances,
"Saul has killed his thousands,
and David his tens of thousands"?'

Chronologically the narrative is 'rewound' here, from a point on the eve of Saul's death (1 Sam. 28:19), to a point some days or even weeks earlier, before the armies have reached their battle positions (1 Sam. 28:4). At this stage the Philistines have mustered at Aphek (from where, years before, they had taken the ark of God; 1 Sam. 4:1), and the Israelites are already encamped some days' march away at Jezreel. But the Philistines are on the move: their officers are marching their troops forward in hundreds and thousands, and David is exactly where Achish said he would be (1 Sam. 28:2): right at the rear, immediately beside the king. But the arrangements provoke some anxiety among Philistine generals. Now that the armies are on a war-footing, their wariness of David and his troops has grown to the point where they cannot keep from challenging Achish: 'what are these Hebrews doing here?'

The phrase 'these Hebrews' is telling. It not only reveals the understandable distrust of the Philistine generals at the presence of Israelite elements in their army; it also betrays something important about the composition of David's troops. The word 'Hebrew' is used quite sparingly in the Old Testament, and usually in contexts which emphasis the origins of Israel in slavery. The use of the word here suggests that David's men still have a reputation for being a band of outcasts, made up of runaway slaves (1 Sam. 25:10), debtors and the dispossessed (1 Sam. 22:2).

Achish attempts to defend David's integrity, somewhat to the amusement of the reader, who knows that the instincts of the generals are truer than those of the king. 'Has David, the servant of King Saul of Israel, not been my associate for years? I've found no fault in him since the day he first deserted to me.'

Yet in seeking to defend him, Achish only succeeds in underlining David's status as a servant of Saul. Far from assuaging the anxieties of his commanders, Achish has only managed to exacerbate them to the point where they become angry with the king and present him with a flat demand. Kings are seldom instructed as forthrightly as Achish's men instruct him here. 'Send the man away', they say. 'He shall not go down with us to battle.' The generals suspect that if David enters battle on their side, he will turn on them and become their adversary. They see that if David is looking for a way to prove his loyalty to Saul, he could find no better way than by presenting Saul with victory. They are not prepared to trust David with the lives of their men. They remember that when David first entered Saul's service, it was to do battle against themselves. They fear that the man who presented Saul with Goliath's head will repeat the gesture with the heads of their men. They know that when the people of Israel sang their song about Saul killing thousands and David killing tens of thousands, it was Philistine deaths that were being celebrated. They had recalled that same song on David's earlier flight to Gath, when the events celebrated were fresh in the mind (1 Sam. 21:11). For Saul, certainly, the song expressed a distance between himself and David (1 Sam. 18:7); but for the Philistine generals, it expresses the solidarity between David and Saul. Moreover they have had bitter first-hand experience of just such a treachery as they fear David will commit given half a chance. Once before Hebrews who had gone to battle ranged alongside the Philistines had turned and joined the forces of Saul and Jonathan (1 Sam. 14:21). They are not about to risk a repeat.

Scene Two (verses 6–11): King Achish dismisses David from the battlefront

> 6 Then Achish called David and said to him, 'As the Lord lives, you have been honest, and to me it seems right that you should march out and in

with me in the campaign; for I have found nothing wrong in you from the day of your coming to me until today. Nevertheless the lords do not approve of you. 7 So go back now; and go peaceably; do nothing to displease the lords of the Philistines.' 8 David said to Achish, 'But what have I done? What have you found in your servant from the day I entered your service until now, that I should not go and fight against the enemies of my lord the king?' 9 Achish replied to David, 'I know that you are as blameless in my sight as an angel of God; nevertheless, the commanders of the Philistines have said, "He shall not go up with us to the battle." 10 Now then rise early in the morning, you and the servants of your lord who came with you, and go to the place that I appointed for you. As for the evil report, do not take it to heart, for you have done well before me. Start early in the morning, and leave as soon as you have light.' 11 So David set out with his men early in the morning, to return to the land of the Philistines. But the Philistines went up to Jezreel.

Achish summons David. If it is no surprise earlier in the narrative, to find Saul (1 Sam. 19:6; 28:10), David (1 Sam. 20:3; 26:10; 28:16), Jonathan (1 Sam. 20:21) and even Abigail (1 Sam. 25:26), swearing 'as the Lord lives', it is startling to find those words on the lips of Achish. Indeed it is a double surprise, firstly because the words are spoken by a Philistine and not a Israelite; and secondly because this is the only reference to the Lord in all the episodes involving Achish (that is, in 1 Samuel 27:1–12; 28:1–2; 29:1–11). There is something pitiful about it, too, as if Achish is trying to ingratiate himself with David, while giving him bad news – especially pitiful in that Achish remains convinced of David's honesty. Personally he would still be perfectly happy for David to join him in the imminent military campaign, as he's found nothing wrong in David since the day of David's defection to him. But the officers won't stand for it. Achish comes over as a weak man: not wanting to displease David, not wanting to displease his generals and even beseeching David not to displease the 'lords of the Philistines'.

It is the height of chutzpah when David says, 'what have I done?' The question seems to be one of his instinctive strategies for dealing with conflict: this is the fourth time in the narrative (1 Sam. 17:29; 20:1; 26:18) that he has protested in this way; but on this occasion with the least justification. The reader knows that if he was only aware of the truth, Achish could reply: 'You have systematically deceived me for months.'

When David continues by asking, further, 'What have you found in your servant from the day I entered your service until now, that I should not go and fight against the enemies of my lord the king?', David's words are again ambiguous. When he speaks of 'my lord the king', is he truly speaking of Achish, or in fact of Saul, the Lord's anointed? Are 'the enemies of my lord the king' the armies of Israel, or those of the Philistines?

There is something comical about Achish's response that David was to him, 'as blameless as an angel of God', and something again pitiful about the way he reports the decision of his generals as something final, that he – though king – is powerless to countermand. So Achish urges David return from the battlefront to Ziklag, to go 'early in the morning' (the phrase is repeated three times in verses 10–11; if there is a reason for the emphasis, it is not clear) and not to take offence. So David set out to return to Philistine territory and the Philistine army made its way to Jezreel (1 Sam. 29:1; 28:4).

Conclusion

The outcome is perfect for David. He is able to withdraw from the field of battle with his honour intact. He does not have to choose between the people of Israel and the king of Gath (his two most necessary allies) and he is not complicit in the ensuing death of Saul and his sons. He does not have to abandon either the policy to which he has held fast until now (by joining in an attack upon the Lord's anointed) or the sanctuary he has enjoyed in Ziklag (by turning on Achish on the field of battle). From a purely political point of view, if he had chosen to fight against Saul and had lost, there would surely have been no prospect of his becoming king in Israel; but even if he had chosen to fight against Saul and won, the challenge of persuading the tribes of Israel to accept him as their new sovereign would have been formidable. Again if he had betrayed Achish, then whether the battle had been won by the Philistines or the Israelites, David would presumably have returned once more to Saul's unpredictable presence. Both options were fraught with risk and David is spared the difficult decision.

As usual in this narrative, the reader is given little insight into how David felt about his predicament and how far the resolution of it seemed to him providential. It may be that having weighed all his options, he was in fact determined to do just what the Philistine generals most feared: by betraying Achish to turn the battle decisively in Saul's favour and so to put beyond doubt his loyalty to the Lord's anointed. In which case it is possible that he felt frustrated in the extreme, as if the purposes of God were further from fulfilment than ever.

Yet, while the outcome is the best possible for David and protects him from the need to make a difficult choice, it is the worst possible for Saul and seals his fate. If David had entered the battle the likelihood is that, with his help, Saul would have been victorious. David's absence consigns Saul to certain defeat and death.

Chapter Fifteen
(1 Samuel 30:1–31)

David at Ziklag

Introduction

Having been, in 1 Samuel 28:4, on the site where battle between the Philistines and the Israelites would shortly ensue, and having moved away from there to Aphek in the previous chapter, the reader is now taken still further away as the narrative follows David first to Ziklag and then on to the open country beyond the Wadi Besor, in pursuit of a band of Amalekite raiders.

At one level it is curious that the narrative devotes such sustained attention to this relatively minor episode while, simultaneously, the armies of Israel are taking the field for what is plainly a major battle. But there are two reasons why it makes good narrative sense. The first is that Saul is frankly no longer significant; David is. The story has made clear again and again that the Lord is with David, not Saul; so now the narrative remains focused on him, not Saul, even at the moment of Saul's tragic defeat and death. The second is that this episode provides a final commentary on Saul's failure. Saul's failure to deal sufficiently ruthlessly with the Amalekites was a symptom of a deeper malaise: his disposition was such that he took himself too seriously and the word of the Lord not seriously enough; he heeded the people, but not the Lord (see chapter 13). Nevertheless, it was in relation to the Amalekites and not, say, the Philistines or the Ammonites, that Saul did not obey the word of the Lord. A lack of ruthlessness was never likely to be the cause of David's downfall (compare 1 Sam. 25:13; 27:8–11). But here (directly before the account of Saul's defeat and death) David is given opportunity, specifically in relation to the Amalekites, to show that he is capable of finishing what Saul failed to do. (In 2 Sam. 1:1, the word translated 'defeating' is the same word as in 1 Sam. 15:3, where Saul is told by Samuel to 'attack' Amalek.) The episode unfolds in four scenes. In the first David returns home from Aphek to find that Ziklag has been burned to the ground, and faces a threat to his leadership; in the second having inquired of the Lord, he sets out in pursuit of the raiders, overtakes and overwhelms them; in the third he ensures a fair distribution of spoil within his own entourage; and in the last he generously distributes spoil more widely to 'his friends, the elders of Judah'.

Scene One (verses 1–6): David in danger

1 Now when David and his men came to Ziklag on the third day, the Amalekites had made a raid on the Negeb and on Ziklag. They had attacked Ziklag, burned it down, 2 and taken captive the women and all who were in it, both small and great; they killed none of them, but carried them off, and went on their way. 3 When David and his men came to the city, they found it burnt down, and their wives and sons and daughters taken captive. 4 Then David and the people who were with him raised their voices and wept, until they had no more strength to weep. 5 David's two wives also had been taken captive, Ahinoam of Jezreel, and Abigail the widow of Nabal of Carmel. 6 David was in great danger; for the people spoke of stoning him, because all the people were bitter in spirit for their sons and daughters. But David strengthened himself in the Lord his God.

It is a sixty-mile, three-day trek from Aphek to Ziklag. When David and his men drew near, they must have been looking forward to a rest; but when they arrive, they find it has been destroyed in an Amalekite raid. From the Amalekite point of view this was a revenge attack. Theirs was one of the cities David himself had attacked so ruthlessly (1 Sam. 27:8). In fact they have proved more merciful than David. When David attacked a city it was his practice to 'leave neither man nor woman alive' (1 Sam.

27:9), whereas in this case the Amalekites did not kill the wives and families of David and his men, but only took them captive, Ahinoam and Abigail included. On the other hand this 'mercy' merely reflects the fact that to the Amalekites, the captured women and children were part of the booty, commodities for acquisition and exploitation. The fear of the Egyptian at the prospect of being returned to his master (in verse 15) offers a glimpse of the harsh reality of his enslavement. Similarly the distress and extreme anger of David's men reflects not only their loss, but their fears for the welfare of their loved ones.

When David and his men see what has happened, they weep until they are exhausted. David then faces a crisis in his leadership. It is not the first time his men have called his role into question. On previous occasions his leniency towards Saul has caused consternation. But this crisis is more severe. The people blame him for what has happened and speak of stoning him. Their grief at the loss of their loved ones turns, as bereavement often does, to anger. As so often in grief, the anger is directed at someone close at hand and not necessarily at the wrongdoer. Had David had made inadequate plans for the protection of the city? At least on occasions (1 Sam. 25:13) it was his policy to leave a third of his men in defence and to set out in attack with the remainder. Perhaps on this occasion he neglected to leave defenders behind. Perhaps Achish gave him no choice.

The upshot is that David is 'in great danger'. The Hebrew means 'a tight place'. The same term is used by Saul in 1 Samuel 28:15, when he says he is 'greatly distressed'. But where, in his distress, Saul finds that 'God has turned away' from him, David 'strengthens himself in the Lord his God'. It is a striking phrase. It presumably implies that he prayed, or called to mind the Lord's promises, or the blessing which has been pronounced over him even by Saul (1 Sam. 26:25). It appears to mean that he took heart from a sense of relationship with the Lord as 'his God'.

It is some time since there has been any glimpse of David's faith and trust in God. He last spoke of the Lord in his final encounter with Saul in 1 Samuel 26, where he expressed a fear that he was being driven out of Israel and would die 'away from the presence of the Lord' (verses 19–20). It was a self-fulfilling prophecy. Since then he has indeed fled to Philistine territory. He has been expelled from Achish's army, when taking part in the battle would at least have taken him back onto Israelite soil; and he now finds himself bereft of his wives and in great danger. But at a low ebb he recovers a sense of God's presence.

Scene Two (verses 7–20): David pursues the Amalekites

7 David said to the priest Abiathar son of Ahimelech, 'Bring me the ephod.' So Abiathar brought the ephod to David. 8 David inquired of the Lord, 'Shall I pursue this band? Shall I overtake them?' He answered him, 'Pursue; for you shall surely overtake and shall surely rescue.' 9 So David set out, he and the six hundred men who were with him. They came to the Wadi Besor, where those stayed who were left behind. 10 But David went on with the pursuit, he and four hundred men; two hundred stayed behind, too exhausted to cross the Wadi Besor.

11 In the open country they found an Egyptian, and brought him to David. They gave him bread and he ate; they gave him water to drink; 12 they also gave him a piece of fig cake and two clusters of raisins. When he had eaten, his spirit revived; for he had not eaten bread or drunk water for three days and three nights. 13 Then David said to him, 'To whom do you belong? Where are you from?' He said, 'I am a young man of Egypt, servant to an Amalekite. My master left me behind because I fell sick three days ago. 14 We had made a raid on the Negeb of the Cherethites and on that which belongs to Judah and on the Negeb of Caleb; and we burned Ziklag down.' 15 David said to him, 'Will you take me down to this raiding party?' He said, 'Swear to me by God that you will not kill me, or hand me over to my master, and I will take you down to them.'

16 When he had taken him down, they were spread out all over the ground, eating and drinking and dancing, because of the great amount of spoil they had taken from the land of the Philistines and from the land of Judah. 17 David attacked them from twilight until the evening of the next day. Not one of them escaped, except four hundred young men, who mounted camels and fled. 18 David recovered all that the Amalekites had taken; and David rescued his two wives. 19 Nothing was missing, whether small or great, sons or daughters, spoil or anything that had been taken; David brought back everything. 20 David also captured all

the flocks and herds, which were driven ahead of the other cattle; people
said, 'This is David's spoil.'

His sense of relationship to God restored, David turns to the priest
and inquires of the Lord what he is to do next. Through the ephod
he asks the Lord if he should pursue the attackers and is told 'Yes:
you shall overtake them; you shall rescue your loved ones.' As in
1 Samuel 23:9–12, it is both David's readiness to turn to the Lord
for guidance and the Lord's readiness to answer so immediately
and plainly that are emphasized. Saul too had turned to the Lord
(in 1 Sam. 28:6). In that respect David's example is not better than
Saul's. But in Saul's case the effort was in vain. The contrast here is
stark: where Saul's inquiries meet with silence, David's meet with
an instant and positive response. He is told what to do and sets out
with all six hundred men. If, earlier on, it would have been wise to
leave a proportion of his army behind to defend the city, now there
is no point; there is nothing left to defend.

When they reached the Wadi Besor, however, the company did
split along the usual lines. Too exhausted to cross the river (partly
on account of their grief and partly on account of the three-day
journey from Aphek), two hundred men are left behind, while four
hundred continue the pursuit of the Amalekites.

On the other side of the Wadi, David and his men come across
a lone Egyptian. He is in a weak condition, but they feed him and
his spirit revives – as Saul was revived in chapter 28. David asks
him who he is. ('To whom do you belong?' is not merely a reflection of the man's lowly status; it also reflects the extent to which
identity in that culture was derived not from occupation, say, but
from community. Boaz asks his men the same question about the
stranger in Ruth 2:5.) The man explains that he is the servant of
an Amalekite master, abandoned three days ago on account of an
illness. He was among those who raided several Judean cities
including Ziklag. David asks the man to lead him to the
Amalekites and (having extracted a promise 'by God' that he will
not be killed or handed over to his master) he agrees.

So David finds the Amalekites one evening ('behold!', hineh
in Hebrew; the NRSV omits the emphatic exclamation) 'eating
and drinking and dancing' and celebrating their success in their
raids. They are portrayed in an excess of self-indulgence,

'spread out' (the word implies a kind of wanton sprawling) on the plain. David attacks at once. In an assault which goes on for over twenty-four hours, he attempts to kill every one of them. 'Not one of them escaped', it says in verse 17 (only to add, 'except four hundred men, who mounted camels and fled', which is a remnant as big as the whole attacking force). David recovers every single thing that had been captured, including his own wives: 'nothing was missing' (like Nabal's sheep in 1 Sam. 25:21) 'whether small or great, sons or daughters, spoil or anything that had been taken'. In addition David acquired flocks which had belonged to the Amalekites themselves. Again there is a contrast with Saul. When he spared the Amalekite flocks (and admittedly their king), it was his downfall (1 Sam. 15:9). Here David does so, even sparing some of the men, and the last clause of the scene applauds rather than condemns the fact: it is 'David's spoil', a mark of his vigour, power and irresistible force. The disparity between the Lord's will for Saul and the Lord's will for David is nowhere more obvious than here and it is entirely unexplained. The narrator is content to leave the matter a mystery.

Scene Three (verses 21–25): David shares the spoil among his men

21 Then David came to the two hundred men who had been too exhausted to follow David, and who had been left at the Wadi Besor. They went out to meet David and to meet the people who were with him. When David drew near to the people he saluted them. 22 Then all the corrupt and worthless fellows among the men who had gone with David said, 'Because they did not go with us, we will not give them any of the spoil that we have recovered, except that each man may take his wife and children, and leave.' 23 But David said, 'You shall not do so, my brothers, with what the Lord has given us; he has preserved us and handed over to us the raiding party that attacked us. 24 Who would listen to you in this matter? For the share of the one who goes down into the battle shall be the same as the share of the one who stays by the baggage; they shall share alike.' 25 From that day forward he made it a statute and an ordinance for Israel; it continues to the present day.

On the return journey David and the men who had performed the rescue reached those who had been too exhausted to cross the Wadi Besor. As they drew near David saluted them. His care for them, which is about to be expressed more practically, is signalled. But a faction among those who had accompanied David is unwilling to share the spoil that has been won. Those who stayed behind can, of course, have their own wives and children back, but they should take those 'and leave' (literally 'and drive them off': to these men as to the Amalekites, the women and children are mere commodities. Is it for this reason, as well as on account of their mean spirit towards their comrades, that the narrator is unusually explicit in the value judgment he passes on these men? They are 'corrupt and worthless').

David intervenes. He regards everything that has been recaptured as 'what the Lord has given us'. It is not by their own strength that they have prevailed: it is the Lord who 'has preserved us and handed over to us' the raiders and their spoil. David's policy is clear: those who fight and those who stay with the baggage will have equal shares, since the booty is God-given. Earlier in the episode it was not in fact stated that those who stayed behind did so to protect the baggage. In verse 10 it had rather appeared that they were just too exhausted to continue in pursuit. In that case it is a nice pastoral touch on David's part to gloss over their weakness and to dress it up as if they stayed behind in accordance with a strategic decision (of the kind that David had made in 1 Sam. 25:13). There is a foreshadowing here of the parable of the workers in the vineyard told by Jesus (Mt. 20:1–16). When David challenges the nay-sayers 'Who would listen to you in this matter?', it is plain that his authority has been fully restored, after the threat to his leadership in verse 6.

'From that day forward he made it a statute and an ordinance for Israel and it continues to this day' (verse 25). This is a new note. David is not just a warrior now. He is statesman, a law-maker, a man ready for the kingdom. And his first law is inclusive in its intent, affirming the weak and the marginalized.

Scene Four (verses 26–31): David shares the spoil with his friends

> 26 When David came to Ziklag, he sent part of the spoil to his friends, the elders of Judah, saying, 'Here is a present for you from the spoil of the enemies of the Lord'; 27 it was for those in Bethel, in Ramoth of the Negeb, in Jattir, 28 in Aroer, in Siphmoth, in Eshtemoa, 29 in Racal, in the towns of the Jerahmeelites, in the towns of the Kenites, 30 in Hormah, in Bor-ashan, in Athach, 31 in Hebron, all the places where David and his men had roamed.

When David got home, he sent part of the spoil to 'his friends' the elders of Judah. It is an interesting phrase, given that David had been about to enter battle against Israel in the company of Achish. He shares with them his spoil 'of the enemies of the Lord'. His largesse was lavish: 'it was for those in Bethel', in various parts of the Negeb, in the towns of the Kenites, in Hebron, and in 'all the places where David and his men had roamed'. Certainly this is generosity and benevolence on David's part; but it is surely also political calculation. He is building up a power base for himself in Judah, making allies who may in due course rally round him as a king. It will become clear in 2 Samuel 2:1–3 that the inclusion of Hebron in this list is especially significant. Given that it is 'the elders of Judah' who benefit, it is worth remembering that David is himself 'the son of an Ephrathite of Bethlehem in Judah' (1 Sam. 17:12).

Conclusion

David's actions are certainly admirable in the opening two episodes of the story, when he is anointed by Samuel, enters Saul's service as a soothing musician, and then fights and overcomes Goliath. But in those early episodes he is the underdog. What is most impressive about David in this episode is that he acts nobly in a position of power. As such, notwithstanding the continued bloody violence, he is a model for leaders in every field.

Early in the episode David faces a crisis. At a moment of great danger, 'he strengthens himself in God'. He inquires of the Lord (as he arguably failed to do before attacking Nabal in 1 Sam. 25 and again before taking refuge with Achish in 1 Sam. 27). With divine direction, he embarks on a decisive course of action. Victorious in battle, he is also generous in the distribution of booty, ensuring all his troops are provided for, including the weak and most easily excluded, out of a sense of what the Lord has given. He makes wise political overtures to the elders of Judah ('making friends for himself with dishonest wealth' as Jesus might have put it; compare Lk. 16:9).

This is the context in which, in verse 26, it is the opponents of David (rather than those of Saul, mustering at this same moment for battle) who are described as 'the enemies of the Lord' – this despite the fact that it is Saul, not David, who leads the armies of Israel in defence of Israelite soil.

Chapter Sixteen
(1 Samuel 31:1–13)

Saul on Gilboa

Introduction

Abruptly the narrative returns to Mount Gilboa (1 Sam. 28:4), where battle is joined between the armies of Israel and Philistine; equally abruptly the outcome of the battle is given.

Just as Saul has been absent from the previous two episodes, since he received his death sentence from Samuel, so David is absent from this episode. Saul's life has for years been defined by the presence of David; but his death is not.

The first scene is dominated by the death of Saul. After a verse of introductory summary, there is a graphic account of Saul's final moments. It is a classic treatment of the kind normally reserved for a hero. Saul dies with dignity.

In death Saul also dominates the second scene. The text reports what happened when the Philistines discovered his body. Indignity is heaped upon indignity. But the scene closes with an account of some men from Jabesh Gilead, who rescue Saul's corpse and those of his sons and bury them and mourn for them so that, at the last, dignity is restored.

Scene One (verses 1–7): The death of Saul

> 1 Now the Philistines fought against Israel; and the men of Israel fled before the Philistines, and many fell on Mount Gilboa. 2 The Philistines overtook Saul and his sons; and the Philistines killed Jonathan and Abinadab and Malchishua, the sons of Saul. 3 The battle pressed hard upon Saul; the archers found him, and he was badly wounded by them.

4 Then Saul said to his armour-bearer, 'Draw your sword and thrust me through with it, so that these uncircumcised may not come and thrust me through, and make sport of me.' But his armour-bearer was unwilling; for he was terrified. So Saul took his own sword and fell upon it. 5 When his armour-bearer saw that Saul was dead, he also fell upon his sword and died with him. 6 So Saul and his three sons and his armour-bearer and all his men died together on the same day. 7 When the men of Israel who were on the other side of the valley and those beyond the Jordan saw that the men of Israel had fled and that Saul and his sons were dead, they forsook their towns and fled; and the Philistines came and occupied them.

Defeat for Saul, when finally it comes, is swift and complete. Battle against the Philistines has been not so much a recurring as a constant feature of his reign; and mostly he has come out on top. But this time 'the Philistines fought against Israel, and the Israelites fled'. The whole story is effectively told in the first dozen words. Many Israelites are killed there on Mount Gilboa – fleeing from the plain of Jezreel, where Philistine chariots were fearsomely effective, to the apparent refuge of the higher ground, only to fall under wave upon wave of arrows.

Then in the second verse the focus narrows from the outcome of the battle and the fate of Israel as a whole onto Saul and three of his sons. Jonathan, Abinadab and Malchishua are killed, as Samuel had predicted they would be (1 Sam. 28:19); it is odd that the text says 'his three sons' and not 'three of his sons'. Ishbosheth is not named either because he was not present, or because, though present, he was not killed. The fighting closes in on Saul and he is found by the archers. By then it is clear to Saul that his end has come. The phrase translated in the NRSV 'he was badly wounded' is equally capable of being rendered 'he quaked with fear'. Saul's fear has been a major motif in the narrative, and his very next words make it clear that he was certainly afraid of what might happen to him if he was found alive by the Philistines; they will not only thrust him through; they will make sport of him. It is a prospect he cannot bear. So – drawing on the tradition of Abimelech in Judges 9:54 – he asks his armour-bearer (a position once held by David of course, 1 Sam. 16:21) to run him through. But Saul is not the only one to be afraid. His armour-bearer is terrified at the suggestion. Given the sequel in 2 Samuel 1:11–16, he was right to be concerned about David's potential reaction, quite apart from other sensibilities. So Saul falls on his own sword; the only surprise is that it isn't his spear. There is pathos here and respect for Saul at the last. For all his fear, Saul dies without self-pity and with real courage. Seeing the king is dead, his armour-bearer, whether out of fear or loyalty, follows suit: he falls on his sword and dies with his lord.

The summary in verse 6 is bleak and its consequence is immediate: Saul and his sons and his armour bearer and 'all his men' (with an appropriate element of licence in the final phrase, presumably) die together on the same day. Then when other Israelites, within sight of the battle, see what has happened, they flee their towns and the Philistines come and occupy them.

Scene Two (verses 8–13): The desecration and rescue of Saul's body

> *8 The next day, when the Philistines came to strip the dead, they found Saul and his three sons fallen on Mount Gilboa. 9 They cut off his head, stripped off his armour, and sent messengers throughout the land of the Philistines to carry the good news to the houses of their idols and to the people. 10 They put his armour in the temple of Astarte; and they fastened his body to the wall of Beth-shan. 11 But when the inhabitants of Jabesh-gilead heard what the Philistines had done to Saul, 12 all the valiant men set out, travelled all night long, and took the body of Saul and the bodies of his sons from the wall of Beth-shan. They came to Jabesh and burned them there. 13 Then they took their bones and buried them under the tamarisk tree in Jabesh, and fasted for seven days.*

The second scene brings first a final humiliation for Saul and then a final dignity. First he and his sons are discovered by looters on the battle field. They are presumably not looking for specifically for Saul. They do not know what they may find. They know they have been victorious and are looking for spoil: they undoubtedly hoped to find wealth or weapons at least. But to find the Israelite king and his three sons, all dead, is more than they could have hoped for. So Saul and his sons are decapitated and stripped. The stripping is a further indignity beyond even decapitation. In

Saul's case, the stripping of his armour completes the symbolic removal of his office foreshadowed when the king stripped himself in a prophetic frenzy in 1 Samuel 19:34. The good news (gospel) of his demise runs like wildfire through Philistine territory – to the people and their idols. This is a theological victory as well as a military one: the Philistines, as well as the Israelites, believe they have seen the defeat of the Lord's anointed. The news is to be taken to the temples ('the houses of their idols') as well as to the people. The narrator mocks the gods of the Philistines: unlike the Lord, who not only knows the future but determines it, the idols of Philistia have to be told not just what is to come but what has happened as well.

Saul's armour is put in one place – the temple of a goddess of war – and his body (and head?) in another. But even the dead king – especially the decapitated king – still inspires loyalty. To deny the dead a burial in the cultures of the ancient near east was a particular indignity. Perhaps if he had not been violated in death, no rescue mission would have been attempted. But when they hear what has happened to him, the 'valiant men' of Jabesh-gilead set out, travelling all night long, and snatch the corpses of Saul and his sons (the narrator had not mentioned that the corpses of Saul's sons had also been desecrated in this way) and take them home. It is not just that these are his kinsmen – fellow Benjaminites (1 Sam. 9:1). The men of Jabesh-gilead are prepared to risk so much, because they are repaying a debt. One of Saul's first decisive acts as king had been to come to their rescue, when they were under siege by the Ammonites (1 Sam. 11:1–15). He risked himself for them then; they risk themselves for him now.

So it is that – in recognition of one of the highlights of his reign – Saul's final resting place is not Gibeah, but 'a tamarisk tree in Jabesh'. There he receives a proper burial and is afforded a week of mourning.

Conclusion

Saul's end is a profound and distressing tragedy. In the first scene he takes his own life. The narrative seems to imply that when he does so, it is in the knowledge that this three sons have already been killed. He dies in the knowledge that his army is also defeated. And after his death in the second scene his corpse is desecrated. Yet in both scenes the narrative also confers on Saul a degree of honour at the end. It's true suicide has traditionally been regarded by the church as a sin – as a premature cutting off of the gift of life. But the narrative seems to side with Saul in scene one in his decision not to wait for an inevitable execution at the hands of 'the uncircumcised', who will surely 'make sport of him', but to take matters into his own hands. And in scene two the action of the valiant men of Jabesh-gilead affords Saul a loving commitment in death that he lacked in life. He belongs.

ACT THREE

David succeeds Saul as king

2 Samuel 1:1 – 5:10

Chapter Seventeen
(2 Samuel 1:1–27)

David laments Saul

Introduction

The break between 1 Samuel and 2 Samuel appropriately marks the death of Saul. But the narrative is barely broken. The story which began with the introduction of David in 1 Samuel 16 is continued seamlessly in 2 Samuel 1 – 4: 'the rise of King David' only ends with his coronation at 2 Samuel 5:1–10.

But Saul's death raises a new question: who will succeed him? There are three possibilities: it might be a member of his family (his son Ishbaal duly becomes king at least over Israel); it might be a member of his own household (Abner is an obvious candidate for a time); or it might be David (but if so, there are considerable obstacles for him to overcome). If Samuel or Jonathan, David or Saul themselves ever assumed David would succeed Saul immediately and straightforwardly, they were mistaken. It is David's gradual and problematic accession which is the theme of Act Three of the narrative.

In this present episode, which unfolds in three scenes, David (returning from defeating the Amalekites in 1 Sam. 30) first hears of Saul's death, then ruthlessly despatches the man who had brought the news (who himself just happened to be an Amalekite), and then laments for Saul and for Jonathan. The outpouring of grief is sincere and in the circumstances generous, and suggests that Saul's hatred did not narrow David, but enlarged him.

Scene One (verses 1–10): David learns of Saul's death

1 After the death of Saul, when David had returned from defeating the Amalekites, David remained two days in Ziklag. 2 On the third day, a man came from Saul's camp, with his clothes torn and dirt on his head. When he came to David, he fell to the ground and did obeisance. 3 David said to him, 'Where have you come from?' He said to him, 'I have escaped from the camp of Israel.' 4 David said to him, 'How did things go? Tell me!' He answered, 'The army fled from the battle, but also many of the army fell and died; and Saul and his son Jonathan also died.' 5 Then David asked the young man who was reporting to him, 'How do you know that Saul and his son Jonathan died?' 6 The young man reporting to him said, 'I happened to be on Mount Gilboa; and there was Saul leaning on his spear, while the chariots and the horsemen drew close to him. 7 When he looked behind him, he saw me, and called to me. I answered, "Here, sir." 8 And he said to me, "Who are you?" I answered him, "I am an Amalekite." 9 He said to me, "Come, stand over me and kill me; for convulsions have seized me, and yet my life still lingers." 10 So I stood over him, and killed him, for I knew that he could not live after he had fallen. I took the crown that was on his head and the armlet that was on his arm, and I have brought them here to my lord.'

The narrator resumes the story, bringing Saul's death and final defeat into relation with David's latest victory. David is where he was when the story last had word of him: in Ziklag. On the third day after David arrived home (compare 1 Sam. 30.1), a man arrives, his clothes torn and dirt on his head. He has fled from the camp of Israel.

When he comes into David's presence, 'he fell on the ground and did obeisance' – as David had done before Saul (1 Sam. 24:8) and Saul before Samuel (1 Sam. 28:14).

The story then unfolds in a series of questions, three asked by David and one (reported) by Saul. It is on the answer to Saul's question that the narrative turns. First David asks, 'Where have you come from?', to which the man answers, 'I have escaped from the camp of Israel.' This is already bad news. Language of escape implies defeat. If Israel had been victorious there would have been no need for it.

So David asks further, 'How did things go?' This is precisely the question that the priest Eli asked the man of Benjamin in

1 Samuel 4:16, and the answer on this occasion is almost identical to the answer Eli received: the army has fled and many have died, including Saul and Jonathan (in Eli's case, it was his two sons, Hophi and Phinehas). There is an acknowledgement of David's particular affection for Jonathan, when the man reports not that 'Saul and his sons also died', but that 'Saul and Jonathan also died'.

Significantly David passes over the outcome of the battle. He has no interest at this point in how or why Israel has been defeated or in how many of its army lost their lives. His attention is focused at once on the fate of the two men. So he asks a third question, 'How do you know that Saul and Jonathan died?'

This prompts this anonymous man (who is twice referred to as 'the young man reporting to him', verses 5, 6) to give his longest speech. He relates that he happened to be on Mount Gilboa and (behold!), he saw Saul (not 'King Saul', let alone 'the Lord's anointed' as David will twice call him in the next scene) leaning on his spear (which makes a final appearance in the story here). The vagueness of his opening words arouses suspicion. What was he doing on the mountain while the battle was still raging? Was he fighting with Israel's army? Or was he a freelance scavenger and opportunist, looking for precisely the kind of spoil he has now brought to David? At any rate he reports that, as chariots (which made the Philistines a particularly terrifying enemy, 1 Sam. 13:5) and horsemen drew near, Saul 'looked behind him', saw this man and called him over.

Then comes the last and critical question. In reported speech, Saul asks, 'Who are you?', and fatefully the man replies, 'I am an Amalekite'. Saul seems content with this answer, but the reader senses that it is ominous all the same. Saul requests the man to kill him. The request is clear and clear-headed: the convulsions of death have laid hold of him and yet he lives. He would rather be despatched by an Amalekite, apparently, than by a Philistine. The young man reports that 'knowing that he could not live after he had fallen', he stood over the king and killed him – perhaps running him through with the spear as Abishai had wished to do (1 Sam. 26:8). Then, the young man claims, he took Saul's royal insignia (a crown and an armlet) and brought them here to David, 'my lord'.

There is a tension, of course, between this account of Saul's death and that in the previous episode, where it seemed that Saul succeeded in killing himself and that his armour bearer then killed himself in sympathy. This may be a fuller and truer account of what took place: if Saul's suicide bid was not entirely successful, perhaps he sensed that just as it took an Edomite to slaughter the priests of Nob (1 Sam. 22:18–19), it might take an Amalekite rather than his own Israelite armour-bearer to slay the Lord's anointed. On the other hand it may be that this young man, in giving his report to David, is exaggerating his own role, seeking to take credit for an act truly requested (but refused) by Saul of his armour-bearer in the mistaken and costly assumption that the act would be pleasing to David. He certainly hopes to gain at least prestige, if not financial reward, from being the person to hand David Saul's crown and armlet.

There is a further irony here, whether Saul actually died at the hands of the Amalekite, or whether it was only by the hands of the Amalekite that his royal insignia were passed to David, given that it was in connection with that people that he lost his right to the kingship.

Scene Two (verses 11 to 16): David commands the Amalekite to be killed

> 11 Then David took hold of his clothes and tore them; and all the men who were with him did the same. 12 They mourned and wept, and fasted until evening for Saul and for his son Jonathan, and for the army of the Lord and for the house of Israel, because they had fallen by the sword. 13 David said to the young man who had reported to him, 'Where do you come from?' He answered, 'I am the son of a resident alien, an Amalekite.' 14 David said to him, 'Were you not afraid to lift your hand to destroy the Lord's anointed?' 15 Then David called one of the young men and said, 'Come here and strike him down.' So he struck him down and he died. 16 David said to him, 'Your blood be on your head; for your own mouth has testified against you, saying, "I have killed the Lord's anointed."'

David's response to the news is two-fold: the first is entirely laudable; the second is more troubling to the Christian reader.

First (in verses 11–12) David takes hold of his clothes and in a customary mark of extreme grief tears them – 'and all the men who were with him did the same'. They mourned and wept and fasted for Saul and Jonathan, for the army of the Lord and for the house of Israel. Laudably David does not celebrate Saul's death or the fact that his path to power is now opening – though the reader also notes that he (and all the men who were with him) 'mourned and wept and fasted' only 'until evening' – whereas the men from Jabesh gilead had fasted a full seven days (1 Sam. 31:13).

David's second response is to turn his attention to the Amalekite who has reported Saul's death. Presumably it is now evening and the man has been waiting around all day, either watching or sharing in the mourning, when David speaks to him and asks a further two questions. It is clear that their earlier conversation is being resumed, because the Amalekite is again described in verse 13 as 'the young man who had reported to him', and because David's fourth question is more or less a repeat of his first: 'Where do you come from?' This time the man replies by emphasizing not his journey from the battlefield as in verse 3, but his origins as an Amalekite as in verse 8. 'I am the son of a resident alien', he says. This is new information. Perhaps, in David's mind, it rendered the man still more culpable. A *ger* (resident alien) had limited rights and responsibilities in Israel and would certainly have been expected to recognize and respect the Lord's anointed.

Then comes David's fifth question, the sixth in the narrative, and the only one for which the young man has no answer. 'Were you not afraid to lift your hand to destroy the Lord's anointed?' The reader is aware that David has not lifted his hand in that way, and that his self-restraint has been a good and noble thing – and that Saul's own armour bearer had also been too terrified to comply with his master's request. This is the exact phrase David has used to speak of Saul on both occasions when it was in his power to kill him (1 Sam. 24:6; 26:9). Is David is giving the Amalekite one last opportunity to save himself by coming clean? But either the Amalekite is telling the truth about what happened (in which case he only killed Saul at Saul's own explicit request); or he is lying, in which case he did not in fact raise his hand against the Lord's anointed at all. Either way what follows seems severe on David's part: he summons one of his entourage to strike the Amalekite down. 'So he struck him down and he died.' It is hard for the Christian reader to sympathize with David when he says, 'Your blood be on your head; for your own mouth has testified against you, saying, "I have killed the Lord's anointed."' Those were not the words of the Amalekite. At most he said, 'I despatched him, for I knew that he could not live.' The most likely reading is that he is lying; for that he dies. Presumably David summons a henchman to perform the execution for him, not because he is not willing to do his own dirty work, but as a mark of contempt.

If David sees calculation and opportunism in this Amalekite, the reader sees it also in David. Whether actually by killing Saul, or simply by claiming to have done so, and then by stripping him of his insignia and bringing these things to David, the Amalekite is certainly hoping to benefit. But Saul's armour-bearer judged his situation well, when he first refused to kill Saul and then took his own life after watching his master do the same. To be asked to kill the Lord's anointed is a no-win situation. David, on the other hand, will not risk any impression that he was complicit in Saul's death or even that he is eager to benefit from it. Politically he will benefit more from maintaining his stance of extreme loyalty to Saul by having the Amalekite executed.

Scene Three (verses 17–27): David laments the deaths of Saul and Jonathan

17 David intoned this lamentation over Saul and his son Jonathan. 18 (He ordered that The Song of the Bow be taught to the people of Judah; it is written in the Book of Jashar.) He said:

19 Your glory, O Israel, lies slain upon your high places!
How the mighty have fallen!
20 Tell it not in Gath, proclaim it not in the streets of Ashkelon;
or the daughters of the Philistines will rejoice, the daughters of the uncircumcised will exult.

21 You mountains of Gilboa, let there be no dew or rain upon you, nor
bounteous fields!
For there the shield of the mighty was defiled,
the shield of Saul, anointed with oil no more.

22 From the blood of the slain, from the fat of the mighty,
the bow of Jonathan did not turn back, nor the sword of Saul return empty.

23 Saul and Jonathan, beloved and lovely!
In life and in death they were not divided;
they were swifter than eagles, they were stronger than lions.

24 O daughters of Israel, weep over Saul,
who clothed you with crimson, in luxury,
who put ornaments of gold on your apparel.

25 How the mighty have fallen in the midst of the battle!
Jonathan lies slain upon your high places.

26 I am distressed for you, my brother Jonathan;
greatly beloved were you to me;
your love to me was wonderful, passing the love of women.

27 How the mighty have fallen, and the weapons of war perished!

The final scene of this episode relates 'the lamentation David intoned over Saul and his son Jonathan'. Perhaps this is what David composed as he 'mourned and wept and fasted' (in verses 11–12). Or perhaps, after he had killed the Amalekite, he returned to his mourning.

This is the nearest thing, in the story of his rise, to a psalm of David (though compare 2 Sam. 22:2–51, which is Ps. 18). Most scholars agree that the 'Psalms of David' include not only 'Psalms by David', but also 'Psalms [in honour] of David', or 'Psalms [in the style] of David'. Nevertheless, it is reasonable to suppose that David was a composer of Psalms, and that some of his compositions have survived in the Scriptures. This possibility is strengthened by the note in verse 18 that David ordered the 'Song of the Bow' (this lamentation presumably; compare verse 22, 'the bow of

Jonathan, the sword of Saul'; and also 1 Sam. 18, where among the things of which Jonathan stripped himself and handed to David was his bow) to be 'taught to the people of Judah'; and that it was 'written in the book of Jashar'. There is a hint here that from the earliest times there was a written collection of at least some compositions by David.

The refrain in this psalm is the phrase, 'how the mighty are fallen'. It occurs three times, at verses 19, 25 and 27. The psalm falls into four parts. In the opening section of the psalm (verses 19–21), the refrain is used in reference to both Saul and Jonathan. The refrain is not used in the second section (in verses 22–23), in which Saul and Jonathan are lamented together, twice over. But it is used again in the third part, which is focused on Saul (verses 24–25a) and again in the final part, which is focused on Jonathan (verses 25b–27).

The poem addresses in turn a series of absent audiences: Israel, Gilboa, the daughters of Israel, and finally Jonathan. The address underlines the absence of the addressee, and climactically, of course, of Jonathan. Nevertheless, the honouring of Saul in verse 21 and verses 24–25 is important: to the end, David remains the loyal subject, not the scheming rival, of Israel's king.

The lamentation is deliberately structured, with some care taken to give due honour to both father and son. If in verse 21 priority is given to Saul (he alone mentioned by name there, his shield is singled out as 'the shield of the mighty'), it is balanced by the fact that the lamentation ends with a climactic emphasis on the love between David and Jonathan. If in verse 22 the reference is to 'Jonathan and Saul' (son and father on the battlefield), in verse 23 it is to 'Saul and Jonathan' (father and son in life and death, heroes likened to eagles and lions). If in verses 24–25a the focus is on Saul alone, with the refrain closing that section, then in verses 25b–27, the focus is on Jonathan alone, with a corresponding refrain.

Verses 19 to 21 are a general introduction, addressed first to Israel and then, which adds to the historicity of the poem, to 'the mountains of Gilboa'. Both Saul and Jonathan are implied by the reference to Israel's glory which 'lies slain on the high places' and to 'the mighty' in the first occurrence of the refrain. The opening section hints at the political implications of the death of Saul and his son: they have symbolized Israel's might, and their loss personifies Israel's vulnerability, not least to the Philistine foe. Yet almost as hard to bear as the loss of these mighty ones in itself, is the inevitable gloating of Israel's traditional enemy. Sometimes it is not so much defeat and disappointment that is hard for us to bear, as the pleasure it brings others. The phrase 'Tell it not in Gath' has particular resonance given the time that David spent there (1 Sam. 27:11).

No new audience is invoked in verses 23–24, in which Saul and Jonathan are treated together and celebrated as warrior partners. When the text says in verse 23 'in life they were not parted', the reader cannot help but think of Saul's sense of betrayal by his son, when David fled from Saul's court with Jonathan's help. If Saul had succeeded in the moment of madness when he sought to kill his own son (1 Sam. 20:33), they would have been parted very dramatically indeed. But in fact Jonathan chose to stay faithfully with his father, supporting him in his kingship, and died beside him in battle. This is part of David's sadness: because Saul and Jonathan were not parted, it meant that he and Jonathan were, to his sorrow.

The daughters of Israel (the ones who had sung of Saul killing his thousands and David his tens of thousands) are then summoned to grieve in the third section of the poem. Finally, in the closing verses, the address is directly to Jonathan. Here the tight structure of the lamentation breaks down, appropriately enough. In the first three sections of the psalm, the grief is formal and public. It expresses love (Saul and Jonathan are 'beloved' and 'lovely'), but in conventional terms. In verse 26, the expression of love is intimate, personal and thoroughly unconventional. Verse 25b belongs well with the rest of the lamentation: 'Jonathan lies upon your high places' is of a piece with 'O daughters of Israel, weep over Saul, who clothed you.' But the repetition of Jonathan's name in verse 26 comes in a completely different voice, 'I am distressed for you, my brother Jonathan.'

The language at the end of the poem is extravagant. Finally, it is clear that David loved Jonathan and also knew himself loved. The phrase 'greatly beloved were you to me' refers to David's love for Jonathan; the words 'your love to me was wonderful, passing the love of women' refer to Jonathan's love for him. The question is inevitably asked, to what extent this mutual love, obviously something intimate and deep, is relevant to the church's current debate about homosexuality today. It undeniably validates and offers a model of same-sex friendship in a way that the church needs to recover. But there is no implication here that the relationship between David and Jonathan was a sexual one. The nearest thing to such an implication in this narrative comes from the lips of an angry Saul in 1 Samuel 20 (verse 30). 'Your love to me was wonderful, passing the love of women', means simply, 'no woman ever loved me as fully and faithfully as you did'. But even that is a startling thing for David to say, and – in a culture like ours in which friendships between men in particular typically struggle to achieve, let alone to express, intimacy – this is something to be celebrated.

Conclusion

In three distinct scenes, this episode records David's reaction to Saul's death. In the first and third scenes, he comes over well; in the middle scene, his capacity for ruthless violence is once again evident.

In the first and last scenes, David offers a model of good grief, desperately needed by our society which no longer knows how to respond to death, or even to the bereaved. The first scene records a series of four actions: he tears his clothes, weeps and mourns and fasts. In these robustly public acts, grief is channelled. What are the contemporary equivalents in the 21st-Century West? A bereaved person might post a poem in a local paper; or with the help of a wise minister, devise an order of service for a funeral. There will almost certainly be an opportunity to get drunk at a wake. But there is unlikely to be anything so vigorous or expressive as the tearing of clothes, or a fasting. Again, our culture knows how to sing songs of triumph in public, and of love – even of sorrow in the face of lost love; but not songs of grief and lamentation. In the face of death our tendency is to respond not with lament and the outpouring of grief, but with denial and distraction: 'Never mind: he's at peace now. Time is a great healer.' Such platitudes are a long way from the raw anguish of David's poem.

Chapter Eighteen
(2 Samuel 2:1–32)

David at Hebron

Introduction

In the first episode after the death of Saul, the drama focuses on David's grief and on his treatment of the man who dared to lift his hand against the Lord's anointed. There is no indecent haste on David's part to grab at the crown which the Amalekite has brought to him. But in this second episode he is duly anointed as king – admittedly, only over Judah.

The references to Hebron at the start (verse 1) and finish (verse 32) of the chapter are telling – this will be his base in the last phase of the story before he succeeds Saul as king over all Israel.

The present episode is made up of three scenes: the first provides a summary of the political arrangements which were established after Saul had died; the second relates the first act of civil war between the houses of David and Saul; while the third homes in on a much more personal struggle between Abner (the leading servant of Ishbaal son of Saul) and the sons of Zeruiah (the leading servants of David).

Scene One (verses 1–11): David is anointed king of Judah

1 After this David inquired of the Lord, 'Shall I go up into any of the cities of Judah?' The Lord said to him, 'Go up.' David said, 'To which shall I go up?' He said, 'To Hebron.' 2 So David went up there, along with his two wives, Ahinoam of Jezreel, and Abigail the widow of Nabal of Carmel. 3 David brought up the men who were with him, every one with his household; and they settled in the towns of Hebron. 4 Then the people of Judah came, and there they anointed David king over the house of Judah.

When they told David, 'It was the people of Jabesh-gilead who buried Saul', 5 David sent messengers to the people of Jabesh-gilead, and said to them, 'May you be blessed by the Lord, because you showed this loyalty to Saul your lord, and buried him! 6 Now may the Lord show steadfast love and faithfulness to you! And I too will reward you because you have done this thing. 7 Therefore let your hands be strong, and be valiant; for Saul your lord is dead, and the house of Judah has anointed me king over them.'

8 But Abner son of Ner, commander of Saul's army, had taken Ishbaal son of Saul, and brought him over to Mahanaim. 9 He made him king over Gilead, the Ashurites, Jezreel, Ephraim, Benjamin, and over all Israel. 10 Ishbaal, Saul's son, was forty years old when he began to reign over Israel, and he reigned for two years. But the house of Judah followed David. 11 The time that David was king in Hebron over the house of Judah was seven years and six months.

At the start of this episode, David is still in Ziklag (1 Sam. 1:1). But with the death of Saul, his alliance with the Philistines holds no further advantage for him and it is safe for him to return to Israelite territory. Indeed if he is going to play a part in the inevitable succession struggle, it is imperative for him to be in Israel. First, however, he inquires of the Lord whether, in principle, this would be a good thing to do; and if so, where he should go. It is of course a good sign that David continues to inquire of the Lord (compare 1 Sam. 23:2; 30:8); but it is worth noting that this is the first time he has done so with a political rather than a military question at stake (though compare also 1 Samuel 22:10).

David asks the Lord, 'Shall I go up into Judah?', and is told, 'Yes, go up.' He asks, 'To which town shall I go up?', and he is told, 'To Hebron.' The city was after all one of the chief beneficiaries of David's largesse after he had defeated the Amalekites and courted the elders of Judah (1 Sam. 30:31). Once again it is not just David's readiness to seek the Lord's guidance which is emphasized by the text, but the Lord's readiness to reply at once and in detail. So when David, his wives (Ahinoam and Abigail), and his men and their families (the whole community, in other words, which had settled with him in Ziklag), move to Hebron, the narrative presents it as an act of obedience to the explicit command of the Lord, rather than as an act of political opportunism.

Then, finally, the shepherd boy is king. For the second time in his life he is anointed. This time it is a public act, not a discreet or even secretive one, for a kingship that is present, not future.

The development is, however, reported in a surprisingly low-key way, given that it represents at least a partial fulfilment of David's destiny, for which he has been waiting for years. There is no detail about any negotiations with elders of Judah which led up to the event, nor about the ceremony itself. If David has come to Hebron in response to the word of the Lord, then when the people of Judah come and anoint him, this is by implication presumably also a response to the guidance of God. Perhaps it is reported quietly partly because he is only a half-king, only king of Judah, only king among his kinsfolk (1 Sam. 17:12). There is certainly more fanfare in 2 Samuel 5 when he becomes king over all Israel. Perhaps the subdued tone of the report reflects some embarrassment that, at this point, there is civil war: the kingdom of Israel is divided, north against south, majority against minority.

Nothing is said about the reaction of King Achish to this state of affairs. Presumably he was neither surprised nor alarmed and assumed that his alliance with David would hold good.

Certainly David still needs allies. So his first act as king in Judah is a peaceful overture to the city of Jabesh-gilead in the territory of Benjamin (Saul's heartland). It is clear from the asides in verses 15, 25 and 31, that the tribe of Benjamin was lined up against David at this point. The people of Judah tell David of the loyalty shown to Saul, even in death, by the men of that city, and David extends a hand of blessing. In verse 5 he prays that they will be blessed by the Lord because they showed loyalty (*hesed*) to Saul. In verse 6a he prays that the Lord will show them steadfast love and faithfulness (*hesed*). He piles on the rhetoric of covenant. But David then also extends the hand of invitation: he wants these men as allies. He wants Saul's most loyal subjects as his own. He promises to do good to this city because it has done

good to Saul. He bids them be strong and reminds them that Saul
is dead – and then reminds them, or informs them, that he has
been anointed king in Judah (the neighbouring tribe). The promise of his reward is coupled with an implicit challenge: 'Whose
side are you on?'

Meanwhile Saul's kingdom is divided – as it will be again,
more permanently, just one generation later on the death of
Solomon (compare 1 Kgs. 12). The tribe of Judah may have
anointed David as king – but the tribes of 'all Israel' (Gilead, the
Ashurites, Jezreel, Ephraim and Benjamin), driven on by Abner
(Saul's right-hand man) have made Ishbaal king at Mahanaim. If
Ishbaal can claim to have the majority of Israel on this side, David
can rightly point out that he was made king by 'the people of
Judah', whereas Ishbaal has been made king only 'by Abner'.
David's anointing had a popular acclaim which Ishbaal's lacked.
Joab may be important to David (and his significance will be
emphasized in the ensuing chapters) but he is no equivalent to
Abner.

It will be seven years (and six months, verse 11) before the
kingdom of Israel is united under David's leadership. There is a
unsubtle judgment on the values of the north in the name of their
king: surely no nation ruled by a sovereign called 'Ishbaal' can
ever enjoy the blessing of Yahweh. The name means 'Man of
Baal'. It is no great consolation if the reading 'Ish-bosheth' is preferred: it means 'Man of Shame'. When the text states that
'Ishbaal, Saul's son, was forty years old when he began to reign
over Israel and he reigned for two years', the implication is presumably that it took Abner five full years to consolidate Ishbaal's
position, before his sovereignty was acknowledged throughout
the northern tribal area. Meanwhile the house of Judah followed
David.

Scene Two (verses 12–17): The servants of David fight with the servants of Ishbaal

> 12 *Abner son of Ner, and the servants of Ishbaal, son of Saul, went out*
> *from Mahanaim to Gibeon. 13 Joab son of Zeruiah, and the servants of*
> *David, went out and met them at the pool of Gibeon. One group sat on*

one side of the pool, while the other sat on the other side of the pool. 14 Abner said to Joab, 'Let the young men come forward and have a contest before us.' Joab said, 'Let them come forward.' 15 So they came forward and were counted as they passed by, twelve for Benjamin and Ishbaal son of Saul, and twelve of the servants of David. 16 Each grasped his opponent by the head, and thrust his sword in his opponent's side; so they fell down together. Therefore that place was called Helkath-hazzurim [Field of Sword-edges'], which is at Gibeon. 17 The battle was very fierce that day; and Abner and the men of Israel were beaten by the servants of David.

Israel is in civil war. Much as David had sought to avoid this situation during the lifetime of king Saul, he appears to accept it during the reign of Ishbaal.

There were however attempts at a diplomatic solution; or at least, attempts to avoid the extent of bloodshed inevitable in all-out war. Abner and some of Ishbaal's men meet with Joab and some of David's men at the pool of Gibeon. One party sits on one side of the pool and the other party on the other side. A formal proposal is made by Abner that some of the young men one each side come forward and engage in a public contest ('Let the young men come forward and play before us'! verse 14) – like some sort of knightly (or more realistically, gladiatorial) tournament. Joab agrees and there is a staged fight, twelve against twelve. But it is not a jousting tournament. It is deadly representative battle. The gist of verse 16 seems to be that all twenty-four of the young men died, so even was the contest: each of the men, in twelve pairings, killed his partner, by running him through with the sword in his side, while grabbing his head in his hand. The incident was so traumatic, the place was re-named after the weapons that shed such blood: 'Field of Sword-edges' (or literally, 'Field of Flints').

If Abner's proposal was an attempt to limit the conflict, it failed. The formal, representative fighting precipitated a more conventional, if particularly fierce, battle – in which 'Abner and the men of Israel' (Ishbaal doesn't even get a mention) suffered a heavy defeat at the hands of Joab's men, who are carefully described as 'the servants of David'. David himself is not present, either at the summit meeting by the pool, or at the subsequent battle – which may reflect the care with which he is being protected not so much from physical danger as from any involvement in violence against the house of Saul. Nevertheless this is the first time in the entire narrative where David appears to sanction violence against Saul's house. He may not be present in person, but three times in six short verses his men are called 'the servants of David'.

Scene Three (verses 18–32): Abner kills Asahel, son of Zeruiah

18 The three sons of Zeruiah were there, Joab, Abishai, and Asahel. Now Asahel was as swift of foot as a wild gazelle. 19 Asahel pursued Abner, turning neither to the right nor to the left as he followed him. 20 Then Abner looked back and said, 'Is it you, Asahel?' He answered, 'Yes, it is.' 21 Abner said to him, 'Turn to your right or to your left, and seize one of the young men, and take his spoil.' But Asahel would not turn away from following him. 22 Abner said again to Asahel, 'Turn away from following me; why should I strike you to the ground? How then could I show my face to your brother Joab?' 23 But he refused to turn away. So Abner struck him in the stomach with the butt of his spear, so that the spear came out at his back. He fell there, and died where he lay. And all those who came to the place where Asahel had fallen and died, stood still.

24 But Joab and Abishai pursued Abner. As the sun was going down they came to the hill of Ammah, which lies before Giah on the way to the wilderness of Gibeon. 25 The Benjaminites rallied around Abner and formed a single band; they took their stand on the top of a hill. 26 Then Abner called to Joab, 'Is the sword to keep devouring for ever? Do you not know that the end will be bitter? How long will it be before you order your people to turn from the pursuit of their kinsmen?' 27 Joab said, 'As God lives, if you had not spoken, the people would have continued to pursue their kinsmen, not stopping until morning.' 28 Joab sounded the trumpet and all the people stopped; they no longer pursued Israel or engaged in battle any further.

29 Abner and his men travelled all that night through the Arabah; they crossed the Jordan, and, marching the whole forenoon, they came to Mahanaim. 30 Joab returned from the pursuit of Abner; and when he had gathered all the people together, there were missing of David's servants nineteen men besides Asahel. 31 But the servants of David had killed of Benjamin three hundred and sixty of Abner's men. 32 They took up Asahel and buried him in the tomb of his father, which was at Bethlehem. Joab and his men marched all night, and the day broke upon them at Hebron.

It will emerge at this end of the scene that there were many casualties on the side 'of Benjamin' and relatively few on the side of David. But the narrative now homes in on the particular conflict between Abner and 'the three sons of Zeruiah'.

It is unusual in the Old Testament period for men to be defined in relation to their mother, and unusual also to find a female character in the Bible with the '-iah' name-ending, which invokes the name of Yahweh. Both the matrilineal designation and the implied relation to the Lord may be explained if, as 1 Chronicles 2:16 suggests, Zeruiah is David's sister or half-sister.

The three sons of Zeruiah are Joab, Abishai and Asahel. Asahel (presumably the youngest, as he is the last named of the three brothers) is quick – 'as swift of foot as a wild gazelle'. In the course of the battle, he sees Abner flee and sets off in single-minded pursuit ('turning neither to the right nor to the left') to kill or capture him. But looking back, Abner recognizes him. The two warriors speak, acknowledging one another. Then Abner seeks to distract Asahel by urging him to capture or kill and loot one of the young fighting men instead. Twice Abner calls on Asahel to give up the pursuit and twice Asahel refuses. In verse 22 Abner effectively accepts that to kill Asahel would be to invite the retribution of at least the older of the other two sons of Zeruiah (who sound, like the later sons of Zebedee, to have been violent men – 'sons of thunder'; Mk. 3:17). In this he is proved right by the course of events: Joab will kill him. But as Asahel maintains his pursuit Abner finally (in verse 23) strikes him in the stomach with the butt of his spear. Perhaps he really did not intend to kill him – just to wound or even wind him. But Asahel is killed ('the spear came out at his back. He fell there and died where he lay'). The solemnity of his death is registered by all who see him: 'all those who came to the place where Asahel had fallen and died, stood still'. The narrative itself stands still momentarily, in recognition of something heroic.

But Abner's challenge is not just to see off Asahel. Joab and Abishai are also in pursuit. They chase him through all that remains of that day until the sun was going down. Meanwhile, the Benjaminites gather around Abner. Taking a stand at the top of a hill he calls to Joab, appealing to him to call off the pursuit. Abner is presented in this part of the story as a man of common sense as well as courage. He stresses that civil war means that the followers of David are engaged in 'the pursuit of their kinsmen'. Joab hears him and 'as God lives' relents. It is even possible to translate verse 27 as if Joab said to Abner , 'If you'd only spoken the word, I'd have called off the slaughter this morning.' But the trumpet is sounded and the battle is called to a halt.

Both Joab and Abner then return to their respective territories. For Abner this means travelling all through the night, crossing the Jordan, and travelling on again the following morning all the way to Mahanaim.

The episode ends with a tally: on David's side nineteen men have been lost, besides Asahel. But 'of Abner's men' (verse 31; not 'Ishbaal's men'), the casualties were three hundred and sixty men. It is 'Advantage David'. He is winning on points but his troops have not delivered a knockout blow. The narrative ends with both armies having marched some distance from the battlefield, to their own territories. Asahel is buried 'in the tomb of his father' at David's hometown; and Joab, marching all night, reaches Hebron at dawn.

Conclusion

There is a subtle development in this episode of the drama which sheds light on what it is like to achieve power.

This is the first episode in which David is a king; admittedly only king of Judah; but a king nevertheless. As such he seems still to be 'a man after God's own heart': he seeks the Lord's guidance before going up to Hebron to take the throne; and his first act as king is a reconciling one, as he reaches out to Saul's valiant champions, the men of Jabesh-gilead. In reaching out to them, he speaks in blessing of the Lord.

But this is also the first episode in which 'the servants of David' represent him in dealings with Saul's house. David plays no active part in the episode beyond verse 7. The sons of Zeruiah act for him. He is no longer the captain of a warrior band. He is a king with captains under him.

This is part of the reality of leadership. Often the more senior a leader becomes the further he or she is drawn away from the front line. This presents new challenges. How is the leader who delegates, to ensure that what is done in the leader's name is done as the leader would wish it? In the very next episode David will find the dilemma is a serious one.

Chapter Nineteen
(2 Samuel 3:1–39)

David and Abner

Introduction

In the previous episode David took two great steps towards becoming king of all Israel: the first was to assume the kingship of Judah; the second was to prove himself (or his servants) stronger in battle than the forces of Ishbaal (or rather of Abner).

In this episode, through a complicated series of betrayals, the process moves forward still further until it is inevitable that the kingdom of Israel will duly be transferred from Saul's house to David. There is a tension in the narrative in this chapter and the next. On the one hand David remains scrupulously innocent of any involvement in the assassinations of key individuals who stand between him and Saul's throne. David does not seize Saul's crown – he is invited to receive it. This is presumably the mode of transfer which most befits the promise of the Lord. But his seizure of the southern tribes demonstrates that David will not relate to Ishbaal in the deferential way in which he related to Saul; and his readiness in the previous episode to allow his servants and those of Saul's house to fight one another in battle turns out not to have been an isolated skirmish, but the first action in a long war. Is David or is he not prepared to wrest the kingdom away from Ishbaal by force of arms?

The narrative is at pains to stress that David is far, far more powerful than Ishbaal. Yet by the end of the episode he is reflecting on his sense of utter powerlessness.

Scene One (verses 1–5): David grows stronger and stronger

1 There was a long war between the house of Saul and the house of David; David grew stronger and stronger, while the house of Saul became weaker and weaker.

2 Sons were born to David at Hebron: his firstborn was Amnon, of Ahinoam of Jezreel; 3 his second, Chileab, of Abigail the widow of Nabal of Carmel; the third, Absalom son of Maacah, daughter of King Talmai of Geshur; 4 the fourth, Adonijah son of Haggith; the fifth, Shephatiah son of Abital; 5 and the sixth, Ithream, of David's wife Eglah. These were born to David in Hebron.

Whatever truce was agreed at the end of 2 Samuel 2, it was by no means a complete cessation of hostilities. On the contrary civil war between the north and south of Saul's kingdom was long and drawn out. Presumably it lasted almost seven years (verse 11) – a period not much shorter than the time David spent fleeing Saul in the wilderness. But from the vantage point of the narrator the outcome was never in doubt. During that time David grew stronger and stronger and the house of Saul (barely worth designating as 'Ishbaal') grew weaker and weaker. The triumph of David may not be immediate but it is inevitable.

To refer to the rulers of the north as 'the house of Saul' is perfectly accurate. To refer to its opponents as 'the house of David' is anachronistic; but one way in which the growing strength of David is reflected is in the birth of his sons. There are six of these, born to six different wives: Amnon, Chileab, Absalom, Adonijah, Shephatiah and Ithream, born respectively to Ahinoam, Abigail, Maacah, Haggith, Abital and Eglah. Of the sons, Chileab, Shephatiah and Ithream are never heard of again. Amnon will feature in 2 Samuel 13–14; Absalom in 2 Samuel 15–19; and Adonijah in 1 Kings 1–2. David is not well served by his sons. On the one hand they are a mark of his virility as a king as well as a man; on the other hand they are also a mark of his vulnerability. Where the sons of a king might be expected to shore up its future, establishing a dynasty, in David's case they undermine his authority and the future of his house.

Of the wives listed in these verses, Maacah, Haggith, Abital and Eglah have not appeared before. Where the latter three have come from the reader is not told. But Maacah is the daughter (and Absalom is therefore the grandson) of a king. Not only that but she is the daughter of a king from the north (Talmai of Geshur). This suggests that during this seven-year period of civil war, David was consolidating his position by embarking on alliances in the area of which Ishbaal was the more obvious sovereign. Maacah is both a mark and a means of David's growing influence and security (although in 2 Samuel 13:37–38, when he flees from his father, Absalom takes refuge in Geshur – with his grandfather's house). The first two wives mentioned, Ahinoam and Abigail, have been with David throughout his wilderness years and have travelled with him to Ziklag and then to Hebron. The narrative has of course mentioned one other wife to whom David was married and she is conspicuous by her absence at this point: Michal, daughter of Saul. But she is about to re-enter the story. Another wife (Bathsheba) and two other sons (Nathan and Solomon) have yet to feature in the narrative. Solomon, born in Jerusalem not Hebron, will be the one success among David's offspring.

The text does not state whether daughters were also born to David – but the outlaw with two wives has become a king with six (a harem fit for a palace). There is no hint here of the trouble that David's wives and children were to him in this bare record of names, and a sense of domestic harmony is hinted at when the text at once goes on to refer to the strife between Ishbaal and Abner over a concubine of Saul's.

Scene Two (verses 6–11): Abner turns against Ishbaal

> 6 *While there was war between the house of Saul and the house of David, Abner was making himself strong in the house of Saul.* 7 *Now Saul had a concubine whose name was Rizpah daughter of Aiah. And Ishbaal said to Abner, 'Why have you gone in to my father's concubine?'* 8 *The words of Ishbaal made Abner very angry; he said, 'Am I a dog's head for Judah? Today I keep showing loyalty to the house of your father Saul, to his brothers, and to his friends, and have not given you*

into the hand of David; and yet you charge me now with a crime concerning this woman. 9 So may God do to Abner and so may he add to it! For just what the Lord has sworn to David, that will I accomplish for him, 10 to transfer the kingdom from the house of Saul, and set up the throne of David over Israel and over Judah, from Dan to Beersheba.' 11 And Ishbaal could not answer Abner another word, because he feared him.

Meanwhile David was not the only one growing stronger. The same is true in the relative weakness of the northern kingdom of Abner. Yet he must surely have seen which way the wind was blowing. He must have recognized that he would one day have to be reconciled to David; and this episode can be read as a transparent ruse on his part – as a deliberate attempt to pick a fight with Ishbaal so as to have grounds for a subsequent overture to David.

Saul had a concubine and Ishbaal accuses Abner of 'going in' to her. This may have been an unjust accusation, reflecting Ishbaal's resentment at Abner's real power in the kingdom. Or it may represent the extent to which Abner had in fact arrogated to himself the power that belonged to the king. The act could be construed as a claim to the throne (which is the interpretation placed by Solomon on a similar act by his brother Adonijah in 1 Kgs. 2:13–25). But Abner protests his innocence: he has been continually loyal to the house of Saul, his brothers and his friends, 'and yet you accuse me of a crime against this woman'. This is an ambiguous protest. It is unclear whether he is denying the act or its criminality. Is he denying any association with the woman concerned or simply any impropriety? His words may amount to a declaration that he is fully entitled, given his loyalty to Saul and his house, to take this woman as his wife. Ominously he points out that he has not handed Ishbaal over to the house of David – implying that it is well within his power to do so. Indeed that is exactly what Abner declares he will now do, so that David will rule, 'from Dan' (in the north) 'to Beersheba' (in the south). If there was no treason in Abner before there is now. The weakness of Ishbaal is reflected in the fact that he cannot say a word against it. He has inherited his father's fearfulness.

Scene Three (verses 12–21): Abner offers to broker peace between David and Israel

12 Abner sent messengers to David at Hebron, saying, 'To whom does the land belong? Make your covenant with me, and I will give you my support to bring all Israel over to you.' 13 He said, 'Good; I will make a covenant with you. But one thing I require of you: you shall never appear in my presence unless you bring Saul's daughter Michal when you come to see me.' 14 Then David sent messengers to Saul's son Ishbaal, saying, 'Give me my wife Michal, to whom I became engaged at the price of one hundred foreskins of the Philistines.' 15 Ishbaal sent and took her from her husband Paltiel the son of Laish. 16 But her husband went with her, weeping as he walked behind her all the way to Bahurim. Then Abner said to him, 'Go back home!' So he went back.

17 Abner sent word to the elders of Israel, saying, 'For some time past you have been seeking David as king over you. 18 Now then bring it about; for the Lord has promised David: Through my servant David I will save my people Israel from the hand of the Philistines, and from all their enemies.' 19 Abner also spoke directly to the Benjaminites; then Abner went to tell David at Hebron all that Israel and the whole house of Benjamin were ready to do.

20 When Abner came with twenty men to David at Hebron, David made a feast for Abner and the men who were with him. 21 Abner said to David, 'Let me go and rally all Israel to my lord the king, in order that they may make a covenant with you, and that you may reign over all that your heart desires.' So David dismissed Abner, and he went away in peace.

Abner at once makes overtures to David. He boldly claims that the land of Israel belongs to himself and that if David will only make a covenant with him, it lies within his power to deliver the kingdom to David.

David agrees to a covenant on one condition: that Abner undertakes to bring with him Michal, the daughter of Saul (1 Sam. 18:20–28; 24:44). (David's words in verse 13 – literally, 'Unless you bring Michal with you, you will not see my face again' – recall those of Joseph to his brothers with reference to

Benjamin in Gen. 43:3.) David simultaneously sends a message to
Ishbaal, demanding that Michal be returned to him, recalling the
price at which he became engaged to her ('one hundred foreskins
of the Philistines') – with an implied allusion to his superior
strength, in that he actually delivered two hundred. This is a
political act, quite apart from any personal affection on David's
side: part of the way in which David can establish his legitimacy
as a successor to Saul is by virtue of his marriage to Saul's daughter.

It betrays the extent to which David has indeed grown stronger
and stronger, and Ishbaal weaker and weaker (especially as a result
of a breakdown in his relationship with Abner), that Ishbaal at once
consents and requires Michal to leave her husband, Paltiel. But
Paltiel apparently loves his wife and in one of the most poignant
cameos in all Scripture, he is depicted as following in the wake of
his wife as she journeys to David, weeping all the way to Bahurim.
They may easily by now have been married for a decade, although
there is no mention of any offspring. The story could scarcely say
less about him and yet the reader sees that Paltiel's reckless love is
at least the match of Michal's (or Jonathan's) for David. The text
does not say what Michal herself thought – whether she was also
bereft at this turn of events, or delighted at the prospect of a reunion
with a man she certainly used to love (1 Sam. 18:20). Significantly, it
is Abner (rather than Ishbaal), who dismisses Paltiel and sends him
home. In this way he has fulfilled the only condition David has laid
on him for the making of a covenant of peace.

Meanwhile Abner has been canvassing support for David. It
transpires that there is a pro-David lobby in Israel and Abner
begins by approaching its members. He reminds them that they
have for some time been considering the possibility of seeking
David's lordship and suggests that the time has now come for
them to act. He reminds them also that the Lord has promised not
only to make David king, but to deliver Israel from the Philistines
by his hand. There is obviously a criticism of Saul implied here:
he has failed to provide this deliverance. Quite why Abner himself has not felt bound before this moment by what the Lord has
so transparently promised, is less clear. But apparently the promise of the Lord legitimates Abner's action: there is no blame
attached to Abner by the narrator.

Having also sounded out the Benjaminites (distinguished presumably because that was the tribe from which Saul had come), Abner lets David know that all Israel is ready to make him king. So a summit meeting is held in Hebron attended by Abner and twenty representatives from Israel. David hosts a feast, at the end of which he 'dismisses Abner in peace' (a phrase repeated with emphasis in verses 22 and 23) to go and rally the Israelites to his cause, so that a covenant might be made.

Scene Four (verses 22–30): Joab and Abishai murder Abner

> 22 *Just then the servants of David arrived with Joab from a raid, bringing much spoil with them. But Abner was not with David at Hebron, for David had dismissed him, and he had gone away in peace. 23 When Joab and all the army that was with him came, it was told Joab, 'Abner son of Ner came to the king, and he has dismissed him, and he has gone away in peace.' 24 Then Joab went to the king and said, 'What have you done? Abner came to you; why did you dismiss him, so that he got away? 25 You know that Abner son of Ner came to deceive you, and to learn your comings and goings and to learn all that you are doing.'*

> 26 *When Joab came out from David's presence, he sent messengers after Abner, and they brought him back from the cistern of Sirah; but David did not know about it. 27 When Abner returned to Hebron, Joab took him aside in the gateway to speak with him privately, and there he stabbed him in the stomach. So he died for shedding lacks the blood of Asahel, Joab's brother. 28 Afterwards, when David heard of it, he said, 'I and my kingdom are for ever guiltless before the Lord for the blood of Abner son of Ner. 29 May the guilt fall on the head of Joab, and on all his father's house; and may the house of Joab never be without one who has a discharge, or who is leprous, or who holds a spindle, or who falls by the sword, or who lacks food!' 30 So Joab and his brother Abishai murdered Abner because he had killed their brother Asahel in the battle at Gibeon.*

The careful reader, meanwhile, is asking what Joab, David's commander, has made of these developments. Not only is Abner a personal enemy of his, responsible for killing his brother; but he is a political rival too. If peace is declared between Judah and Israel, and if Abner is credited with the peacemaking, he will inevitably be a rival to Joab for David's ear. But Joab knows nothing about these developments. He has been away on a raid. (Raiding used to be David's occupation; now it is undertaken by others on his behalf.)

Joab and his men now suddenly return with 'much spoil' (compare 1 Sam. 30:30; such raids – whether against the northern tribes or against Philistine and other cities to the south – are evidently still an essential part of the way in which David secures political and economic advantage, part of the way in which in the words of the opening verse, he is growing 'stronger and stronger'). When he arrives, Joab is told that Abner has been 'and has gone away in peace'. Joab is (or at least purports to be) wholly suspicious of Abner and his motives and warns the king of the danger that Abner has only come to him to spy on him. He remonstrates with David for failing to eliminate him while he was in his power (as others had previously remonstrated with David for failing to eliminate Saul when opportunity presented itself). Joab does not add, 'And besides, Abner's the man who killed my brother', but the reader knows. Nor does Joab remind David that Asahel was his own flesh and blood (1 Chron. 2:16). For whatever mixed motives, Joab the hawk is furious with David's dove-like stance. 'Why did you dismiss him', he asks, 'so that he got away?' But David does not answer. To answer would be to choose between Joab and Abner, and David is not ready to do that.

At once, Joab sends emissaries after Abner to bring him back. He does not want Abner's peace. He does not want to be in partnership with the commander of Israel. He wants him dead. When Abner comes back, Joab takes him aside as if to impart some important message to him, and then stabs him in the stomach and kills him. (There are echoes here of the killing of King Eglon of Moab by Ehud in Jdgs. 3:15–26.) The explicit reference to Abner's stomach looks like a plain statement of Joab's revenge for the death of Asahel (2 Sam. 2:23). The deed is briefly recorded and swiftly done.

The narrator is careful to record that 'David knew nothing of this' (verse 26). This means that when David hears the news that Abner is dead, he can protest his own innocence of blood-guilt:

just as he was innocent of the deaths of Nabal and Saul. Yet David's first words are not words of grief (as they were, for example, when he heard of Saul's death), but of self-justification. David is hyper-aware of the political ramifications here. His instinctive reaction is not 'How awful. Good Abner is dead', but (almost comically, Homer Simpson-like), 'It wasn't me! It was like that when I got here!' The negotiations with the elders of Israel are at an especially delicate stage and Abner's violent death is the last thing David needed: it might precipitate a change of mind on the part of 'all Israel and the house of Benjamin', if they suspect that Abner has been killed at David's instigation or with his collusion. But it also matters to the narrator to present David as innocent of any blood-guilt; as if that in itself was a threat to his legitimacy as king.

So as quickly as David previously turned on the Amalekite who slew Saul, he now turns on Joab and his descendants and curses them. On the other hand, he conspicuously doesn't slay Joab on the spot in the way that he did the Amalekite. He doesn't even dismiss him from his position. In fact, Joab apparently continues in David's service just as before (2 Sam. 8:16; 10:7; 11:1; 12:26; etc.). Joab is family, after all, and almost as indispensable to David as Abner himself had ultimately become to Ishbaal.

The third 'son of Zeruiah', Abishai, has not been mentioned until this point (verse 30), but was apparently complicit in Joab's murder.

Scene Five (verses 31 to 39): David grieves for Abner

> 31 Then David said to Joab and to all the people who were with him, 'Tear your clothes, and put on sackcloth, and mourn over Abner.' And King David followed the bier. 32 They buried Abner at Hebron. The king lifted up his voice and wept at the grave of Abner, and all the people wept. 33 The king lamented for Abner, saying,
> 'Should Abner die as a fool dies?
> 34 Your hands were not bound,
> your feet were not fettered;
> as one falls before the wicked
> you have fallen.'

And all the people wept over him again. 35 *Then all the people came to persuade David to eat something while it was still day; but David swore, saying, 'So may God do to me, and more, if I taste bread or anything else before the sun goes down!' 36 All the people took notice of it, and it pleased them; just as everything the king did pleased all the people. 37 So all the people and all Israel understood that day that the king had no part in the killing of Abner son of Ner. 38 And the king said to his servants, 'Do you not know that a prince and a great man has fallen this day in Israel? 39 Today I am powerless, even though anointed king; these men, the sons of Zeruiah, are too violent for me. The Lord pay back the one who does wickedly in accordance with his wickedness!'*

There is an almost ludicrous stress in verses 31 to 37, intended not just to absolve David from all responsibility for Abner's demise, but to make clear that his innocence was universally accepted at the time. David instructs Joab and 'all the people' to mourn over Abner. A state funeral is organized and 'King David' follows the bier. This is a new departure, shoring up David's authority at a moment when it was in jeopardy. David has previously been identified as 'the king' (2 Sam. 2:4, 7, 11; 3:17, 21–24), but this is the first time that the narrator has put his name and his office together. Abner is buried in Hebron, David's capital; his body is not returned to the northern kingdom. Again, there is obvious political benefit for David here.

David weeps and 'all the people' weep with him. As David had mourned for Saul and Jonathan, he now mourns for Abner in a poetic lamentation. As Jonathan and Saul had fallen, so now Abner too has fallen. He laments not just the fact of Abner's death, but the manner of it: he was too great a man to die, as he did, a fool's death, at the hands of the wicked. When they hear this noble lament, 'all the people' weep again.

Such is the extent of David's personal distress, that his health becomes a concern: 'all the people' come to him to persuade him to eat. But he will not; on oath to God, he swears that he will not. And 'all the people' took note of it and it pleased them, 'just as everything the king did pleased the people'.

Those words 'all the people' comes six times in verses 31–36. When it recurs for the seventh and final time in this section at the beginning of verse 37, the point is clear. 'All the people – and all

Israel – understood that day that the king had no part in the killing of Abner son of Ner'. All the people apparently meant not only those of Judah, but those of Benjamin and all Israel too. David's handling of the death of Abner, and his evident sense of personal loss, has saved the day: the alliance with Israel will hold. All are convinced that David had truly sent Abner away in peace.

David's shrewdness is further demonstrated in the conclusion of the episode. It was evident in the earlier scenes of this episode that Ishbaal was king of Israel only in name – Abner was the real power holder. David first acknowledges this reality ('a prince and a great man has fallen this day in Israel') and then acknowledges the extent to which he finds himself in a similar position. 'Today I am powerless', he says. The death of Abner has revealed to David the limits of his control: he was not able to save Abner from death or to restrain the violent sons of Zeruiah. 'They are too violent for me.' For the second time, he curses them, praying that the Lord would pay back their wickedness in wickedness. It might have sounded to some of his hearers as an invitation to assassinate Joab and Abishai.

Verse 31, and still more verse 38, come as a belated response to verses 24–25, when Joab challenged David in the strongest possible terms and David made no reply. But David will continue to rely on the sons of Zeruiah, and this will not be the last time that he finds himself simultaneously dependent on and yet at odds with them (2 Sam. 15–16, 19–20, 21).

Conclusion

Power-holding is seldom straightforward. On the one hand this episode finds David as powerful in worldly terms as he has ever been. King of Judah, he is apparently about to become king of all Israel. He can certainly dictate terms to Ishbaal. Since the death of Saul, he has acquired a throne and a capital city. It has become possible to speak of 'the house of David' and 'the servants of David'.

On the other hand this episode depicts David as more vulnerable than ever – and depicts him as recognizing the fact. 'Today

I am powerless,' he says, 'even though anointed king.' His servants, who act in his name, are beyond his control. Many a leader in many a different field (politics, business and church for certain) has lamented this dynamic. To have responsibility without control is a nightmare. Yet it is rare for the person with ultimate responsibility to have unilateral power. The art of effective leadership is to create a sufficient sense of shared vision, of shared ethos, to ensure that throughout an organization power is exercised in ways that further the desired goal.

David and Ishbaal

Introduction

In the previous episode, when Abner left David in peace to go and rally all Israel to his side, it seemed that David's accession to Saul's throne was imminent. At almost any earlier stage, Abner's death would have been a further convenient step in the process. But in these particular circumstances, the loss of Abner is a setback. Given his committed stance of loyalty to Saul's house, his steadfast refusal to condone the violent overthrow of Israel's leadership, how is David now to overcome Ishbaal? Until and unless Ishbaal is dead or defeated, David cannot be king of Israel. Yet he cannot take any initiative to hasten matters.

In this final episode before David is finally king of Israel, Ishbaal dies. In relation to this death, as in relation to the deaths of Saul, Jonathan and Abner in previous episodes, David is innocent of any involvement – he is the passive beneficiary of other people's actions.

Scene One (verses 1–3): Ishbaal's courage fails

1 When Saul's son Ishbaal heard that Abner had died at Hebron, his courage failed, and all Israel was dismayed. 2 Saul's son had two captains of raiding bands; the name of one was Baanah, and the name of the other Rechab. They were sons of Rimmon, a Benjaminite from Beeroth—for Beeroth is considered to belong to Benjamin. 3 (Now the people of Beeroth had fled to Gittaim and are there as resident aliens to this day).

It was Abner who made Ishbaal king (2 Sam. 2:8–10) and Ishbaal feared him (2 Sam. 3:10). Given the breakdown of relationship between them and Abner's recent defection to David (which, if not common knowledge, was at least known to many of Israel's elders) it might have been thought that news of Abner's death would be the best possible tidings to Ishbaal. Does it not offer him a fresh opportunity to establish his authority over Israel? But instead, when Ishbaal hears that Abner has died, his courage fails him (literally, 'his hands grew weak'; that is, 'he lost his grip'). If Ishbaal was weak with Abner at his side, he is still weaker without him. All Israel knows it.

Two new characters are then introduced into the drama: two captains of Ishbaal's raiding bands, Baanah and Rechab. They are brothers and Benjaminites. Nothing more is said about them at this point except that their people had fled to Gittaim 'and are there as resident aliens to this day'. The abrupt change of scene after verse 3 alerts the reader that something significant has been introduced, but at once deferred. The fact that Baanah and Rechab are announced as captains of raiding bands and resident aliens recalls how David – resident alien in Gath, captain of a raiding band ostensibly loyal to Achish – betrayed his lord; the reader waits to see if Baanah and Rechab might not do likewise.

Scene Two (verse 4): The introduction of Mephibosheth

4 Saul's son Jonathan had a son who was crippled in his feet. He was five years old when the news about Saul and Jonathan came from Jezreel. His nurse picked him up and fled; and, in her haste to flee, it happened that he fell and became lame. His name was Mephibosheth.

Then a third new character is introduced and at once the dramatic focus moves on again. This is Ishbaal's nephew, the son of Jonathan. The first thing we are told about him is that he was disabled. We learn his age and the circumstances of the accident that caused his disability: he was five years old when the news came of the death on the battlefield of his father and grandfather. His nurse picked him up and fled. In her haste he fell and was so injured that he was left permanently lame. Then at the end we learn his name: Mephibosheth. His story will not be resumed until 2 Samuel 9:1–8; but the note does play a part at this point in the narrative. The house of Saul is about to suffer a further grievous blow. Before that happens Mephibosheth is introduced to the drama, because it will be in him, as its last representative, that David is able to fulfil his promise to Jonathan to show mercy to Saul's house. Moreover the point is being made that with the imminent demise of Ishbaal, there will be no adult, or indeed able-bodied, successor left to Saul.

Scene Three (verses 5–12): The death of Ishbaal

> 5 Now the sons of Rimmon the Beerothite, Rechab and Baanah, set out, and about the heat of the day they came to the house of Ishbaal, while he was taking his noonday rest. 6 They came inside the house as though to take wheat, and they struck him in the stomach; then Rechab and his brother Baanah escaped. 7 Now they had come into the house while he was lying on his couch in his bedchamber; they attacked him, killed him, and beheaded him. Then they took his head and travelled by way of the Arabah all night long. 8 They brought the head of Ishbaal to David at Hebron and said to the king, 'Here is the head of Ishbaal, son of Saul your enemy who sought your life; the Lord has avenged my lord the king this day on Saul and on his offspring.'

> 9 David answered Rechab and his brother Baanah, the sons of Rimmon the Beerothite, 'As the Lord lives, who has redeemed my life out of every adversity, 10 when the one who told me, "See, Saul is dead", thought he was bringing good news, I seized him and killed him at Ziklag — this was the reward I gave him for his news. 11 How much more then, when wicked men have killed a righteous man on his bed in his own house! And now shall I not require his blood at your hand, and destroy you from the earth?' 12 So David commanded the young men, and they killed them; they cut off their hands and feet, and hung their bodies beside the pool at Hebron. But the head of Ishbaal they took and buried in the tomb of Abner at Hebron.

Now the spotlight moves back, after a dramatic pause, to Rechab and Baanah; and this time it remains on them. They understand

and seek to exploit the situation. They come to Ishbaal's house, to which as captains of his raiding bands it appears that they have free access. The king is taking a siesta in the early afternoon. To those whose courage has failed, bed can be a tempting place to stay; sleep can provide a kind of refuge. But it provides only a temporary refuge from the need to act and to face the future; it cannot provide a permanent refuge from violence.

Under the guise of collecting provisions, Rechab and Baanah embark on one more raid – only this time their master is their target. They enter his room while he is still asleep and attack him. Ishbaal is quite literally caught napping. First Asahel, then Abner and now finally Ishbaal is stabbed in the stomach. Killing him, they then decapitate him before escaping with his head. First Goliath, then Saul and now finally Ishbaal is beheaded.

Rechab and Baanah travel from Israel to Judah overnight, with the head as their trophy and present it to David at Hebron. 'Here is the head of Ishbaal, son of Saul your enemy who sought your life; the Lord has avenged my lord the king this day on Saul and on his offspring.' Clearly, like the Amalekite who either witnessed or expedited the death of Saul and brought to David the news of it, they believe they have done a laudable thing politically, even theologically, and will be bountifully rewarded for their decisive intervention.

It is hard to imagine a greater misjudgment. They had evidently not heard how David had responded to that Amalekite – who only brought news of the deaths of Saul and Jonathan and not their heads. David makes the connection: 'When the one who told me, "See, Saul is dead", thought he was bringing me good news, I seized him and killed him – how much more when wicked men have killed a righteous man on his bed in his own house!' It is not clear from the story that David has learned this culpable detail (that Ishbaal was killed in his sleep) from the assassins themselves. Perhaps he has received intelligence from another source and is therefore prepared when Benaah and Rechab arrive. David once again distances himself from a death of which he is the obvious beneficiary. 'Shall I not require his blood at your hand and destroy you from the earth?' he warns them.

Just as he had done in that earlier episode, David turns to the young men among his followers (again it is an act of contempt on his part not to deliver the fatal blows himself) and commands them to kill Rechab and Baanah. The men die a bloody death, with their hands and feet amputated and their bodies hung out in public disgrace. But Ishbaal's head is given a dignified burial in Abner's tomb. The head is retained not just with Abner's body, but like Abner's body: in Hebron and away from the house of Saul. David is politically astute enough not to provide his opponents with a totemic focus for their opposition.

Theologically, the crux of this episode comes in verses 8 and 9. In verse 8 Baanah and Rechab claim that through them the Lord has avenged David on Saul ('your enemy, who sought your life') and on his family, through the death of Ishbaal. David rejects this interpretation of events. Even if it is true that Saul sought to kill him, David finds no need to avenge himself, for (verse 9) the Lord 'has redeemed my life out of every adversity'. As David told Saul at their last meeting (1 Sam. 26:24) 'the Lord rescues me from all tribulation'. For this reason David does not regard Saul as his enemy. Rather he regards Saul's enemies as his own. To the bitter end he remains loyal to the family of Saul and refuses to see in the untimely demise of Ishbaal, the hand of the Lord at work. David does not cause the deaths of Saul's people and he does not celebrate them either.

Conclusion

From the moment he slew Goliath, David's has demonstrated a capacity for ruthless violence against both individuals and communities. It is a dreadful capacity in one to whom great power will be entrusted.

The story of David's rise is in part a story about his capacity to manage this impulse to violence. There are certainly plenty of less restrained men in the narrative. Against the Lord's anointed, he is scrupulous not to raise his hand. He commits no violence against Saul, Abner, or Ishbaal.

But whether he killed Goliath with the sling (1 Sam. 17:50) or the sword (1 Sam. 17:51), the decapitation which followed was an act of violence. Against Nabal, he was saved from himself by Abigail (1 Sam. 25:31). Against the Geshurites, the Gerzites and the Amalekites, his aggression was unrestrained (1 Sam. 27:8–11). He was ruthless in despatching the Amalekite who sought to profit from Saul's death (2 Sam. 1:15), and now these two warlords who sought to profit from Ishbaal's – whose bodies are violated after death in much the way that Saul's had been by the Philistines.

Chapter Twenty One
(2 Samuel 5:1–10)

David at Jerusalem

Introduction

There are two scenes in the last episode in the story of David's rise. The first sees David graduate from being king of Judah to being king of all Israel. The second sees him move his base from Hebron to Jerusalem. Between them the two scenes encapsulate the enigma of his character: his capacity for faith and trust in the living God on the one hand and his capacity for calculation and political cunning, on the other.

In the first scene, then, David at last becomes king of all Israel. But even now with Ishbaal dead, he does not seize Saul's throne. Even now he waits to be invited. Just as he refused to speed the day of his accession by harming Saul, just as he sought to remain loyal to Saul's house, so now he is presented not as grasping at power, but as receiving overtures from others.

In the second scene David leaves Hebron and takes Jerusalem from the Jebusites by force. It may be that Hebron was simply too far south to serve as an effective base for a king of all Israel, or that it was too closely associated with the initial phase of David's kingship and that a new phase of his reign demanded a new base.

Scene One (verses 1–5): David is anointed king over all Israel

> *1 Then all the tribes of Israel came to David at Hebron, and said, 'Look, we are your bone and flesh. 2 For some time, while Saul was king over us, it was you who led out Israel and brought it in. The Lord said to you:*

It is you who shall be shepherd of my people Israel, you who shall be ruler over Israel.' 3 So all the elders of Israel came to the king at Hebron; and King David made a covenant with them at Hebron before the Lord, and they anointed David king over Israel. 4 David was thirty years old when he began to reign, and he reigned for forty years. 5 At Hebron he reigned over Judah for seven years and six months; and at Jerusalem he reigned over all Israel and Judah for thirty-three years.

The result of Ishbaal's death (following the deaths of Saul, Jonathan and Abner) is that David finally assumes the throne of Israel. But to the last David does not snatch at power: it is presented to him. 'All the tribes of Israel' come to him in Hebron, and they make for him his case to be king on three distinct grounds. First they tell him, 'we are your bone and flesh' (compare Gen. 2:23, 29:14; Jdgs. 9:2; 2 Sam. 19:12–13). Israel and Judah are family; it is a violation of their kinship that they should be divided, let alone at war. Secondly they concede the fact (and the speech does have the character of a concession about it) that even while Saul was king, it was in fact David who led Israel – at least 'for some time'. Thirdly they acknowledge that even then, the Lord promised he would one day become shepherd not of Jesse's flock but of the Lord's. The allusion to David's shepherding origins in 1 Samuel 16 is neat. It indicates that the narrative begun there is now nearing conclusion. They acknowledge that David is destined to be 'ruler' over Israel.

David's credentials for royal office in all Israel are three-fold: he is family, he is a proven, successful military leader, and he is God's chosen one. The case is so obvious and unanswerable that reader might be forgiven for wondering why the strength of these arguments was not apparent to the elders of Israel at the death of Saul. If hereditary right held sway then, so that it was right for one of Saul's sons to succeed him, does it not still do so? Should Mephibosheth or a son of Ishbaal not succeed to the throne? If hereditary right is not an established pattern, ought this embassy not to have been sent to David seven years previously, with some saving of bloodshed?

Nevertheless all the elders of Israel now come to David at Hebron. Verse 3 is phrased with great care. 'All the elders of Israel come to the king at Hebron:' this manages to convey at one

and the same time both the initiative of the elders, and their sup-
plicant status. 'King David made a covenant with them at Hebron
before the Lord.' There is a shift of power here: the statement
implies an initiative on David's part. The elders of Israel have
issued the invitation, but in accepting it, David assumes power
and exercises it. There is no doubt now who is in charge. But
'they anointed David king of all Israel'. Still the elders of Israel
have an important part to play. This is the third and final anointing of David's life (1 Sam. 16; 2 Sam. 3). Again, the contrast is
with Ishbaal, who was 'made king' by Abner alone. David is
authorized by the leaders of Israel.

The first scene closes with a rare chronological detail: 'David
was thirty years old when he began to reign and he reigned for
forty years' (verse 4). In a sense, it is odd to find this information
placed here, since the very next verse clarifies that it was over
Judah (in Hebron) that he reigned for the first seven of those forty
years; he was king of Israel in Jerusalem for only the last thirty-
three years. But in another sense, this is exactly the right place for
such a note: it underlines that it is only now that David's kingship is fulfilled.

Scene Two (verses 6–10): David captures the stronghold of Zion

> 6 *The king and his men marched to Jerusalem against the Jebusites, the
> inhabitants of the land, who said to David, 'You will not come in here,
> even the blind and the lame will turn you back'—thinking, 'David can-
> not come in here.' 7 Nevertheless, David took the stronghold of Zion,
> which is now the city of David. 8 David had said on that day, 'Whoever
> wishes to strike down the Jebusites, let him get up the water shaft to
> attack the lame and the blind, those whom David hates.'.Therefore it is
> said, 'The blind and the lame shall not come into the house.' 9 David
> occupied the stronghold, and named it the city of David. David built the
> city all around from the Millo inwards. 10 And David became greater
> and greater, for the Lord, the God of hosts, was with him.*

The previous scene ended with the statement that as king of
Israel David reigned from Jerusalem. So the final scene in this the

story of David's rise ends with an account of the capture of the city.

Hebron has been an entirely appropriate and effective base while David has been king over Judah alone. But now that he is king also over the north, for pragmatic and for diplomatic reasons, a new centre of power is required.

So David's first act as king over all Israel is to mount an attack on the Jebusites. They are defiant. So convinced are they of the impregnability of their stronghold that they say, 'David cannot come in here.' The narrative provides no detail of the assault (although there may be a clue in verse 8 that it involved a stealthy infiltration via the water shaft). It simply states, 'David took the stronghold of Zion.'

The interpretation of verse 8 is vexed. Three times in this final scene, there are references to the blind and the lame – and the phrase seems to mean something a little different in each case. In verse 6 it seems to mean that the city is so well fortified that even the severely disabled could defend it. In the second, in verse 8a, David seems to be turning the complacency of the Jebusites against them by insulting them: for all the good they will be as warriors in the forthcoming battle, they might as well be lame and blind. But the third reference is the most difficult to understand. It seems (not necessarily at the time of the siege, but at some later point before the writing of this narrative) to have become a proverb that 'the blind and the lame' be excluded 'from the house'. This has a more ritual feel, as if it refers to the exclusion of the blind and the lame not from the city of Jerusalem, but from the temple (compare Lev. 21:18). If such an exclusion later developed and was grounded theologically in the Jebusite taunts of David and his rejoinder, then Matthew's telling of the story of the triumphal entry of Jesus into Jerusalem, as the son of David, is masterful: it ends with the Saviour's inclusion of the blind and the lame (compare Mt. 21:5, 9, 14).

David did not merely take the city. He renamed it (calling it after himself, 'the city of David') and he rebuilt it.

The conclusion brings to a perfect end the story of David's rise: 'David became greater and greater, for the Lord, the God of hosts, was with him'. In 2 Samuel 3, David – as king of Judah – was growing stronger and stronger. Now – as king of Israel – he is growing greater and greater. Why? Simply because 'the Lord, the God of hosts was with him'. Early in the narrative, the phrase 'the Lord was with David' was used (including three times over within a single episode) to underline David's emergence and his overshadowing of Saul (1 Sam. 16:15; 18:12, 14, 28). But this statement is unmistakably climactic: not just 'the Lord', but 'the Lord, the God of hosts', was with him.

Conclusion

Early in the narrative, in the lead up to his battle against Goliath, David asks some bystanders an intriguing pair of questions. The first betrays his self-interest and political ambition: 'What shall be done for the man who kills this Philistine?' The second reflects his faith: 'Who is this Philistine that he should defy the armies of the living God?' The two questions neatly capture the two dominant – if conflicted – sides to David's personality. He is at once both a humble and devout believer, eager to serve his God and ready to trust in his providence; and he is a cunning and ambitious politician, eager to achieve greatness and ready to exploit others in the process.

For all the years of endurance and patience in the wilderness – the years of David's maturing – at the end of the story of his rise, these two competing aspects of his personality are still evident. On the one hand even with his destiny so near to fulfilment, David refrains from snatching at the crown, but (in scene one) waits to be approached by his people. In this, David exemplifies the faith and trust in the Lord which have been characteristic of him since at least the days of his battle against Goliath (1 Sam. 17:37, 45–47; compare his other confessions of faith in 1 Sam. 24:12; 25:32; 26:23–24; 30:23). There is a Christ-likeness about a victor who refuses to snatch at the prize. Yet on the other hand David is astute enough to move quickly after his anointing against the Jebusite stronghold. When he captures it, it becomes 'the city of David' – a symbol of his power and success. In the process he exemplifies the kind of shrewd and decisive manoeuvring which has equally been characteristic of him since at least the days of his battle against Goliath (1 Sam. 17:40–43; compare his other examples of cunning or even deceit in 1 Sam. 20:5–8; 21:2; 21:13; 27:8–12).

The faith and trust in God exercised by David are an indication of the nobility and godliness which are possible even in those who possess great power. But his cunning and self-interest serve to illustrate what every reader of the Bible knows: that God also exercises faith and trust in calling ordinary men and women, in all their ordinary limitations, to be the ones in and through whom his providence is worked out.

Concluding Reflections

David is one of the great heroes of the Bible. He alone is designated 'a man after God's own heart' (1 Sam. 13:14; Acts of the Apostles 13:22). But what does this mean? What is it about David that justifies the expression?

Perhaps it is his achievements? His victories are especially evident in the first and last acts of the drama. In Act One he not only conquers the Philistines and their champion, but wins the hearts of the people of Israel – even vanquishing the black moods of king Saul. In Act Three he not only conquers the Jebusite stronghold, but wins the crown of all Israel – even overcoming the reservations of the elders of the northern tribes. These achievements are all the more remarkable in the light of David's origins. He begins the story as an obscure shepherd boy and ends it as a mighty king. It is a classic rags to riches tale. Moreover for Christian readers, David's victories prefigure those of Christ Jesus, who defeated sin, death and the devil on the cross; and his humble origins hint at the Saviour's birth.

Alternatively does the phrase 'a man after God's own heart' relate simply to his status as God's chosen? This chosen-ness, too, is emphasized in Acts One and Three: the story begins and ends with his anointing. While the reader might instinctively suppose that it was because he was 'a man after God's own heart' that he became chosen, it is truer to the pattern of grace which runs through the Scriptures to suppose that he became 'a man after God's own heart', because he was chosen. It has been noted that in Act One David's success is attributed to the fact that the Lord is with him; and that in Act Three the narrative culminates in the declaration that his increasing greatness is due to the fact that the

Lord, the God of Hosts, is with him. The Lord is not with him because he is successful; he is successful because the Lord is with him. Perhaps by the same token his chosen-ness accounts for, rather than derives from, the fact that he is 'a man after God's own heart'. Certainly, just as David's victories are contrasted with Saul's defeats, and his successes with Saul's failures, so the fact that he is chosen is contrasted with the fact that the Lord rejected Saul. For Christian readers it is also in his chosen-ness that David foreshadows Jesus, the Messiah, the Chosen One.

Yet by far the longest of the three Acts in the story of David's rise is the middle one. Act Two is considerably longer than Acts One and Three put together. Presumably, 'a man after God's own heart' has a heart which reflects the heart of God. There are at least three ways in which, specifically in his wilderness years, David's innermost nature reflects that of Christ Jesus, in whom (as Christians believe) the heart of God is ultimately revealed.

In the first place it is in Act Two that David suffers. In exile, he grew acquainted with his own frailty. When he first fled the court of king Saul, he came (via Nob and Gath) to Moab. There he requested the king to take care of his parents, 'until I know what God will do for me' (1 Sam. 22:3). The chronology is not clear but it is fair to assume that it was something like a decade before David's uncertainty was resolved. That is a long period of waiting – sometimes in extreme vulnerability, in agitation, fear and doubt. He faced the loss of his wives and children, and the loss of others' confidence in his leadership. It was a period in which he surely discovered, as the Apostle Paul would later do, that the power of God is made perfect in weakness (2 Cor. 12:9). The David who fought Goliath had never, so far as the narrative tells, been chastened. Through his struggles as an outlaw, David learned contrition and humility (notably in 1 Sam. 22:22) and a reliance on the deliverance of God altogether more profound than the naïve (though admirable) faith he demonstrated in that fight (compare 1 Sam. 26:24, 2 Sam. 4:9). It was presumably this period of David's life which the Psalmist had in mind when he wrote, 'O Lord, remember in David's favour all the hardships he endured' (Ps. 132:1).

Secondly, and quite possibly consequently, it is in Act Two that David shows compassion for the vulnerable. He does so most obviously when (in 1 Sam. 30, returning from his pursuit of the Amalekites after the destruction of Ziklag), he sides with the exhausted 'baggage-watchers' against the self-righteous warriors (though his offer of refuge to the newly bereaved Abiathar in 1 Sam. 22:20–23 is also as much an expression of compassion as it is of penitence).

Thirdly it is in Act Two that David learns (or demonstrates) restraint. This may in fact be the key characteristic of David as 'a man after God's own heart'. Certainly, the contrast between David and Saul in this respect is considerable. Saul is quick to anger; his temper flares up easily. David, like God himself, is slow to anger (compare, for example, Ex. 34:6; Ps. 86:15 – inevitably, a psalm 'of David'). Saul never showed restraint. Indeed, his lack of restraint was his downfall. Even before David arrived on the scene, Saul could not restrain himself from offering a sacrifice (which it was Samuel's prerogative to offer, 1 Sam. 13:8–12) or from 'swooping down' on Amalekite spoil (which he was categorically forbidden to do, 1 Sam. 15:1–31). After his rival appeared, his capacity to restrain himself only diminished. He could not restrain himself from lashing out at David or even at Jonathan (1 Sam. 18:10–11; 20:30–33). He could not restrain himself from slaughtering the priests of Nob (1 Sam. 22) or from visiting a medium he himself had banned (1 Sam. 28). David, by contrast, restrained himself repeatedly – most obviously, precisely in relation to Saul. He not only restrained himself from lifting his hand against the Lord's anointed; he resisted the temptation to snatch at Saul's crown prematurely (2 Sam. 1:10; 2 Sam. 5:1–5). In the wilderness David learned patience and endurance – unglamorous but vital expressions of power.

Of course there are occasions in the story when David is unrestrained in violence (compare 1 Sam. 27:9; 30:17). On one occasion, he has to be restrained by someone else (1 Sam. 25:34). But specifically – and this is significant – in relation to his calling, David shows consistent restraint. Specifically in relation to his destiny to be the king of Israel, David resists all temptation to snatch or grab or give the providence of God a helping hand. It is above all in this respect that he shows what it means to be a man after God's own heart.

If the world is yet to be 'a world after God's own heart', it needs desperately to recover restraint. In the first decade of the twenty-first century, examples of its absence are not hard to find. In retrospect even the main protagonists are increasingly conceding that the invasion of Saddam Hussein's Iraq by the US and its British allies in 2003 betrayed a regrettable lack of restraint. In Zimbabwe, Georgia and Iran at the present time, what a difference a period of restraint might make. Beyond the sphere of military action, there are increasing calls for concerted restraint currently not only in relation to the 'carbon footprint' made by the richest nations of the world but in relation to their 'water footprint' too. Moreover after thirty years of rampant consumerism and unfettered market forces, it seems that a global recession in the second decade of this century might be about to introduce an unexpected element of restraint even into international economics.

Meanwhile the continued 'individualization' of western society and its consequent lack of social cohesion create new challenges. One of the questions raised by the recent escalation in knife-crime in the UK, is where and how restraint can be fostered in increasingly diverse and multicultural communities. Similarly the almost infinite opportunities opened up through the internet (not least, but not only, for pornography) place new onus, as well as new strain, on individual powers of restraint – exercised in private.

Again if the church is to be 'a church after God's own heart' it needs to recover restraint. Church leaders are under huge pressure these days to make difficult decisions quickly. An instinct for competition and an expectation of instant success (both derived from contemporary culture and not from the Scriptures) make it hard for leaders simply to hold their nerve, to show restraint, and not to be rushed into this or that course of action. Sometimes within the good will and purpose of God, our destiny and vocation cannot be hurried into fulfilment, but must be awaited patiently. It may be that the 2008 Lambeth Conference of the Anglican Communion will prove in time to be a prophetic model of restraint for the whole church. There is of course every chance that those who choose the path of restraint will find themselves, like David himself, accused of cowardice or at least of dithering – of a failure to seize what God has promised.

And if Christians desire to be, like David, people after God's own heart, there is little doubt that their discipleship (their spiritual journey) will require the cultivation of restraint. This story in which spears and swords feature so prominently shows that if waiting is the anvil on which God hammers out holiness in the believer, then restraint is the whetstone on which sharpness is honed. To have power and yet to renounce the use of it for personal gain is both a mark of and a means to mature holiness; for to be slow to anger and not to lash out, to be patient and not to snatch and grab are the attributes of God himself.

The story of David's rise, then, is the story of 'a man after God's own heart'. And of all the virtues he demonstrates in the course of his journey from Bethlehem to Jerusalem, restraint was the key. When Christ Jesus – having himself journeyed from Bethlehem to Jerusalem – was hit, he did not hit back; when he was spat upon, he did not spit; and when he was cursed and vilified, he held his tongue. He was the one who, 'though he was in the form of God, did not consider equality with God a thing to be grasped' (Phil. 2:6).

The same restraint and vulnerability will characterize all who 'walk before the Lord, as David our ancestor walked' (1 Kgs. 9:4).

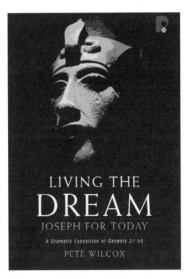

Living the Dream: Joseph for Today

A Dramatic Exposition of Genesis 3–50

Pete Wilcox

In a lively and gripping way, Pete Wilcox unfolds the story of Joseph in fourteen dramatic episodes. With a light touch and the sensitivity of one who has listened carefully to the biblical text, Wilcox allows the narrative to give up its treasures, and enables his readers to set their own stories alongside it. In this the way the ancient tale is made fresh for a modern western generation. The Joseph cycle is a story about coping with adversity and disunity and this makes it a useful text for the Church to hear again today.

'This book takes a well-known story and draws out of it any number of new things. The unfolding drama of Joseph's story, one of the most unforgettable narratives of the Old Testament, is revealed as a clue to the depths of Christian living – to the tangles of self-deception, the slow evolution of truthfulness, the cost of reconciliation, and, above all, the patient working of God through all the messy byways of human sin and conflict to bring about fresh hope. Readable, practical and profound.' – **Dr Rowan Williams,** Archbishop of Canterbury

'A powerful and engaging retelling of the classic story of Joseph, bringing out its power to illuminate and transform the life of faith. Wilcox will help many to rediscover and live out the "dream" in our postmodern times.' – **Alister McGrath,** Professor of Historical Theology, Oxford University

Pete Wilcox is the Canon Chancellor at Lichfield Cathedral.

978-1-932805-555-9

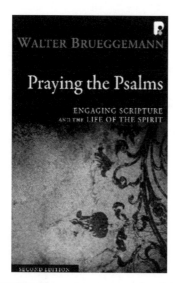

Praying the Psalms

Enaging Scripture and the Life of the Spirit

Walter Brueggemann

Walter Brueggemann pushes his readers to recognize the full gamut of passions reflected in the Psalms: joy and exultation but also disappointment, sorrow, anger, resentment, even the desire for vengeance. We are invited into a daring relationship with the God who calls us to pray with *honesty*. In this spiritual classic readers are guided into a thoughtful and prayerful encounter with God through the Psalms. This new edition includes a thoroughly revised text, new notes, and new bibliography.

'Few persons have so lived in and with the Psalms as Walter Brueggemann. Here he takes us into their depths, which are so clearly the depths of our human existence. The piety of the Psalms is strong medicine. Brueggemann bids us take it for the cure of our souls.' – **Patrick D. Miller**, Professor of Old Testament, Princeton Theological Seminary, USA

'In *Praying the Psalms*, Brueggemann carefully guides us away from the bland colours of contemporary culture and into the ancient and extreme world of praise and lament. This is essential reading.' – **Ian Stackhouse**, Senior Pastor, Guildford Baptist Church, England

Walter Brueggemann is William Marcellus McPheeters Professor of Old Testament Emeritus at Columbia Theological Seminary, Decatur, Georgia.

978-1-84227-555-9